Self Initiations

A Manual for Spiritual Breakthrough

The Companion to *Living Mastery*

by

Joanna Cherry

Little White Buffalo Publishing Cottage

Self Initiations: A Manual for Spiritual Breakthrough

by

Joanna Cherry

Published in 1999

Copyright © 1999   Joanna Cherry

01 00 99   0 9 8 7 6 5 4 3 2 1

Published by

Little White Buffalo Publishing Cottage
12345 Lake City Way NE #204
Seattle, WA 98125
(425) 673-9325

Cover design by Eric Akeson, Akeson Design

ISBN: 0-9658545-3-1

Printed in the USA

Dark and light
Love all as divine
Thus to ascend.

Table of Contents

Acknowledgments

I thank from my deepest heart spirit within me for guiding me through the release of long-held limitation. I thank Babaji, the immortal master of the Himalayas, for his love and vital assistance. I thank Divine Mother for being the greatness she is, and helping me draw closer to her. I thank my other beloved master friends for each giving me his or her unique gifts.

On the physical plane, thanks once again to Tony Stubbs for his expert assistance with editing and formatting. Thanks to Shahan Jon for helping me embrace a higher quality of writing. And thanks to Janeanne Narrin of Little White Buffalo Publishing Cottage for her love, encouragement and expertise.

Introduction

What is my intuition here? How does spirit guide me? What does my heart say? What is my joy?

Simple questions like these are signposts of a great revolution. For many centuries, human decisions have been based upon questions such as, "What will my family accept?" "What does my minister say?" "What will give me food and shelter?" or, "How can I earn the most money?"

In other words, we were looking outside for our answers. Now, more and more, we are looking within and moving as our heart dictates.

We are beginning to remember that we are part of divinity. We are expanding spiritually in tiny steps, middle-sized steps, or giant leaps.

An initiation is a change of mind and heart, a significant step in spiritual expansion. It is an opening into a deeper experience of divinity. In certain teachings, initiations are guided by a teacher or guru. In the past, this help was needed.

With the great awakening taking place, many of us are ready to touch our own inner wisdom and follow it into every initiation. To forge our own path, to discover how the divine *we* are does things, and express the individuality of *this* god/goddess. We desire this—I would say also that we need it. Marching, meandering, sailing, or flying to the beat of our own spirit-drum empowers us. It brings us fulfillment and joy.

When an initiatory path is guided from within, there is no set order of evolvement. Things do tend to happen in a certain order, but it is helpful to not know it. Then our openness and spontaneity may invite a surprise expansion.

An initiation may be a giant step, a life-turning event. Or it may be such a small step that we don't recognize it as such; but with other small steps, we gradually climb to the heights of our being.

In this time of finding your own path, receiving initiations from your own spirit, how could a book of someone else's initiations be helpful to you?

Initiations leading to the experience of divinity are a required course. Certain things need to happen for each and every one of us: feeling safe, loved, worthy and empowered; forgiving and releasing the past; opening to the love within us and expressing it; trusting God and life; creating the life of our heart's passion; learning to be present in timeless, indescribable reality.

As we each take these steps, we have gifts to give. We are not lone wolves; we are helping one another. We are interdependent. The ones who have gone before are giving us a hand up, and we are assisting the ones coming along after us. A helping hand can come through activity, but doesn't need to; it also happens as a function of consciousness. We are part of a great oneness.

As a friend says, "Every healer needs a healer." No matter who we are or what our realization, there are times when we need a perspective on life different from our own; connection with different wisdom and different gifts. It isn't that our spirit is limited—it is that until we experience its vastness, our perspective on life is limited. We learn from each other.

The initiations here are all from spirit, and nearly all from my own divinity. They have been effective for me, and for the people I have worked with in two decades of giving sessions and workshops. They will work for you if three conditions are present:

1. You are ready for a particular initiation.
2. This way of evoking it works for you.
3. You actually do it.

I trust these initiations will serve you, as they have served me and others, in a good and powerful way.

1
The Power of Initiation

My yearning heart stretches toward the star of my spirit.
My spirit reaches down ten times as far
to let me know I am already itself.

Life is a hologram of consciousness. The outside reflects perfectly the inside. We choose—consciously or unconsciously—everything that happens to our body, every thought and feeling, every relationship, every situation, every event from the grand to the minute. It is an almost unbelievable play, a dance of oneness in which all that happens is perfect for us.*

Because everything in our lives is a reflection, we are presented with unlimited opportunities to see what we believe, what we expect from life and other people—and to use that knowledge to choose a happier reality. That is why it can be said: "All is well, all is good."

When we are able to use anything that comes our way for such a positive cause, we are evolving consciously and purposefully. That is what this book is about.

In this period of transition into the age of light, opportunities for self-knowledge are coming thick and fast! The frequency of everything is speeding up. (Frequency is the measurable rate at which something vibrates. Everything has vibrational rate or frequency, not only objects but thoughts and emotions. The faster or higher the frequency, the more it resonates with the divine.)

---

* Those under the control of others—children subject to their parents' creations and trees destroyed for human purposes are two examples—may not choose difficult events; but at some level they are agreed to.

The Earth herself is rising in frequency, as is all of nature, humanity, and man-made creation. This causes a tremendous speed-up in the changes taking place—a great challenge for all of us! Initiations have increased in number and intensity to such a degree that what used to take us five or more lifetimes to accomplish, we are now accomplishing in one.

What is the Nature of Initiation?

It isn't easy to closely define or analyze initiation. It is ultimately a mystery. The Life of our life is the divine—the divine which is all of everything. It is infinite mystery. It may be called the Tao, universal Isness, God, the Force; what you will. This Life is ever on the move to higher levels of being and expression. As long as we believe we aren't fully divine, part of the great One, our initiations will take us step by step into the knowing that we are. But even the greatest of masters such as Jesus and Buddha still have initiations; life unfolds eternally.

Initiation is an expansion of consciousness from inner experience. It may be a little teeny shift or a life-turning shift, and it may come in myriads of ways. You get an Aha! when you're crossing the street or cleaning up the kitchen. You forgive someone who hurt you. Tentatively, you open to trust. A new purpose is born through life-threatening illness. Big initiations shake us, change our relationships, give us new work, lead us to or away from a teacher or lead us to teach—you name it.

Initiation may have little or nothing to do with events of the moment. When my mother was six, sitting one ordinary day at her desk in school, the room suddenly turned golden—and she was in paradise. Enlightenment struck one fellow as he drove across the Golden Gate Bridge. Others have been suddenly and inexplicably overwhelmed by the bliss of oneness with all things. An old ceiling can open up anytime to a new level.

Initiation may have everything to do with what is happening around us. An earthquake or flood may literally shake or flow our life into a new direction. (No matter how many people a "natural disaster" affects, each elected from some level to experience it and have the opportunity to grow from it. It isn't random or accidental. The day before a huge earthquake in

Mexico City, a woman said "I don't know why, but I have to go to Mexico City. I'm flying there today." Of course, she may have gone to help.) Relationships at home or work, activity we are involved in, anything may bring initiation.

Often initiation is messy and inconvenient. It grabs us by the scruff of the neck and drops us into white water, sweeping us along willy-nilly. We flail around to keep our nose above water and scramble for the further shore. When we resist knowing, or moving upon, a deep inner truth, we invite white water initiation. A long relationship ends unexpectedly; our home burns to the ground; we're fired; we're visited by cataclysmic illness— this is life taking drastic steps to help us do what we need to do. The more consciously we cooperate with life, the more we do our best to accept and move with our truth, the easier our initiations are likely to be. And more fun.

Many powerful initiations are set up. In shamanic initiation, elements of mystery serve to confound logical, linear mental process. Such process is oriented in human conditioning and time, which do not invite transformation. Spirits may be called in. Darkness, strange surroundings, fire, objects held or worn, painting the body, chanting and drumming, dancing— any of these invoke an open and willing heart. The change itself usually comes through an inner journey guided by spirit.

Elements of mystery need not be present. Initiation may be as simple as gathering your desire and intention to change, sitting down and opening up to spirit. Then you are not only in the mystery, you *are* the mystery—and things start happening! Your desire to expand beyond your former limits—"push the envelope"—is the fuel that feeds the alchemical fire. You may fully feel this desire or not, but it opens you to change, to think and feel in a new way. Your passion to change may be so strong that your initiation is accomplished through that alone. You have invited your divinity to replace limited with unlimited, hate with love, addiction with freedom—and it has accepted your invitation.

The shift itself is a new and deeper oneness with spirit. This may feel like joy or bliss, freedom, a surrender. Thought is not part of it; there are no words. The shift is beyond mind:

magical, timeless, of God Itself. "You"—your personality, your outer thoughts and feelings—do not do this. The divine within you does it. You are alive with the new way of your spirit, which brings a new life and changes little or large.

We in the West usually need to work a good bit with our mind, to become aware of the prison of limited thought and consciously re-choose unlimited thought. That is why most of these initiations work with mind. But mind is *in itself* a kind of prison. Working with it only points the way to a greater and deeper truth, it doesn't take us there. "A finger pointing to the moon" is how Zen Buddhists describe this. Who we are, the Universal I Am, lies beyond ego and mind. Thus the goal of all initiation is to move more deeply into unfathomable, indescribable reality.

About the Initiations

Each chapter of *Self Initiations* corresponds to a chapter in *Living Mastery,* the first volume of this set. *Living Mastery* provides deeper understanding on each subject and gives examples of personal accounts. In this book, subjects are briefly explained to simply introduce the initiations. If you find yourself unclear, it will be helpful to read the corresponding chapter in *Living Mastery.*

The chapters are loosely ordered, on purpose, and include initiations from the nitty-gritty to the transcendent. They are like a buffet from which you may choose whatever feels right to you; you'll be drawn to some and not others. We each have wisdom in some areas and can use assistance in others. As you continue with the book, you may find yourself ready for an initiation that didn't attract you earlier.

If you have trouble sensing which initiations are right for you, know that your spirit can be sensed through your heart, your feeling. A sense of rightness, or *Yes!* about a certain initiation, is your spirit guiding you. If you want clearer guidance from your spirit, higher self, inner self, God, master, guru, guides—whatever you choose to call your divinity—you may work with the next chapter first.

Benefiting from the Initiations

The initiations are possibilities upon which your spirit may build. You may be guided to make changes, add or leave something out. It may be that just the first step of your personal initiation follows the one in the book, and then your guidance takes you in a whole new direction. When a process is suggested, do it your way. If a visualization is suggested, for instance, and you do better with words or feelings, use words or feelings. The best way to do it is the way that is easiest for you.

Some of the sections are not so much initiations as catalysts for initiation, especially the spoken word statements. If you'd like to break a pattern, you can begin by speaking the freeing statements for several days or weeks. This will automatically bring up the beliefs and emotions within you which resist this change. Then you may choose to transform them. The spoken word sections also help keep the new shift in place.

What is the best time for initiation? As your life unfolds you notice the sticking places—things aren't working. This is a great opportunity to make discoveries and go to work. Find the initiation here—they are all named in the Table of Contents—that most closely matches your desired change.

I'm at the end of my rope. I feel hopeless. This may be the perfect time for initiation. This dynamic is known in Alcoholics Anonymous. A leader in AA once told me the most dramatic success comes from those who hit bottom. The Chinese have one ideogram for both "crisis" and "opportunity." Hitting bottom may open doors to change. It is a most powerful time.

The place to do initiations should be private, preferably where you can talk aloud (loudly!), cry or laugh or even scream. Nature can be a perfect setting for initiation: not only does it have fewer limited thought forms (the energies of thought and emotion that stay behind in a place) than you find in buildings, but being away from your usual environment opens a door to change. Nature accepts you exactly as you are, and encourages freedom and upliftment.

Before you do an initiation, call upon the love and wisdom of your spirit to assist you, as well as guides, master friends, angels you love. This is an important key. Throughout the initiation, move with your spirit. Listen, listen to your inner wisdom, and follow where it leads.

You may hit a feeling of pain, anger, sorrow, or other strong emotion. Your spirit may lead you there so you can release it and move on. But don't allow yourself to get stuck in drama; move *through* old feeling into forgiveness, joy, and love. Revel in drama for the fun of it for a while if you wish; or cry or rave if you need to. But the goal is *release*. If it takes some time to release, keep your balance; cry every *other* day.

Be really aware of what you are doing. Old feelings delved into can become circular. The angriest man I ever met was a primal scream therapist who helped people release anger! Once you have uncovered a deep source of pain, *don't identify yourself with it*. When that happens, you may be processing it thirty years later. Determine to move *through* it to the place *in you* where it doesn't exist, and never has existed. See more about this in the "Clear!" chapter, Break the Loop.

Do not attempt to control your initiation, for that keeps you in your mind; change doesn't easily happen. Initiation involves a leap, big or small—a leap in faith, a leap in spirit. Though it is not easy to define, you will recognize it.

Remember the element of desire, fueling your energy, intention, determination, patience and perseverance to change. And remember spirit. Spirit is the mystery, the grace, the upliftment, the joy, the light, the new! *You* are spirit.

A single initiation can take more than one sitting, maybe several hours of concentrated inner activity spread out over a few days. Some projects are huge; complete forgiveness of yourself and everyone and everything, for example, is likely to take many sittings over a number of years. The time an initiation takes is not important. What is important is that you throw yourself into it wholeheartedly and with determination.

You can set a time to fully receive or accomplish a particular initiation. Forty days, or six weeks, seems a universal time frame for significant change. Or, create your own: three, six, nine, twelve or twenty-four months, and accomplish a portion of the initiation each week or month. It may be helpful to get a notebook and record your experiences. Just remember that *you* chose the time frame, and if you do not accomplish your intention within it, remake it to fit *you.* Never think that you have failed; you were simply not in full realization of what it would take, and now you know more. Always encourage yourself! You may choose to take some down time before you begin again.

Integrating the energies of an initiation is equally as important as the time of receiving it. Don't get too serious; let yourself rest, have fun, breathe, relax, and find your own good rhythm. "Slowliness is holiness," Herakhan Baba once said.

Most initiations work best when you are alone. If you and a friend are ready for the same initiation and desire to assist each other, and you each have the balance and wisdom to do that, working together can be excellent. One could read an instruction from the book, and give enough time for both to complete that part. Or you could listen to the tape together (see below), or create your own way.

The power of the spoken word is undeniable. In many initiations you will find truthful words. It is suggested that you stand in a powerful position: feet hip-width apart, knees loose, back straight, head tilted neither forward nor back but perfectly level, eyes straight ahead. Speak the words with clarity and power, loudly or softly as feels best. Change them any way that empowers you.

Initiations involving deep inner work have been taped by the author and are available for every chapter. You simply listen and do the process. In the back of the book, you will find the address to write to for tape information.

If you are not working with the tapes, you may record a particular initiation yourself. Then you more easily remain in the deep inner space of greatest effectiveness.

All blessings to you with your self-initiations!

2
Contact! Your Spirit

Contact what you are. Become what you are.
Be what you are—fully divine.

What is your divinity? Your master self, inner self, divinity or divine self, the father within you, your higher self, your I Am Presence, the Christ within, your true self—what you call it is yours to choose. Your divinity is perfectly one with God—the divine, the Tao, spirit, universal life force, all-that-is—and aware of this oneness. It is an individualized expression of God/Goddess.

There are many aspects of individual divinity. Various teachings name them differently. Connection happens with the right one at the right time. An aspect often called the Christ bridges the purely divine—which knows nothing of limited human experience—with the human. It is the Christ level that many of us connect with now. Above this is the great master self or I Am Presence, and on beyond there are others—cosmic level presences. Each aspect has its own frequency and sound, or name.

A guide, which many have now, may actually be an aspect of one's own divinity. It may also be a master, a friend we've known in a past or present life, or other possibilities. A guide can come from any level: one close to the human, like one's grandmother who has passed, to the highest levels.

There is no natural separation between what we call "myself" and our divinity. The only separation has been in our mind: our belief. After our ancient decision to believe in matter rather than in the spirit that created and infused it, we began to lose the awareness that we *are* our divinity.

The days of separation are ending now, and we are—at long last!—returning to our experience of divinity. We say this calmly, but in fact it is a mind-blowing, belief-trampling, life-turning and sometimes hair-raising transformation. A return from death to life.

The initiations in this chapter lift us over Separation Gulch to paradise on the other side.

I gratefully acknowledge the Teaching of the Inner Christ (see References) for some of the major techniques here. (I used to be a minister with the Teaching. My work has expanded into its own uniqueness, yet there remain priceless tools from TIC.)

How's Your Relationship with God?

Before we begin contact initiations, it is important to understand how you feel about God and your own divinity, which is one with God.

Most of us project our parents and grandparents onto God. But few of us experienced divine love in childhood. Human love is usually conditional: I will love you if _____ . And if a parent both loved and punished harshly, we may understand love as including harsh punishment, or whatever condition existed.

Trusting divine love comes quietly, gently over time. Forgiving our parents and grandparents for their shortcomings and healing our relationship with them is a vital step.

The love of the divine for Itself-as-us is infinitely vast, eternal, and unconditional. From the human perspective we get only a shadow glimpse of this love. The more we merge with our divine self, the more love we can feel. We are divine love ourselves. Trusting divine love is trusting ourselves. We are love, lover, and beloved.

Initiation

Go into a quiet space, and call your divine self. If you desire, call also a master you love or any other being of God love and light.

Prepare for love: go into meditation, think of a loving or happy event, dwell upon a beloved master—find something that awakens love in your heart.

When you're ready, ask to feel and receive divine love. It's here! Open to it. Be open as a little child. Let the love in just as much as you can.

If there arises pain, sorrow, fear, anger, skepticism, or hardness, love it. Ask that it be lifted from you if you are ready. Ask a golden flame from your divinity to blaze through every level of your being: your subconscious mind, your conscious mind, emotions, body and aura. Breathe deeply. Use your hands to sweep up your body as you breathe in, and up above your head as you breathe out. Give up this old emotion! Let it go as much as you are able.

This is usually a layer release, over time. What you do today may bring up more to forgive and release. But you will succeed.

Now, open again to love. As you receive more of it, it intensifies. If you are not feeling love, or not much love, know that the effort you are making now will come back to you a thousand-fold. For every step we take, our divinity takes ten.

Below is a statement you can say aloud or silently.

I am one with the divine. I myself am divine love. The divine loves Itself as me. I am safe to receive, bask in, and trust divine love and guidance. Divine love is my love for myself. In the innocence of a child, as I am ready, I open like a beautiful rose to love. The rose is nourished with sunshine and rain and earth. How could I, the very image of the divine, be less cared for? I am infinitely and eternally loved. I am love, lover, and beloved.

Clear Your Space

When you commune with spirit, the first thing to check is your "receiving space." Is it clear? A clear space means you are the only energy occupying your aura, *and* your own energy is clear enough to commune with spirit. We can, of course, be influenced by other energies, and all of us have experienced this whether or not we've put labels to it. Even the most sincere and practiced of us needs to pay close attention to the receiving space.

The way to do this is usually very simple. Speak these words, silently or aloud, with conviction:

My aura is now only the Love and the Light of my divine Presence I Am.

Remember that you may use the Christ, God, or any term you choose rather than the one given. Now you will simply intend to connect deeply with spirit.

If you feel unclear, unreleased belief and emotion may be clogging your channel, or you may be allowing other energies in your space, or both. You may need to dissolve psychic cords with another person; see the relationships chapter. Or you may need to heal thought and emotion; see the clearing chapter. To release thought forms or an entity (a person whose spirit is here with you), see the service chapter. Don't be concerned—all is forthcoming! For now, simply do your best.

The Contact Initiation

Meditation

Create space in the activity of your day to open the door to your true nature and invite your higher self to step through. Meditation is probably essential, at least in the beginning, to connect and merge with your divine presence. It's the space to receive guidance from within. Here is a basic meditation that deeply relaxes the body, mind and feelings. When we're relaxed we're closer to being our real self and more easily connect with it.

Sit comfortably with your spine straight. Close your eyes and begin to breathe deeply and gently. Feel your groundedness from your root chakra (the energy center at the base of your spine) and your feet down into the center of the earth. Feel the support of Mother Earth, your oneness with her. Breathe and relax.

Invite the love energy from Divine Mother (or Mary, Quan Yin, Saraswati, your own goddess self or another aspect of the Goddess) to flow up from earth's center into your feet, filling every atom with love. This wonderful rose-gold, liquid love light energy is the love nature of God or the universe. Let your feet feel this love. If you don't feel it don't worry about it, simply continue. This energy flows upward now into your ankles and calves, slowly, and then into your knees and thighs. Take two deep breaths of this love, and let your legs and feet deeply relax.

Invite the divine love energy to flow gently into your lower torso, including your genital area, and slowly on up into the solar plexus and middle back, and your chest, upper back and shoulders. Again, see if you can actually feel the love. Take three deep breaths of this energy, and let your whole torso relax completely.

Continue on in the same way, allowing the love to flow down into your arms and hands, then up into your neck, face and head. Wiggle your chin and jaw to help them relax, and let the social persona fall away. Let your mouth and cheeks fall, your eyes and forehead really relax. Feel the love. Take two deep breaths.

If you wish, invite light energy from Divine Father to flow from the top of your head down your body, merging with the Goddess energy.

Continue to breathe deeply as you release tension from all body parts, relaxing more and more. Bless your body. Say silently or aloud:

I bless this beloved divine body. This body is formed and maintained each moment by God/Goddess love, light, intelligence and will.

Tune more deeply now into awareness of mind and feeling. Thoughts and feelings are like our children; we created them, and they need our love and understanding to expand into divine freedom. If you have a judgment for instance, or a fear, loving it lifts it into a lighter state. And love yourself for having it!

Choose now an old pattern you'd like to release. Love and bless it. Embrace it! Love yourself, with all you heart, for choosing it. Say:

I love myself for thinking this thought, and feeling this feeling. I embrace it now in love. I bless all my thoughts and feelings. They lift into my natural expression of love, joy, light, wisdom, knowing, oneness and power. So be it.

Tune more deeply now into the awareness of your spirit. Call upon it to come. If you have guides or a favorite master you work with, you may call them now. A master or angel you know something about, or have a picture of, can be a point of focus and a wonderful aid to deeper connection with spirit. Or simply ask God or your inner self to be with you, be *as* you.

You may affirm and feel truths about yourself, such as:

I am the love of God/Goddess. I am the light of God/Goddess. I am a divine master, remembering who I Am. I am beautiful. As part of the divine, I am eternally innocent and good. I am infinitely loved, supported and provided for. I am the knowing and wisdom of God-I-Am. I am the freedom and the power. I am the joy! I am divine, unlimited abundance. I am one with all.

Now be a receptive vessel, intent upon receiving from your spirit. You may hear, feel, or see what your spirit gives you. If distractions arise, witness their passing without giving them your attention. Remain in this state for twenty minutes or half an hour.

Meditation twice a day is beneficial.

Hear an Inner Name

If you would like to receive an inner name from an aspect of your divine nature, ask for it now.

An inner name may be a familiar one, such as that of a master you know, or entirely new such as Ama or Rata-Joriah. In listening for the name you may get it all at once or piece by piece.

Begin to listen for it. Be relaxed, patient, open, and focused on love. Give it some time. If there seems to be difficulty, ask for it letter by letter. It is easy here to start fooling ourselves and hear names from the mind. If what you receive feels right to the core of your heart, it's likely to be from your spirit. If it doesn't, it is probably not. Be discriminating in your openness. Take all the time you need.

A name can be wonderful, but you do not need one to attune to your spirit. You can use simply God, my I Am Presence, my inner self, my divinity, my guide(s), my Council of Light or Council of Twelve, or whatever feels most natural for you.

Receive Your Signal

Whether or not you are working with a name, you can ask for and receive a "signal" through your physical body. You may receive a signal spontaneously, such as rocking gently back and forth in meditation, or a thrill up the spine when you hear truth. The benefit of a signal is that you are receiving spirit *directly through and as your body.* This helps you be more clear about a message you are receiving. It also helps your body!

A signal can be almost anything. You may see light in your third eye (your sixth chakra between your eyebrows), or colors or a vision. You may smell a beautiful fragrance of flowers. A signal can be movement of some part of your body, such as your head, thumb, or arm; a feeling of love or well-being in your heart; a tingling—even a change in your breath. It is often accompanied by feelings of love and joy.

If you like, ask for a signal. Again, be patient, relaxed, and focused on love. If you receive something, test it out. Ask for it to become stronger. Ask for it to stop and start again. If it is really a signal from your spirit, these tests should be met. If you are not getting anything, remember that spirit never withholds; it is an unreadiness in you, usually a mistrust of God. As you develop greater trust and openness, a signal can come. In your sincere asking, you are opening the door.

A movement signal has the benefit of being definite and clear. If you would like one, ask for it. My head turning—and more recently a delighted smile—have been movement signals for me. The one drawback of a movement signal is that your mind can get into it, more easily than with subtler signals, and move your body. *The single most important thing in receiving from your spirit: stay attuned to love.*

Whether or not you receive a name or signal, you are able to receive messages, and answers to your questions, from your higher self.

Guidance from Your Spirit

Messages

Now you are ready to ask for a message, an answer to a question, or other guidance.

Messages from your spirit are usually given in abstractions, rather than words or pictures. We translate these abstractions into the form we best receive them. That is why two people who receive the same message express it in different ways.

Following are the three most common ways we translate the abstractions of spirit into what makes sense to us:

1. **Words.** You can "hear" words in your mind. This may be just like someone talking to you, word for word. Or you may hear key words bridged with a sense of the meaning that connects them. For instance, suppose the full message were: "This relationship is right for you.

You have been waiting to come together until you were both ready. You are ancient soulmates." You could receive the words: "Relationship ... right ... waiting ... soulmates," and feel the meaning that connects them.

2. **Pictures,** or a **vision.** Here you see a picture within your mind's eye that communicates a message. The only catch: you may not understand the meaning of the picture. If you don't, ask "What does this mean?" and become clear.

3. **Feeling,** or **knowing.** This is a way of sensing that needs no words. Knowing or feeling from spirit is direct intuition, closer to what's being given than either pictures or words. People sometimes feel direct intuition lacks specificity, but it is a wonderful way to receive from spirit.

4. A **combination** of any or all of these. This occurs frequently, and adds depth and verification to what you receive.

It may help you receive messages to look deeply into the eyes of a master you love. Use a physical picture, or see her or him before you in your mind's eye. (And don't be surprised if, with a physical picture, the expression changes!)

If you ask for a message, you'll likely receive one of love for you, how wondrous you are, or to love yourself more.

Answers to Questions

Knowing what questions to ask is indicative of a loving, effective relationship with your spirit. Questions important to your heart, to the big scheme of your life, are most appropriate. Trivial questions are generally not the best use for your divine connection. Occasionally, if I've lost something and have looked everywhere, I've cried in frustration *"Where is it, God?!"* and usually it's in my hands within thirty seconds. Anything you really want to know, even if it seems small—understanding an event you were part of, the health of your cat, need for financial input—is all fine. There is no judgment about what to ask. It's just that with such a loving, powerful energy present, you want to both honor it and use it to greatest benefit.

How to ask reflects the nature of God/universe. You are not a puppet with God pulling the strings; and life as you experience it is created from your conscious and unconscious thought and feeling. Questions such as *Am I to do this?* or *Is a relationship coming to me?* imply that you are being done **to**—not your highest truth. Even questions like Is there going to be a big earthquake here this year? deny one's own creative power.

Here are some examples of questions asked from deeper understanding: *I Am a co-creator with God/universe, one with everything and everyone. What is truly best for me is best for all.*

1. Is it my true desire—the desire of my heart, most right for me at this time—to _____?
2. Is it my highest choice to call a relationship to me at this time? (If yes:) How shall I go about this?
3. Is an earthquake here likely this year? (If yes:) Is it possible to divert this energy? Is this wise? How shall it be done?

If you are one who desires to serve the masters and God, then a question such as *What can I do now?* may be good. Even then, a spirit of co-creation honors your human self and allows you to say "No" if you need to. That is healthy and balanced.

Something interesting and important to know about answers to questions or specific guidance: spirit may tell you something that turns out another way. I once planned a one-day visit to a friend on the Oregon coast whose little town, far from any city, was an eight-hour drive away. As I don't enjoy driving that long in one day, the short visit would have taken four days of my time—time that was increasingly precious to me. I hit upon the idea of hiring a private plane to fly me there. I asked spirit, "If I put a notice up at the local airport, will that bring results?" "Yes." A solid, no-nonsense "Yes."

I drove the fifteen miles to the tiny airport and taped my notice where it wouldn't fail to be seen. Later that day, I mentioned what I did to a friend. "Oh," she said, "Richard who works at Truck Village is a pilot. Ask him."

I called Richard, and my flight dates didn't work for him. But he referred me to another pilot who could take me.

Spirit knew—as it knows everything—that posting my sign was not the direct route to getting a flight, but that it *led* directly to success.

A message or idea you act upon may turn out to be a facet of a whole mandala of guidance. James Twyman's idea to give a peace concert in Bosnia was such a message. (See his book, *Emissary of Light,* in the Bibliography.)

Not all guidance takes us into uplifted or joyful experience. A friend visiting India was once guided to spend the night alone in a Benares temple. In the early morning hours he was robbed of everything, including every shred of clothing! He had to run out naked to get help.

Telling me about this later, he said he realized spirit was helping him learn something he needed to know: with *nothing,* he was whole and fine.

So guidance may look like one thing and turn out to be something more or something different—even *entirely* different and seemingly unrelated. Gradually we are able to completely trust the flow of life, so we don't need to know *why* we are moved to do something. We do as we feel from our heart, and that is always right.

Feeling, Spirit and You

Deep feeling from your heart is united with spirit. In this sense, it is simple to feel one with your spirit and know your guidance is correct. What is the passion of your heart? What do you *not* want any longer? The desires of your heart are *from* your spirit. If you long to live by the sea, study massage, or chuck your job for something more creative, that is your spirit saying "Yes!! Do this!" You might ask only how to proceed.

Your body also responds to life choices. If you get a shrinking or contracting sensation in your body, for instance, it's obviously part of a "No" answer. (Always discernment, however! It may be a "Feel the fear and do it anyway!" scenario.) If you get a sense of expansion and joy—you guessed it.

Other Ways to Get Messages

You don't have to be in meditation to get messages from your spirit. Everything is a great oneness, and messages come in many forms.

Have you hit upon a wonderful idea? It's from your spirit! If you are open, helpful ideas for every area of your life will come—so many you can't use them all. Spirit is infinite creativity!

Any time, day or night, you can receive a message, an idea or a revelation. You may sleep on a problem and wake up with the answer. You may get a message through a dream. Someone may speak a truth for you, a human messenger. You may use runes, Tarot cards, the I Ching, Medicine Cards, angel cards, Course in Miracle cards, or any other tool. Any form works if you approach it with a sincere heart. You may find a message in a book you are browsing, receive one from a bird or animal—the possibilities are endless. Just be open and aware.

Is This Message from Spirit?

Spirit is for your *emancipation:* your freedom, enlightenment, joy, creativity, play, abundance, peace, power, godliness—and nothing less! Does your message resonate with these elements? Does it come from love, unmistakable *love?* Does your heart resonate with it? Does it inspire you? Bring you joy? Empower you? Open you to new possibilities? Awaken your creativity? Does it feel right to you, all the way down in your belly? Is it *completely* devoid of judgment toward you or anyone else? Then it is likely to be from your true self. A message can take a stern tone, "tough love," but even then you will know the truth of it.

It is easy to think that messages from your mind are coming from spirit. This happens to experienced people, too. For instance, if you ask a question and the answer is what you *thought* it would be, you want to be especially cautious about it. Determine to get the truth. Tune more purposefully to your spirit. Feel its love, light, and clarity, and ask again. If you wait a couple of days before re-asking, that can help. Make sure the answer comes from that clarity. Messages can even come from "higher mind," closer to spirit but not spirit; this difference is harder to discern. Many people channel from higher mind. And be aware that another energy can come in and give you a false message. Be determined to accept messages only from your spirit, and you will succeed.

Often, especially in the beginning, you may get both spirit and mind messages together. I was working with a woman whose great desire was to study art. She got this message: "Yes, be an artist! But first go to law school to please your parents." She didn't realize that the "law school" part was from her mind, her sense of "should." *There are no shoulds in spirit.* It knows that parental and social expectations are not usually your truth. (Occasionally, though, there is a *must* which is irresistible!)

If you get a message or answer that is unexpected, confusing, or spectacular, put it on the shelf and ask again later. The truth will out. In 1988, I was living in San Francisco and expected to be there a long time. That summer, I spent a week camping on Mt. Shasta in Squaw Meadow, an incredible spot 8,000 feet up. When I got back home, I began to feel very confused. Finally I exclaimed, *"All right!* What is this about?" and immediately I saw myself living in Mt. Shasta.

"No, that *can't* be right!" I thought. "After all, spirit *brought* me to San Francisco!" Over the next several days I tuned in again and again, and each time I saw the same vision. I knew then that against all expectation, it was right. And I moved to Mt. Shasta. So be open to the new! Today's freedom is tomorrow's prison. Your spirit knows what is best.

What's for Today?

Ask spirit: "What's for today? Is there a new thought? Is this action I'm considering best for all? What is the reason for _____? How shall I proceed in this relationship?"

With a daily check-in, it's easier to keep abreast of ourselves—and our lives *work.*

Genuine openness is important. A particular guidance may not seem logical, because spirit sees and knows *everything* and our personas do not.

Once Mahatma Gandhi, in his enduring passion to free India from British rule, planned a big parade. Shortly before it was to happen, he cancelled it. To the people vehemently protesting, he answered: "It is not the purpose to have a parade. It is the purpose to follow the will of God."

Do You Want to Channel?

When we connect with our own spirit, or a being other than ourselves, we can bring messages through. This is called channeling. Anyone can learn to channel. For some, channeling is part of true purpose. Through dedicated channels, great beings have accelerated the coming of the age of light.

If you are channeling, or receiving the channeling of another person, you must bring forward the D-word: **discrimination.** You notice Archangel Michael has channeled an article. Maybe you've liked other channelings through this same person. But each message must stand on its own; maybe it's right for you, and maybe it isn't.

I learned to channel in 1980, during my training with the Teaching of the Inner Christ. Channeling was easy for me, and I enjoyed it. Babaji and other masters came through me with messages of light and love, information that felt true in the heart. I became confident as a channel.

I was assigned a paper based upon my channeling. I was doing a lot of entity healing at that time, assisting people who had passed over to go into the light. I decided to do my paper on this subject. Magnificent information came through!—how to call in entities from Russia, and more. I sent the paper to TIC headquarters. A week later, I received a letter. "We understand this as mental channeling," wrote the TIC leaders. "Try again."

I was stunned. I had gotten "Yes" on everything I had written. The "facts" seemed so wonderful, so exciting! How could I possibly have gone wrong?

I sat down to meditate upon this dilemma. I was taught from my spirit that one can be focused within an *entire framework* that is not from spirit, which is limited or downright false, and never know it because everything within that framework is logical to itself. I learned that the *one primary key* in channeling is this: it comes from the **love** of spirit, and you can *feel* this love as you channel. Other beings or your own mind can give you misinformation, but *they cannot duplicate love.* I have never forgotten this.

Since then I have learned that even when the connection with spirit is truly there, the channeling entity cannot bring forth something that goes against the belief of the channeler. For instance, in the "green books" of the St. Germain Press, Guy Ballard channeled that one should forget the lower chakras completely, just cut them off. But in recent years he has given a message to both me and others that this was his bias at that time and thus what he heard. It did not come from spirit.

It is possible for a channel to go "in and out" within the same transmission, connected with spirit *and* disconnected (connected with other levels of the psyche), and not be aware of it. Thus it is easily possible for one sentence to be "off," and the sentences before and after to be perfectly "on." It is logical and good for us to accept certain *pieces* of a particular channeling.

Even if we perceive an entire channeling to be one with spirit, one part may be right for us and another not, or none of it may apply to us. We are divine beings, creating our reality as we choose, and we receive spirit in our own way. The key here is: *never, ever give away your authority!*

A practice of mine is to be extra careful about any channeling that would arouse fear. If a channeling we feel is accurate concerns something we do not want to happen, *it may be possible to change it.* Most prophets of earth changes are clear about this: their job is to let us know where we're headed, so that we change direction and avert the earthquake or whatever. Thus the best prophets make themselves "wrong"—and deserve extra thanks for this!

Even the most sincere channel may open, unaware, to a lower level being, or mental messages—both "full body" and conscious channels. A channeler must *objectively* evaluate what has been received, and check with his own spirit about it. And the receiver must check with *his* own spirit, and accept *only* what feels right within his own being. Here are some "channeling checks" for both channeler and receiver. They are the same as for messages:

1. Do I feel the infinite love and honoring of all life that spirit is in this channeling? Is it completely free of judgment?

2. Does it feel right to *me*, within my heart and being?

3. In accepting this channeling, do I feel empowered? Does it increase my sense of integrity? Does it strengthen my path in life? Does it give me a sense of joy and upliftment, at least in the longer term?

If you have a strong desire about something, or strong emotion, your channeling about it has about a 50-50 chance of being accurate. I once fooled myself for *several years* about a certain man I wanted in my life. I thought spirit was agreeing! Even if an accurate channel looks into an emotional issue with you, the information may be iffy. I have found for instance that channeling for someone regarding a strongly desired relationship is least likely to hold true. Am I pregnant? Do I have a serious illness? Questions like these are better farmed off to someone clear and objective. Even then, do not lean upon the answer; it may be best for you to discover what's going on in third-dimensional terms such as consulting a doctor.

Whenever we channel, we are doing it within a perceived matrix or framework of life, though it may be quite an enlightened one. As life expands, so expands our field of perception. When we step from a smaller matrix into a larger one, channeling from the old one may need to be adjusted and integrated into the new. The new matrix may invalidate an earlier channeling completely, as the expansion opens up new and different information. The great truths such as, "All is divine" are not subject to this so much as, for instance, a channeling on life's activities.

A note here for those of us who perceive ourselves as givers or servers. Many of us have been serving for lifetimes, and we may have a kneejerk response about helping or giving in a certain way. The suggestion to give may truly come from spirit— after all, it is a joy to give what is rightfully ours to give. But let us be aware of a possible vulnerability to misinterpret a situation. Take the example of Kathryne, who was given an exquisite amber necklace—and this she cherished! The same evening, she wore the necklace to a seminar, and the woman leader immediately exclaimed, "What a gorgeous necklace!" She gazed at it often throughout the evening.

"Give it to her," came a voice in Kathryne's ear, over and over. "Give it to her." She had not had the chance to enjoy her beautiful gift, so she resisted. But as she was leaving, at the last second, she took off her necklace and put it over the other woman's head. Kathryne cried all the way home.

Kathryne later realized that the "Give it to her" message came from a part of herself that desired to always be a giver. It was a "should" message. In a similar circumstance, such a message could be true. But the things we cherish are with us rightly because we cherish them, and there is nothing wrong with that.

The broader learning here is that the most accurate channel, if locked into a self-definition of "server" (or any other), may well misunderstand spirit's direction. She may receive messages to serve in ways unharmonious to her and follow them anyway. One major pattern is running hither and thither to serve others, long after one needs to stay home and rest. Flexibility, humor, not taking oneself or one's mission too seriously, a balance of energy and activity in life, all help to make a truly accurate channel.

Channeling regarding another person, even by their request, deserves very special care. It is not our job to tell anyone else what to do.

A wise teacher once described truth as a huge bouquet of flowers. Each of us sees the bouquet from a different angle, coalescing colors and shapes into an image that is ours alone. Though the discrete images may at times contradict one another, our various visions intermesh to form a kaleidoscope of incredible richness. The more clear we become, the less our personality colors what we see, and our images are more alike— but never exactly the same. Therefore we cannot see another's truth as clearly as their own spirit does.

The divine never orders anyone around. Our higher self and any true master respect, *always,* our individual perspective and free will. We may receive a suggested course of action. If we do it, good. If we don't do it, so be it. If we channel by request or receive a spontaneous message for another—even if we feel the message is vital for their good—we put it forth for consideration, not as a mandate. How could we do anything less?

One last—and vital—consideration on channeling. We have been inclined, from limited perspective, to think a high being is greater than ourselves. Nothing could be further from the truth. We are all equal, beloved, divine god/goddess. It is serving us for the moment to hear those who have *realized* their godhood, and are assisting us to do the same. But the direction we are headed is to be our own wisdom, our own authority, to "channel" *our own master self.* And even that is on our way to *being* our godhood, and expressing it completely—right here in the world.

Cosmos Contact

Here is an inspiring initiation of oneness with divinity that came when I needed it. As always, make it your own by changing it as you choose:

Imagine yourself on the top plateau of the Grand Canyon, or anywhere in beautiful nature. It is a glorious day! The sun is shining joyfully, the sky is a deep clear blue, and a cooling breeze caresses your cheek. You are relaxed and happy. Do you hear the sounds of nature about you?

Looking before you, all you see is this natural setting. You look behind you, to your right and left, and above. No one here but you!

Feeling completely peaceful, you begin to float gently upwards. The earth falls away beneath you. You float higher, and soon you can see for many miles. You continue upward; now you can see the curve of the earth, and now the continent you are leaving, surrounded by its oceans.

You go up and up, and now you are leaving the planet's atmosphere. She becomes the size of a basketball in your vision, and now the size of a baseball. Now she's just a tiny marble—and now she disappears! You fly on.

Finally, you arrive at the center of the universe. Peacefully you sit in space and look in all directions at the nearby stars and galaxies.

Now, you notice a brilliant light that is not a star, moving your way. As it gets closer and brighter, you realize it is a beautiful divine being, glowing like a sun. You recognize your own divine presence!

You embrace in great joy! You share what you wish, you're wordless, you receive gifts or messages, you fly around the universe—whatever comes. Gradually you notice your own body beginning to glow with the same light.

If you have questions or problems you want help with, present them and listen for answers.

Are there other gifts to receive at this moment?

Now you and your divinity may merge into one, if you desire.

When you are replete, begin to float back toward Earth. Finally you see her, a pinpoint in the distance! She grows larger in your vision: now like a Ping-pong ball, an orange, a soccer ball. Now she fills your entire vision. You locate the spot you floated up from, and float back down.

When you arrive, look deeply into yourself and your life. Are there changes to make? New paths to take? Be with yourself until all is clear.

You may go back any time.

Sacred Space

If you are feeling troubled, small, all too human, the following method of contact/oneness is especially helpful.

From a meditative space, become aware of the grounding cord between your root chakra and the center of the earth. Slide down this cord into the protective, nurturing womb of the mother. Adjust to this space in comfort. If you would be more comfortable, place yourself in a beautiful spot in nature and adjust the rest of the process accordingly.

You notice, some distance away, a light. You begin to move easily toward this light. When you arrive, you see that it is a beautiful space created just for you, exactly as you would want it. Look around and take note of the details. If it's underground it can be full of light, including windows. Is it a cave? A palatial room? A dome or tent?

Does it have comfortable furnishings, cushions, fragrance, candles, plants, music? If you see anything you'd like to change, change it now by your thought.

No one may enter here without your permission. Your divine self, or a favorite master of your choice, would very much enjoy coming to you when you are ready. As you feel ready, call this being: and here it is! Beaming a smile of welcome, he or she moves to you with open arms.

You embrace in joyous reunion! Share anything you wish.

Sit now in the lap of your divine friend, who lovingly holds you, rocks and caresses you. He or she speaks wonderful truths to you, such as "You are so beautiful. You are the beloved of God, a divine aspect of God. You are good and innocent. You are the worth of the divine. You are infinitely and eternally loved! I love you." What other loving words are you hearing?

As this continues, a change takes place. In the lap of this divine presence, your body has begun to shine.

Now you realize that you are the master as well as your old self, holding you, loving you, caressing you, speaking to you.

Suddenly, you *are* the master, and there is no "you" lying in your lap. *You are the divine.* Take your time and feel this with deep clarity.

Into this space now, with your permission, may come your old friends: fellow masters. You recognize some of them perhaps, and others may feel new to you. Again, a joyous reunion.

With these masters, create any kind of exchange that you enjoy.

This space is here for you at all times.

Oneness

After you have been receiving messages for a while, it may seem hard at times to get one—an odd development! I've realized it is because my spirit wants me to **be** itself, to simply know from being the divinity I Am. This is the merging we are all headed for, being one with our divine master self.

May the love and light of spirit you are infuse and bless you infinitely.

3
Clear!

Clear away what you are not.
What you are will shine its infinite light
throughout the universe.

What is there to clear? Spirit/God is everything. It is all-loving, all-powerful, and all-knowing. We are the exact image and likeness of God. As such, how can we appear so different from that?

The answer lies in our belief that we are separate from God and from others. We think we are contained within a body, a speck in the dust of the universe. We think we haven't enough money, time, or energy. We feel powerless to stop aging and death. Because we are divine, these limiting beliefs are all powerful and manifest in our lives. Then we give them still more power.

The experience of separation has caused all of our difficult "karma," the energies from every life that circle out and return to us. This chapter could be called "Clear Difficult Karma;" that's what we're doing. But our ego, that fragment of consciousness we call "I," believes separation is real. Its life and identity hang upon keeping separate.

Our true being is like a magnificent diamond shining like a million suns through all the universe. Our light is one with the light from all other diamonds. Over this wondrous, luminous, eternal diamond is caked the mud of limited belief and experience. This has made it awfully hard to see who we really are.

As we focus upon our divine diamond, or simply gain wisdom, bit by bit the mud washes away. More and more our truth shines out. Our mind, heart and body reflect the unlimited possibilities of the divine.

Life shows us where we have "bought" limited human thinking. Are there people we haven't forgiven? Do we feel less love and joy than our heart yearns for? If we are not completely happy, healthy, immortal in form, with exquisite relationships, creating the life passionate to our heart, then we have stuck places to clear. Stuck places are things we haven't completely forgiven. To clear means to release, quickly or gradually, these places from all levels of being.

Borrowing from *Living Mastery,* the first book of this set, here are possible stuck places to clear:

☆ Powerful, terrifying emotion (trauma)

☆ Lasting circumstances, like growing up in poverty

☆ Situations of the moment

☆ Beliefs, especially believing limitation is real

☆ Relationships

Readiness to clear unfolds organically; it cannot be rushed. Closeness with our inner self gives us strength to face—and love—our stuck places.

Clearing becomes a process of conscious evolution. Unresolved issues from the past appear as situations in life, or emotions arising for no apparent reason, so that all may be cleared.

Elements that assist clearing:

☆ You desire to clear.

☆ You intend to clear.

☆ You are willing to love all you find within yourself.

☆ You are willing to release the past (to forgive).

☆ You are willing for your life to change more quickly.

☆ You focus upon spirit to assist your clearing.

☆ You harness passionate emotion, both in releasing and affirming the new.

☆ You are willing to re-define yourself in new and positive terms.

☆ You replace the vacuum of something released with your new truth.

☆ You have patience, discipline and perseverance in creating the new; you choose it again and again.

☆ When you are ready, you rise above—transcend—the old, to the place in you where it has never existed.

Above all love yourself, nurture yourself, be patient and kind with yourself, and flow with your own path. Perfectionism and pushing yourself are simply more to release.

God in the Belly

A master's presence, whether in person or in a picture, radiates a serenity that encompasses the whole being.

Most of us, myself included, have felt serene from the chest up. We have largely suppressed or denied pain, fear, sorrow, anger and confusion that reside in our lower three chakras. We have feared these feelings and judged them unspiritual and unworthy of allowance.

I once had a hidden fear: if I truly felt my sorrow and hopelessness, I would fall into them and be lost forever. But when I dived all the way down into these depths, and breathed in them and was simply aware, I realized there was nowhere to be lost. My fear had no basis.

Here is a way to look at the relationship between differing aspects of self:

The head is Father, the mind, light, heaven. The heart is the Christ within—our own individuation of God/Goddess' only begotten Son/Daughter. Our lower three chakras are Mother, earth, feeling, darkness. Darkness in this sense does not mean difficulty or pain but rather the sacred womb of creation, the void from which all springs. The lower three chakras can also be called our human self, which is on earth and full of feeling.

Both Father and Mother, mind and feeling, darkness and light, heaven and earth are needed for creation to happen, for life to exist. Both are needed for *us* to exist.

The heart, the Christ within, is the savior of our human self. It is here to heal our sins. Sin here means separation; sin is our error in believing we are separate from divinity.

When we judge ourselves or our thoughts, feelings, actions or non-actions, an extraordinary thing happens. We replace the all-loving Christ with Jehovah, the angry and judgmental God. Jehovah is also the ego. *We betray ourselves;* we separate our different aspects one from another. This self-betrayal manifests in life as situations or people who abandon or "betray" us.

The Christ loves everything about us unconditionally. It does not fear or deny any of it. When our anger, for instance, can feel that it is loved and accepted, the energy falls out of it. It transforms into love itself. It then takes its place as a *realized* part of divinity.

It is time to recognize judgment of anything about ourselves as part of the problem, not the solution. To go into light—to ascend—by trying to leave judged areas behind does not work. We have descended into a body on earth for a purpose: to experience and love *everything* as divine. The divine includes not only all our emotions, but our body as well. The integration of the dark and light within us is part of our ascension path. Indeed, it *is* our ascension path.

We have all we need to recognize the divinity of our entire being. The Christ we are is fearless and totally loving. It already loves all that we are. When we stay tuned to this love which is the greatest truth of our being, and send love down to God in our belly, we are well on our way to mastery.

The initiations below offer a good number of choices in what and how you clear. Certain elements, such as forgiveness and self-empowerment, are common to many of them. I have fought a desire to be more concise, because each initiation has a unique slant for particular clearing.

So here we go. As always, do what feels right to you and follow your wisdom throughout.

Accepting Change

When you make a pivotal inner turn such as these initiations foster, it's likely you will create major shifts in your life. You may outgrow a relationship, for instance, and move to a time of solitude.

Also, your life may change around you. One woman took a huge step in consciousness one evening. She walked into her office next morning and was fired on the spot!

The problem is, change is a most challenging dynamic. Long after we're dead tired of an outworn way of being or an insufferable situation; after we've declared our intention to change; after we've taken steps to change; it can be a mind-boggling discovery that something inside is keeping a drowning man's grip on the old way.

The fear of change is deeply rooted in humanity, largely as a survival fear or fear of death. We may not be aware of this fear, but it is almost always present. If we are to live a full life, it needs to be overcome.

If you are taking one step forward and two back in an area of desired change; if you're procrastinating; if you're saying one thing and doing another; if in spite of all your efforts little is happening; you are almost certainly in fear of change. Here is an initiation to help release this fear.

Initiation

Settle back comfortably in your chair, and attune to your spirit.

Think of this change you want which is eluding you. Now give the gift of it to yourself. Immerse yourself in it. See yourself enjoying it to the full.

Do you notice fear? Where is it? Ask:

What will happen if I allow this change? What is the danger?

Listen closely and deeply to yourself. Pictures may arise, or words or other emotions. Become as clear as you can about the holdup. Staying attuned to the love in your heart, if possible, feel the emotions and be with them. Breathe with them. Do not get caught in thoughts and reactions about them; just be with them. If you cry or rage, so be it; be a witness to it. A witness is calm and in a sense detached. If you can, also love the difficult thoughts and emotions. You may need to work with this more than once. But there will come a point where the emotion fades of its own accord and you will be there, calm and whole and at peace.

Here are statements to help the process along:

I am safe to change in every way that serves my expansion. My spirit, and my true friends, support my changes. I attract to myself people who have made the changes I am making, and enjoy empowering me to do the same. I am loved as I move in new directions and leave old ways behind. My life is harmonious. I know that whatever I leave behind is replaced by something better. So be it.

You may choose to refer often to these words as you move through the initiations.

Dear Ego, Come In from the Cold

In relation to other people: if you feel better or less than; if you judge, fight with, compete with, try to please, feel afraid of, feel arrogant, obligated, or hard-hearted toward, feel victimized by another person, that is ego. It is wise to note that any self-judgment, guilt, or feeling of unworthiness is also ego.

Ego, believing in separation from God and other people, is invested in keeping us in that illusion. Moving into oneness is a change so deep that ego couldn't recognize itself. This would mean its "death."

Many of us have declared ego the enemy, and fight it. This is a separative tactic that simply strengthens it. Ego has done its best with what it has understood. It has served us well. It deserves our love; that may be the only way it can transform into enlightened energy.

Here are things you can say to your ego when it is being inappropriate:

My beloved ego, hello! I love you.

For a long time I believed I was separate from God. I thought I needed defense against others. Thank you for wanting to defend me.

Now I have realized I am part of the divine, one with spirit and one with everything and everyone. Spirit is so wonderful! It is all-loving, all-knowing, all-powerful, a great will-to-good for me and for everyone.

Spirit is our source, our very being. Without it we would not have a body, we wouldn't have awareness, we couldn't think or feel or see or hear. It is spirit that does the trillions of transactions every second between the cells of our body, and keeps it living. Without spirit there would be no creation whatsoever—no earth, no people, no trees or plants or animals. It is the isness of all existence.

Spirit is joy, abundance, light, ease, freedom! It is everywhere, as everything. To be one with this is the most wondrous way things could be.

We are individual too, because that's how God expresses in creation. Feeling one with spirit, we never lose our individuality. In fact, our uniqueness is enhanced as we express our divinity. There is no need to fear divine power, because we are that power, part of it. Power and love, love and power are one.

I invite you to come in from the cold. We don't need defense any longer. We are safe in oneness. It's our only real safety because oneness is the truth. We are totally loved, protected and cared for by spirit. You can relax now, and be in joy, because your job is complete. You can feel warm and happy and loved. You can have fun! I love you. Come on in and be part of things.

Notice how your ego responds. Does it feel ready to do what you ask? It may greet this message with suspicion, especially at first. If so, love it as it is. But persist. It will come in from the cold.

Clear Karma

This whole chapter is about clearing difficult karma, the stuck and unhappy energies of the past. Karma we are ready to release and transform may be cleared by commanding that this be done.

Go into a quiet space and call your spirit, a favorite master or other guide. Become aware of your desire and intention to let go of anything that no longer serves you, is no longer "yours." Say with power and conviction:

I command to be removed from me now any karma I am ready to release, any karma I am ready to transform. (Now breathe, deeply and freely, and send this karma up to your spirit through your out-breath.) *Any karma I am not ready to release, I ask assistance to do this in all harmony and speed. I choose to be completely clear of karma. So be it!*

Remind yourself over the next weeks that you've done this. Take some time to feel and own it.

The Magnificent Violet Flame

The violet flame is a forgiving and purifying energy from spirit. You can lighten any problem with it, or completely clear whatever is ready. It is especially effective when you feel passionate about clearing. I also call other flames at the same time: the blue flame of Archangel Michael, the rose flame of Divine Mother, the golden flame of my own divinity, and the diamond flame of Mother/Father God. It is excellent to use the violet flame frequently, even daily, to stay clear.

Bring to mind an issue you want to clear, or a general clearing of everything that no longer serves you. Intend to clear from your entire being: subconscious mind where all past life and other buried memories are stored; emotions, mind, physical body, and aura. Intend that all the clearing you can handle takes place today.

Call in, if you wish, Archangel Zadkiel (who gave the violet flame) or the ascended master St. Germain (its strongest activator), or simply call the violet flame from within your own heart and spirit.

See the flame rise from the center of the earth in a great blaze of powerful energy and intention. Let it blaze through every level of your consciousness! Breathe! See it, feel it! See it rise a mile and more into the sky. Consciously give up limitations to be dissolved in the flame! Form an energy ball of them in your hands before you, lift this ball until it gets above your head, then swoosh your hands out and up, letting go with great out-breaths. Intend to be free! If you are releasing a pattern, say these statements with feeling:

I now let go of all causes of this pattern. I let go of all memories, of this and any life, associated with it. I let go of all limited thought around it. I let go of old emotions about it. I let it go from the cells of my body. I release it from my aura. I have released all I can at this moment. I forgive myself. I forgive all. I am free! I am clear!

Now, take a look. Is there something more to do? The first clearing may not be complete, or it may have uncovered the need for another. If so, and you are ready, work with that.

Finally, choose what you want. See it, feel it, *be* it. Your new reality is like a little seed wanting to grow. If you go back to the old thoughts, it will perish. It needs nourishing, watering, the light of your love and attention. Also be patient—there may be deep reasons for changing an old pattern gently, step by step. Let yourself unfold.

The Rebirthing Breath Initiation

The rebirthing movement was inspired by Herakhan Babaji (see the pictures in the back of the book) and discovered in the 1970s by the founder of the movement, Leonard Orr. Rebirthing is more aptly called "conscious breathing," because while it was first conceived as clearing birth trauma (see below), it is one of the most powerful means of clearing anything. In a mysterious way, the rebirthing breath creates a bridge between mind, body and spirit so strong that you experience wholeness.

Rebirthing is a way of breathing that dovetails the inhale with the exhale, the exhale with the inhale, so there is no pause whatever between breaths. You breathe through your nose, as that more deeply benefits your nervous system and thus your whole being. The breathing is energetic but not forced, with particular focus upon a relaxed exhale. It seems vital to breathe into the chest, the area of the heart, where we armor against painful emotion. It can also be helpful to breathe into other chakra centers.

The idea is simply to breathe, and accept whatever you notice. If difficult feeling comes up, don't get stuck in it; breathe *through* it. When strong emotion is present, breathe through your mouth awhile. Cry for a bit if crying is a release; then begin breathing again through your nose. If your nose gets stopped up, it's okay to breathe through your mouth.

A rebirthing is a cycle of energy usually lasting forty-five minutes to something over an hour. At the end of the session one is almost always in profound joy, even bliss.

"Rebirthers" have been trained to facilitate a rebirthing by "holding the space" for clearing and transformation (and keeping the breather awake if need be!). The breather and rebirther together create an exponential power and intention for good. But if you've had some sessions—or even if you haven't—you may benefit by breathing on your own.

From my first rebirthing sessions under Leonard's tutelage, I felt my "solid" problems become transparent. Also, one day I suddenly began to breathe out ether. I had heard of anesthesia lodging in the body and then exiting through rebirthing, and gave it no thought. But here it was, unmistakable! It had to have come from my tonsillectomy when I was six years old.

Rebirthing can be a powerful force in physical healing, as well. I used to lead group rebirthing sessions in my workshops. Once a woman with a sprained leg muscle came in on crutches and left without need of them. Another had a malformation of the vertebrae in her neck. The evening after the rebirthing she was at a party and her chiropractor came up to her. "It's time for another neck treatment," he said. "Feel it," she replied. Amazed, he said, "The problem is gone!"

There are many offshoots of rebirthing now, such as Holotrophic Breathing which is done with music, and they are probably all good. I would just be alert about rigid rules with any of them, as there are no rules about what works best with each breather.

To experience rebirthing, look in any new age publication for rebirthers.

The Power of Forgiveness

Innocence I Am

Think of one incident in which you did or said something you afterward regretted and blamed yourself for. Go into a quiet space. Call your spirit.

Think about the time leading up to this incident that had a bearing on what happened, be it years, weeks or moments beforehand. How were you thinking? What were you feeling?

Now think of the moments just before this took place. What was happening? How were you thinking and feeling? Let this lead into the incident itself. See if you can realize that *at that moment, you did not truly feel another choice. You did your best.* Even if what you did was the result of a considered decision on your part, feel that the choice you made was your best at the time. Really feel this, really *know* it. Take time here.

Finally, forgive yourself. Ask yourself, What was I trying to teach myself here? Have I learned it? Can I learn this more deeply now?

Contemplate, and be honest with yourself. One thing you were teaching yourself is that judging yourself or another isn't happy. What else is there?

If you need to forgive others, or the incident or situation, forgive now to the best of your ability.

Now you are prepared for the deeper work below.

As you say these or similar words, pause often to feel, breathe, release, and forgive specific things you have held against yourself. Remember, forgiveness comes from your heart. It is an *emotional* release. *Breathe* through it.

Complete forgiveness will probably happen over time; if it feels beneficial, schedule this process for a few times a year, once a month, once a week, as feels right for you.

Here are the statements:

I Am created the very essence of God/Goddess. I Am guiltless and free of sin, innocent forever and forever. (Feel, breathe! Release on the outbreath!) *Nothing I have ever done, said, felt, thought, or seemingly failed to do has ever changed my essential innocence. I have always done my best in the moment with what I have truly learned, and I always will. I have never harmed the inner being of another, for that is inviolate.*

When I know my innocence, I cannot blame. When I have fully forgiven myself, I have forgiven everything.

I forgive myself for doubting God and doubting myself.

I forgive myself for causing my mother trouble during my infancy and childhood. (If your mother or other family member became ill or died, or your parents got divorced, forgive yourself—we usually blame ourselves for such things.) *I forgive myself for _____ .*

I forgive myself for anything I have done that hurt someone's feelings, body or life. (Think of specific people. Feel, breathe, release!) *I forgive words I have spoken in anger. I forgive myself for untrue words. I forgive myself for blaming, and for holding resentments. I forgive myself for any fears I have felt. I forgive myself for attachments that have clouded my experience of spirit. I forgive myself for the times I have allowed my ego to run things. I forgive myself for anything less than one hundred percent commitment to myself, my life, and those around me. I forgive myself now, as deeply and completely as I can.* (Add anything you choose.)

I begin to see myself in the light of love and innocence and divinity, as I Am. I begin to see all others in this same light. Everyone and everything my eyes light upon is blessed, and blesses me. I live in a forgiven world, where all is well. There is nothing to fear. I love this oneness. The world is at peace because peace is in my heart. I live in heaven on earth. So be it.

As an "innocence test," see if you can feel the oneness of these twosomes in your heart:

☆   Innocence and me
☆   Innocence and wealth; innocence and money
☆   Innocence and strength; innocence and power
☆   Innocence and sex
☆   Innocence and joyous freedom; innocence and ease
☆   Innocence and beauty
☆   Innocence and fame

Of the following pairs, we are not talking about anyone being a victim; someone who is harming the lives of others should be stopped. We are talking about the essential *being* of each person. A challenge! Can you do it? Think in terms of individuals. See a boy's innocent babyhood; imagine what caused him to turn to such activities.

☆   Criminal and innocence
☆   Murderer and innocence
☆   Drug pusher and innocence
☆   Politician on the take and innocence
☆   Corrupt cop and innocence
☆   Nazi and innocence; Hitler and innocence
☆   Rapist and innocence

All blessings in recognizing your essential innocence, and in forgiving yourself and others.

Co-Creators We Are

If you find yourself in a confusing situation, or you are blaming someone or something, these statements are powerful. Call your spirit and focus inwardly upon the person or situation. When you are fully focused, say these words and take time to feel them:

You and I are one. I and this situation are one. We have co-created it together for self-discovery. I become aware of love and of what needs love. Thank you for assisting my growth. I am willing to grow. I accept you where you are, and forgive you. I bless this. I learn from it. With its help I move into a new consciousness.

Clear Fear-Based Energy

Break the Loop

It is one thing—a very good thing—that we learn what wants clearing and get on with it. It is another thing for this to actually work.

On the clearing path, what waylays most of us is becoming so mesmerized—like a mouse with a cobra—by the memory of a particularly traumatic event or series of events, such as molestation, abuse, or violence, that we start running around in circles. It becomes our story. We focus on it, talk about it, chew it to pieces, define ourselves by it even as we are "working to clear" it. Did you ever meet someone and learn all about their trauma in the first five minutes?

It is not that clearing isn't a serious activity, worthy of honor. But over-seriousness often takes over, and this kind of loop may result. Oops! Here are my own tracks—I've made another circle!

I once led a session with a woman who was greatly concerned about poisonous residues in well water she had drunk, years earlier. We discovered that she had actually been *creating the poisons in her body!* That is the power of our mind to create whatever is being focused upon. In this case, her mind instructed her body's chemist to manufacture the poisons in obedience to her "command:" her belief that they remained.

Why do we do this? Often we believe the earlier event is continuing to harm us. And thus, it is. Or we fear it will be repeated, and act as if it *were* a cobra which can be kept from striking if we just keep looking at it. In either case, though the event(s) is in the past, we are back there with it. And so is part of our energy.

Another possibility regarding focusing upon an old trauma is that we have come to thrive upon the drama of it. It can be quite handy for getting attention or manipulating others if they feel sorry for us.

How can we release what we are constantly dwelling upon, talking about, and feeling bad about? It is futile as Lady MacBeth crying "Out, damned spot!"

To create a life of joy, we forget and forgive our past and focus upon our heart's desires. These are the fertile ground for a full, creative, happy, powerful life.

The kind of loop which is based upon a particular difficulty we will call a Specific Loop.

There is another kind of loop: the biggest, most dangerous, and hardest to see. It is unconscious negativity—expecting life to be difficult and thus continually creating it so, not realizing we are doing it. This comes most often from family and social conditioning, but can be from difficulties either conscious or buried. We'll call this a General Loop.

This initiation is to break the loop: awaken from self-hypnosis so we can really clear a hard thing or the habit of negativity, and move on.

If you have already realized that you are in a loop, and are determined to break free, skip to the Initiation below.

If you are wondering whether or not you're in a loop, think over recent conversations. (You might record some of these on a pocket recorder.) What did you talk about? Were you sharing a wonderful development in your life, or something you were looking forward to? Were you complaining about how bad things were?

If the latter has predominance, look at this now. What were you saying, exactly? Jot down a few things. You may want to take a few days or weeks for this. Really become aware of your habits of thought and speech.

How do you feel about patterns you see? Do you choose to change? If not that's fine; skip the initiation below. If you feel a deep despair or boredom with the old ways, let these emotions come forward. Let them assist your choice for change.

Once you feel clearly determined to make a change, here you go!

Initiation

Go into a quiet, private space and call your spirit. Breathe deeply and freely for awhile. Feel your determination and choice for a new way. Ask for help from your spirit to make this change. Be open to a message, feeling, knowing, or pictures from within you.

If the loop you've been in is a General Loop, skip down to the words beginning *I now break the loop of negativity* and say these silently or aloud. For a Specific Loop, here are statements you can use or change as right for you. Take time to feel each statement you choose, and breathe with it:

When this happened, I felt powerless. I love myself that that I felt so thrown by it. I love myself that I continued to think I was being harmed. I love myself that I was trying to protect myself, and keep it from happening again, by focusing upon it. I love myself that I loved drama, attention or manipulation.

I realize, deeply, that I am different now. I am no longer powerless; I am powerful. Nothing can cause me to lose my power, ever again. I have grown beyond that situation. There is no reason for it to be repeated. It is in the past, and I am in the present. If it ever were repeated, I would handle it.

I choose to break the loop! I cut the cord with this event or series of events, or this situation. I disconnect from it. I no longer define myself by it. It is gone, and I do not create it anew. I give the memory no power. I bring my energy back now to the present. So be it.

(If you've been in a General Loop, join in here:)

I now break the loop of negativity. I am not now and never have been a victim. I've created my life from my beliefs. I choose to forgive and forget.

I choose a positive, joyful, creative, effective life. I choose to focus on and expect the good in life, one with the divinity I am. I choose to speak positively about my life, and about others' lives. I choose to love and honor, as best I can, myself and others. I choose to encourage myself to know I can do, be and have anything that is my heart's desire. I choose to encourage others as well.

I am patient with myself and others in making this shift. I do my best each day, and know I am expanding into oneness with my spirit.

If big changes happen in my life, I welcome them because it demonstrates that I am truly changing from within. I know that anything that leaves my life is being replaced with something better for me and for everyone. So be it.

Now, you will probably want to decide on specific changes in your way of speaking and thinking, your relationship with yourself and others, and other changes. It helps to write these down. You may choose a 40-Day Process (see the chapter "Empower Yourself"), setting certain goals and manifesting them.

Your spirit may also show you a life shift now, or something else pertinent to your decision.

If yours has been a great trauma, you may do the Trauma or Past Life Clearing initiation below to clear the trauma still more deeply. But you have broken the loop! Congratulations!

Clear your Birth

Most of us had traumatic births, even if everything "went fine" according to the medical staff. There are many variables: not being wanted in the first place (and perhaps abortion attempts made); our mother being "out," not able to help us make the transition from her soft womb into the world; knowing we were causing our mother pain; the umbilical cord wrapping around our neck; entering a cold, blinding and deafening hospital room; knowing our parents wanted a certain sex child and we were the other; being hurt or damaged by forceps; having the cord cut before we were able to breathe; our first breath taken in pain and fear as we were slapped; many of us being premature, whisked away from our mothers (I was taken away from my mother for the first twenty-four hours because it was the *custom*); being born to a mother on alcohol or drugs; our mother died giving birth to us; not being recognized as a divine one being born; and more. Any of these could give the psyche a painful wound, and virtually all of us experienced a number of them.

The infant we were, a great being in a helpless, tiny body, had no words and no defense. The terrifying experiences of birth are usually frozen into our psyches. Often we feel unworthy, or angry with ourselves for being alive. These feelings are so deep that we rarely become aware of them.

How to clear these things? It is usually a long process that gets clearer through the years. Here are suggestions:

1. Ask your spirit to help you remember your birth, or remember it more clearly. Memory often comes piecemeal. See if you can remember some of your feelings. A rebirthing session can help you remember, or help you clear what you remember (see above).

2. Forgive yourself if need be; self-blame for birth trauma is illogical, but common all the same. Remember to breathe and release. Here are words of self-forgiveness:

   I forgive myself for causing my mother pain. I forgive myself if my mother died giving birth to me. I forgive myself if I wasn't wanted. I forgive myself if a different sex child was wanted. I forgive myself for being here. I release all anger and blame toward myself for being alive. As part of the divine, I am innocent forever. I am loved. I choose to love myself.

Add anything you choose.

3. Forgive all others (and breathe!):

   Though the divine being I am was not recognized at my birth, I know now that I am part of the divine. I am powerful now, and I can forgive.

I forgive my mother for not wanting me, trying to abort me, or wanting a different sex child. I forgive my father for anything I have held against him. I forgive doctors, nurses, and everyone who was present. I know all were doing their best with what they knew.

I, in the full divinity I Am, now choose to release the fears from my birth which have kept me from being fully alive in the present. I will succeed. I will bring all my energies into now! So be it.

4. Use any other initiation you are guided to: trauma clearing, violet flame or anything else.

5. Create a new birth for yourself, the birth of your heart's desire. This will literally change the past. You may be your own midwife, or designate a trusted friend or master. Here is a possible scenario; change it as you choose.

The space for your ideal birth is warm and softly lit. Lovely music fills the air, and people are speaking in soft tones. Just the people you choose are there, lovingly supporting your mother and awaiting your arrival.

A divine being is coming to earth! Everyone is thrilled that you are being born, especially your mother.

A water birth is planned. You will enter the world into water that is the exact temperature of your body.

Be with yourself in the birth canal, stroking, loving and encouraging yourself. Correct any difficulty with the birth position or the umbilical cord. Magically expand the birth canal so that your mother is comfortable and relaxed. When you are ready, take yourself through the gateway to your new life! As you emerge into the world, each person greets you in great joy—often to see you again.

In the comfort of the water, you rest quietly from the intensity of your passage. When you are ready, lift yourself from the water and gently clear your breathing passages. After your first breaths, cut the cord. Place yourself on the outside of your mother's womb, her arms wrapped lovingly around you. She draws you to her breast to suckle her warm, sweet milk.

You immerse yourself in this environment of safety, love and welcome. You know all is well. You know this life will be a happy one, and a great step in your reunion with God.

You may want to re-experience your ideal birth many times to make it your memory, your history.

Now you may say:

I love myself. I love the infant I am. I love myself for being. I am worthy to be here, to be alive. I am a great and wonderful, divine being. The world is not complete without me, and I am welcome here! In a great new way, I welcome myself to life! So be it!

Feeling, I Embrace You

Neither a thought of limitation, nor the feeling such as fear which accompanies it, are based upon reality. They are like a dragon mask. When we dive deeply enough into such a thought-feeling, it gradually transforms—often through a number of metamorphoses—into an unlimited thought and its accompanying feeling of love, joy, freedom or the like.

Go into a quiet space within yourself and call your spirit. Relax your body and mind, and begin to breathe deeply.

Locate a feeling and its accompanying thought that you have a hard time with. Possibilities are fear of someone or something known or unknown; anger or resentment, loneliness, confusion, or feeling victimized. If you associate this feeling with a situation, don't bring the story in. Focus only upon your feeling, and welcome it. Let it come in. Find it. Where is it in your body?

Look into this feeling. Feel it. If your mind wanders—a big temptation here—just bring it back. Explore it. If the feeling jumps around in your body, follow it. You may see pictures from childhood, infancy or a past life which give a deeper cause for the feeling. *Breathe, breathe deeply!* What is the thought within this feeling?

Welcoming your feeling will begin to transform it—but maybe not yet into something wonderful. Feelings are often multi-layered; you may move from anger, for instance, to sorrow or fear that lie beneath it. This is excellent! You are moving!

Deep attention to your feeling is love. If you can love it more, do that now. Picture it and put your arms around it. See it fill with light, perhaps a pink light or flame of love. When you really love it, your feeling will begin to transform.

Do you need to forgive? Begin that now.

Now love yourself for feeling this way. You chose it to teach yourself something. You deserve only love, understanding and forgiveness in feeling it. If this is hard, just do your best. Cross your palms over your heart and rock gently.

Finally, affirm truth about this feeling. Is it one of these?

I Am divine god-goddess I Am.

I am loved, infinitely and eternally loved.

I am protected everywhere, all the time.

I am always in power and choice.

I am infinitely abundant. God is my ever-present source.

I am the peace, the love, the joy, the clarity, the knowing, the power, the wisdom, the light, the oneness, the freedom of my divinity.

Don't underestimate this simple process. It can bring profound transformation. Loving everything within and about you is a freeway to enlightenment. As you feel and love difficult feelings, they will gradually transmute into the joyous feelings of your divine nature.

What Haven't You Said?

We come into life on earth with the memory of the celestial realm we left behind. Life there resonates with truth, because the divine is recognized as all there is.

Earth life is largely a denial of this prime truth. Even belief in God is fraught with limitation because of humanity's distorted definition of itself and of God. So here we are as little tiny children, knowing the truth and seeing it denied all around us. At first we can't speak, and when we can we feel unsafe to speak truth in the teeth of the heavy beliefs operating around us.

In the ups and downs of human relationships, especially with people in authority over our young lives, there come many times when we feel unable to speak or to express our feelings.

Uncommunicated words and feelings clog our energies. They lodge in our throat, chest, or another area of the body. They can pull our shoulders forward, cave in our chest, put a frog or stronger blocks in our throat. When blocks are present, anything we speak has to go around them to get out.

It is a great gift to discover what hasn't been expressed and let it out! We keep our expression safe for ourselves and others, such as doing it alone. And as no one is to blame, we also do it responsibly.

With the help of a healer friend, I discovered that I had a wad of unexpressed stuff around my throat. When I looked at that in meditation, I suddenly found myself yelling at the top of my voice, "Don't you know that God is *real*? You ignoramuses!" Enlightened communication it wasn't, but yelling got it out of my throat and unstuck my energies.

I realized there was more to let go, and got busy discovering it all. What a relief! I feel that virtually all of us need this release.

Get to a place where you can yell if need be. Go into meditation and tune with your spirit. Ask the question:

What haven't I said that I need to say? What feelings do I need to express?

Then wait, patiently; these things have been buried since childhood or longer and may need time to come to the surface. If it doesn't work today, come back to it.

When things come up, let yourself express them as you do. You may rage or cry, beat a pillow, speak or yell—all is good! Notice how your freedom opens up as you let these old energies out! Some statements:

I discover everything I need to say and haven't said. I say them! I discover all the feelings I need to express. I express them! My energies are freed! I am joyously alive this moment in the fullness of my being! So be it.

Complete Your Project

This initiation is helpful when you are working to create something but find yourself stymied.

Imagine you have succeeded with this project, and it is now part of your life. See or feel it clearly.

A feeling will probably rise from deep in your psyche, fear about having this. Here is a way to get to the thought—often several big thoughts—behind your feeling, and help transform them.

Call your spirit. Connect up. Go into your feeling. Again, where is it in your body? How exactly does it feel?

Ask it, *What would you like to tell me?* Be open to any answer from your feeling-voice, no matter how illogical it may appear to your mind. Honoring the answer is vital to the process.

Your voice may tell you a number of things, such as "This is impossible. You're just fooling yourself. It will never happen! You'll fail and then you'll be devastated! Besides, it's wrong to have so much good. And it isn't safe to have that much power." Accept calmly whatever you hear, and write it down.

When your voice stops, go deeper. For instance, if it said your project is impossible, ask why. You may hear something like, "Because life just isn't that wonderful!" You'll want also to address such beliefs. Try to discover all major thoughts within the feeling.

These emotions and thoughts are here for a good purpose. They think they are protecting you from punishment, being unloved, dying, or the like.

Ask your feeling, *What is your purpose here? How are you serving me?* Again, listen with an open mind.

Whether or not you have discovered its service, take the next step: *What do I want to learn here?* If you learn that you fear being powerful, for instance, your self-honesty becomes a force for clearing.

When you understand your limiting thoughts and feelings on this project, say to them:

I love and accept you. You are an old thought-feeling, based on limitation. That is okay.

I choose to move into the divinity which is my truth. I am unlimited. I can do, be, and have anything I choose. I am able to complete this project.

Now invite your feeling-voice to respond. It believed your project was a danger to you. Dialogue as long as "both of you" seem to be getting somewhere. Then ask, *Are you willing to help me have what I choose?* Don't insist that it change on the spot; give it time to absorb what you are saying and change of its own accord. Continue each day to feel your project is complete. You may do a 40-Day Process to bring it to success. Take the necessary steps to secure your goal. Your old thoughts and feelings may continue to arise; talk with them when you feel prompted.

With this kind of dialogue, you gradually align all aspects of yourself with having and accomplishing the passions of your heart.

Hey, Magical Child!

Much of the pain we are clearing comes from the children and infants we have been in many lives. The composite of these children we'll simply call our child. It has numerous sides and personality traits.

Our child often feels it cannot speak. Usually, it doesn't feel safe to speak because it doesn't feel valued. Creating an honest relationship with it is usually up to "us," the adult. The pain of the child may be difficult to face, but wonderful gifts flow from clearing it.

Go to a quiet space within. Make up a name for your child, either one you were called or another that feels better. Call him or her to you. Say:

I love you so much. You're part of me, and I value you greatly. I need you. I need your passion and aliveness. I need your honesty. I need your joy! I need to know any pain you feel so we can both be happier. I need your creativity and I need to play! Will you come?

Just be there, patiently, and see what happens. You may not hear any words, but eventually you will get a feeling you can recognize as from your child. Ask what it would like to tell you, in feelings or words or pictures.

If your child is in pain, love it and embrace it in your heart. Does it want help to clear something? If so, begin to assist with that. To forgive, the child often needs the Come Even process (see the relationships chapter).

If your child yearns for joy and adventure, honor this communication. Joy and adventure are a *need* in life, not just a luxury. What have you always wanted to do that you haven't done? Who would love to come with you? Make plans, and stick to them!

What else is your child telling you? Listen, honor and follow up.

Ask if your child would like to spend time with a master or angel you love. It will probably say Yes! Call this being to you. Your child may jump into his or her arms and stay a long time.

Ask your child what it wants, and what it wants to do—frequently. If you're particularly busy for awhile and know you're ignoring this beautiful and important part of yourself, make amends:

I know I haven't given you much attention lately, so tomorrow I'm setting aside time for fun. You're the leader! What shall we do?

May the magical gifts of your magical child blossom into fullness, infusing your life with magic.

Elementals

Thinking something creates an energy or thought form, also called an elemental. Take, for example, the thought, *I lack money.* The longer you think lack, the stronger your lack elemental becomes. It actually takes on a life of its own. It is invested in *staying* alive by your continuing to think you lack money.

Elementals have a cyclic nature. They seem to disappear for a while, and just when you think they're gone, bam! they're in your face again, creating something weird.

When you recognize a limiting pattern, realize that the elementals you've created are with you, keeping that pattern in place.

Call in your spirit and connect with it. Say in no uncertain terms:

All elementals connected with this pattern are now dissolved in the Light and the Love of Truth! So be it! Repeat as necessary, until you feel complete.

Don't be discouraged if you feel the pattern come around again. This is out of habit. It will become weaker every time you do this release.

What thoughts do you now choose? Write them down. Begin to think and feel them.

When you catch yourself in the old thought, don't react. Don't judge either yourself or the thought. Simply change it to the new thought. The old one will be more and more easy to catch. You are beginning to support the emergence of a new, unlimited pattern.

Nurture your new pattern for at least six weeks.

If this work brings up deeper issues that are still stuck, use an initiation geared to clear them.

Persistence cannot be over-estimated! If you persist, you will eventually succeed.

Trauma or Past Life Clearing

A trauma is your crystallized reaction to a difficult event of this life or another. It's usually something that happened to you, or someone "did to you." It can also be something you did to another, for which you may feel guilt and fear of power.

Throughout many lifetimes we've played the roles of both victim and perpetrator. We've been both abused and abuser. If one has played only the victim role, it seems to make clearing more difficult. At least in being the doer rather than the done-unto, one feels some power.

Until a trauma is cleared from your psyche, it runs you. It also leaves energy stuck in the past, unavailable for life.

If the trauma is from a past life, a general idea of what happened, once or serially, is a big help. If you're aware of a strong fear but don't know the cause, see if you can discover what it's about. You may need help from a good practitioner. Since you're feeling it, you're probably ready to deal with it. If you already know what the trauma is, you're ready to begin.

Here is a process to clear a trauma from any life:

Go into meditation. Ask your inner self to assist, protect and love you while you are clearing. Feel this connection.

Realize that from some level you chose, or at least allowed, this event. Though you felt so, you were not in truth disempowered.

I, _____, know that I was in my power and choice to experience this event.

Now, forgive yourself as deeply as you can for inviting or allowing it:

I forgive myself for allowing or creating it. Take time with this, forgiving from your heart.

Next, make a declaration that you will never create this situation or event again. Stand up, plant your feet hip-width apart, unlock your knees, and speak passionately. Say:

I have grown beyond this experience. I never choose it again. It will never happen again. I am free of it forever! So be it!

If you have feared that the trauma will happen again—which most of us have—an odd logic takes place. Holding blame against others feels like protection. When you declare an end to trauma, it assists your forgiveness of all involved.

Before you can forgive those who "did you wrong," you may need to do a Come Even process (relationships chapter). Also, you may want stronger certainty that you are protected. The Invincible Protection initiation is below if you'd like to do that now.

Recognize that others did their best in the situation. If they were cruel, they were learning that cruelty isn't enjoyable and that it comes back to them. You were learning to protect yourself psychically or physically. You were helping one another, *in love* on your deepest levels, to grow in wisdom.

When you feel clear about this, take time to forgive them. Again, forgive from your heart. This may be a layer process; some traumas are really deep.

I now forgive all others involved. I know they did the best they knew. I helped them learn and grow, and they helped me as well.

Finally, see what it is you were choosing to learn. Feel deeply into the whole event, and understand it. Learn from it now, or learn more deeply:

I learn now what I wanted to learn then. My learning is _____. I accept it.

I am completely done with this old event or situation. I am not subject to any repetition of it whatsoever. I am more powerful now. I am wiser.

I retrieve my energy that was stuck in the past. I bring it now fully into the present. So be it.

As the days go by, see how your release and learning affect your life. What changes do you notice? Nurture these changes. You may say:

I replace what I have released with positive new ways. I know what I choose to create in my life. I am creating it! So be it.

Spiritual Teacher's Special

This clearing is dear to my heart. I very much needed it in the beginning of my spiritual work, but I had no idea *what* was needed, let alone how to do it. I gradually came to see all the terrible stuff I'd been through in former lives as a spiritual teacher, and was able to clear and forgive. Because I've completed this for myself, I've been able to serve many others with it.

If you feel you have a spiritual mission of some kind but you haven't seen it, haven't begun it or haven't allowed it to blossom, this clearing is probably for you. It is the same as the one above, except for specifics.

If you are aware of past life traumas as a teacher, you're ready to begin. If you aren't, connect with your spirit. Ask:

Have I been a spiritual teacher in the past?

If yes: *Did I experience trauma in this role?*

If yes: *Please show me what I am ready to clear.*

Hold on to your hat, because what you see will probably shock you. When you understand what to clear, proceed with the Trauma or Past Life Clearing above. Recognize your power to create, forgive yourself and all others involved. To close:

I recognize that you, my co-creators in this event, felt afraid to hear my truth at that time, and reacted out of fear. You served me by helping me see that I was open to a difficult situation. I have expanded beyond this kind of event (or, I expand beyond it now). I served you by helping you realize that fear and violence are not joyful, and by planting in your mind a seed of greater truth. I know most of you are now more open to the truth within you, and more peaceful toward others.

*I declare for myself that I will **never** again experience abuse of any kind in sharing my truth. I have expanded into a protected, peaceful, inviolate space. I Am completely protected and safe wherever I* *share my truth. I attract to myself **only** those who desire to know what I have to share, and who appreciate and benefit from it. From this time forth I share my truth in perfect harmony, peace, joy and love with all others. So be it!*

Addiction

Realizing we are loved by that which is unseen—especially if we don't have loving relationships with people—is a great help in releasing addiction. Even one clear and loving relationship can bring release. Love can clear the cause of addiction.

Alcoholics Anonymous and other well-known groups can support you in breaking addiction. If you choose support from an individual, make it one with compassion and know-how, not an "enabler."

Conscious attention can break the back of an addiction. An addicted over-eater became fascinated with food and taste, and concentrated upon his eating. Within weeks, he left his addiction behind. Smokers may stop and write with each cigarette: What am I feeling before I smoke? What do I feel as I smoke? How does my body feel?

Drugs may be pleasurable at first and then become addictive. There is help available to de-tox and get on with life. It may be important to discover why you were vulnerable to drugs in the first place.

Serious addiction can be so all-consuming that you may need a new and positive focus to turn your life around. One possibility: discover how you can serve others, perhaps those who are wrestling with what you have overcome.

Realize why you are here: to discover and express your innate divinity.

In a nutshell, here are suggestions to break addiction:

1.   Get help from a wise, compassionate person or organization that *empowers* you.
2.   Realize the love and power of God. Know you are loved.
3.   Become conscious of your addiction process.

4. When you are ready, allow the cause of pain or self-hatred to come forward and be released.
5. Forgive yourself. Love yourself.
6. Forgive others.
7. Make amends, for the good of all.
8. Find a way to help others.
9. Recognize yourself as part of and one with the divine, all that is. Fulfill your purposes for being here.

Invincible Protection

This initiation is for physical protection. (For an initiation to clear accident karma, see the health chapter.)

Call your divine presence and/or a powerful master. Archangel Michael is a powerful protector; also Jesus, Babaji or any true master.

Stand and place your body in a powerful stance, feet hip-width apart, knees loose, spine straight, head level. Feel your divinity as a beam of golden light from above your head through all your body. Also feel connected to the core of the earth.

Envision a protective, invincible energy in a color you choose. (Archangel Michael is known for a strong electric blue.) Let this energy begin as a circular motion below your feet, spinning slowly upward to encompass your entire body and aura, and ending above your head.

Speak these words:

In the name, and by the power, of The Lord God of My Being, I declare that protection is with me from this moment and forever. I am absolutely safe at all times and all places. I am safe in all circumstances. I am safe with all people. I am safe now and forever. This protection is absolute. So be it.

Feel this protection. Get a clear sense of it. Know that it is *always* present. Remind yourself of it during the day. Call upon it in any moment of fear, and you will realize it is there.

A master you love is instantly available to protect you. Simply call, silently or aloud.

Lightworker's Syndrome

If you are helping lift humanity and the planet, you're what we call a "lightworker." Thank you!

Many lightworkers demonstrate a pattern that could benefit from some light! Here are its common threads:

☆   I take care of everyone but myself.

☆   I receive with hesitancy gifts from other people.

☆   It isn't right to rest or play—I'm carrying the burden of my service.

This syndrome usually comes from many past lives as lightworkers. We've often felt we were the only one carrying the ball, the only one caring about the state of humanity. We have often been perceived as "the strong one" by our family and others, and been expected to take care of things. In other words, we've often felt alone and burdened.

But the lightworker syndrome is simply another form of separation. If I am taking care of everyone except myself, I am feeling separate from those I care for. If I'm not open to receiving the worthy gifts of others, I have a wall up. If I can't play, I'm setting myself up as different from or better than others. And a gift from a burdened person is not the greatest gift; giving comes from an overflowing cup, not a drained one.

Initiation

Look into your thoughts and your life. Do you have Lightworker's Syndrome? If so, here are thoughts:

I recognize that now there are millions of lightworkers here, and I am re-joining my ancient spiritual family. I'm not alone any longer. I choose to form deep friendships with my peers. I choose to both give and receive freely. I choose to have fun! I relax, breathe, rest and enjoy. From my happiness, I give a much greater gift to our awakening planet. So be it.

Troubleshoot a Situation

The situation represents thoughts you have (conscious and/or unconscious) that are being mirrored back to you. It is serving you perfectly, and you are one hundred per-cent responsible for your experience of it.

When you change your thoughts, you will experience the situation differently. It will either change around you or leave your life. When you love yourself, others are more easily able to express their love for you. And when you are able to love those around you and see them as beings of love, strength, joy, freedom and light, you invite them to shift in your presence.

If there is another person in the situation who would work with you on the situation, that will increase exponentially the power for good.

First, consciously release the way it has been. No one and no situation is bound to its past. If you feel bothered by a particular individual, do a Relationship Healing from the relationships chapter.

Now, consider very deeply: what is wanted *for the good of the whole?* Be careful here!—it is all too easy for we humans to think selfishly. You may want to enlist the help of a wise and impartial friend. Put yourself in the shoes of others involved. What do they want? What would you want in their place? Are you making unfair demands? Are they? What is fair? Can you see a way to come into accord?

If it is appropriate, consider humanity and the planet as part of the situation. What is best for the greater whole?

When you have arrived at your best understanding, it is time to build the inner foundation that supports outward change. Do not underestimate the power of this inner work, no matter how complicated the situation. Miracles can happen. Miracles *do* happen.

First, forgive yourself. Love yourself. Forgive the others involved. Affirm and feel their forgiveness of you—the forgiveness from their real self, their divinity. If prayer feels right, pray about the situation.

If you choose, write a letter to the divine self of one or more involved. Write of your love and honor for them. Tell them how you feel. Ask them to fulfill their part in what is best for all. Keep this letter private.

Send your love to all others. See each person as divine. Bless each one, bless the whole situation, and surround it with light. When you are with the others, give your love silently or openly as works best.

Affirm: *Divine love fills this situation and brings it into perfect harmony now.*

See your vision—or better—of what is best for all actually happening. See understanding and love between everyone. Ask God within each of you to be in charge of making the changes.

Now, is it appropriate to say something? You will probably want to share your vision of what is best for the good of the whole, keeping aware that this is *your* vision, not the be-all and end-all. Listen and honor the thoughts of others. Is there give and take that can work for everyone? Are you able to come to a harmonious resolution?

Your words may not be what others want to hear. In some situations it is much easier to compromise and keep the peace than to stand up for what is right within your heart. Speak your truth. That invites others to share their own truth and is ultimately best for everyone. Then "divine right action" can take place.

It may be that others weren't open to your words, or talking produced no results of value. Then, act from your heart.

A vital key: do your best, and don't be attached to the results. With your intention and love, the situation will unfold as best it can given the consciousness of all involved. Even if what looks like unfairness rules the day, take responsibility for co-creation and be at peace with it.

In emotionally charged situations such as money settlements, divorce or politics, opposing demands may be too strong to allow harmony. In that case, your job is to come to harmony and forgiveness within yourself; give up demands that would compromise the integrity of another; communicate preferences aligned with your integrity; work for the good of the whole; and remain unattached to the outcome. If the situation is ongoing, it is likely you will want to go elsewhere.

Personal Un-Conditioning

Give yourself a few weeks or months to contemplate your past. Examine carefully everything you've been taught by your family, your friends, your co-workers—everything. Does this still serve you? Does that? Do you want to choose a new way? Say at any point:

My beloved family: thank you for choosing me as part of your life. Thank you for doing your best to love me and bring me up. I respect your chosen ways as right for you. I admire and keep (name the things).

I choose a new path in these ways: (Name them. For example, I choose to stop the aging process and move into rejuvenation.) *In the name and by the power of the Lord God of My Being, I will manifest as I choose. So be it.*

Of course, moving into new ways requires energy and intention. Work with the initiations as you are guided.

A New Social Agenda

Here are thoughts that counteract "normal" beliefs:

☆ *Spirit I am. Divine I am.*

☆ *I love myself. I am my own best friend.*

☆ *I invite the winds of spirit to blow through my life, bringing all the changes best for me.*

☆ *I am clearing my karma from every life.*

☆ *From my thought and feeling, both conscious and unconscious, I create my entire reality.*

☆ *I can do, be or have anything.*

☆ *I am completely protected and safe at all times. There are no harmful "accidents" for me.*

☆ *I do not "catch" colds, flu or other illness. Harmful germs and viruses don't exist for me: I ignore them, and they ignore me. I create illness only through my thought and feeling. No illness is terminal. I can create health whenever I am ready.*

☆ *Life is joy! Life is light!*

☆ *Matter is illusion.*

☆ *I fulfill all my purposes for being here.*

☆ *The universe lovingly and effortlessly supports my doing what I love to do.*

☆ *Angels are real.*

☆ *The more I give, the more I receive and the more I have to give.*

☆ *Everyone can be abundant.*

☆ *Fairies are real.*

☆ *God and love are the realest of the real.*

☆ *Life is meant to be easy—so I take it easy!*

☆ *Magic is real.*

☆ *I have wonderful true friends. I am a true friend.*

☆ *My friends support my spiritual expansion and my joy.*

☆ *I have the love and courage for intimacy.*

☆ *Everyone in my life is a divine, beloved god/goddess.*

☆ *Time doesn't exist. We made it up.*

☆ *We are not the victim of time. Time is our servant.*

☆ *Corporations built on love along with know-how become the richest of all.*

☆ *Lawyers and undertakers will be out of a job.*

☆ *We have already transcended doomsday scenarios.*

☆ *I see perfection in all things.*

☆ *All is turning out wonderfully!*

☆ *Earth is paradise, waiting for us to remember it.*

☆ *Spirit and matter are one.*

☆ *My body lives forever in ever-greater life, health, and beauty.*

☆ *I stay on earth as long as I choose. When I leave, I take my body with me into light. I leave no form behind.*

☆ *Rejuvenation is possible, and it can be easy and fast.*

☆ *When I accept my ability I may travel by thought, taking my body into light and setting it down wherever I choose.*

☆   *I may step back and forth between dimensions.*

☆   *I may manifest anything I need or want right from the air.*

☆   *I am becoming an ascended master on earth.*

Make up your own unlimited thoughts. Let them become your truth. Be patient with yourself; remember that you're also changing emotional patterns and working with deeper layers of consciousness. Persevere!

My New Life!

Here are affirmations to bring into reality or give thanks for:

I am clear! All my karma is cleared. I have forgiven all old wounds.

I now define myself as spirit. I am strong. I am happy. I love. I follow my heart's path in a fulfilled life. I express my divinity more and more completely. So be it.

Tremendous blessings to you!

Clearing Initiations in Other Chapters

"The Peak of Health" chapter:
- ☆ Genetic Chain Busting
- ☆ Clear Accident Karma
- ☆ Clear the Cause

"Empower Yourself" chapter:
- ☆ Release Fear of Power

"Lighten Relationships" chapter:
- ☆ Come Even
- ☆ Dissolve Psychic Cords
- ☆ Relationship Healing

"Rejuvenation and Immortality" chapter:
- ☆ Clear Barriers to Rejuvenation.

"Goddess, Awake!" chapter:
- ☆ Heal the Feminine

"Serve the One" chapter:
- ☆ Astral Healing

"Rejuvenation and Immortality" chapter:
- ☆ Clear the Unconscious
- ☆ I Release Death!
- ☆ Clear Barriers to Rejuvenation
- ☆ Reverse the Death Hormone in the Pituitary

4
The Peak of Health

Your body is not only a temple for the divine,
it is the divine.
How could it be otherwise than perfect?

The Body Divine

The human body is divine because everything is divine, part of God/Goddess. The body is made of divine substance—particles of energy—none of which is solid. Divine intelligence formed our body in our mother's womb in the greatest perfection our soul's path could allow. Divine intelligence maintains our body by managing six trillion transactions per second.

Part of our job, as humans, is to recognize the divinity of our body and allow that to be expressed. When that happens, the body will be immortal; able to travel by thought; able to step through to other dimensions and return; and may be eternally youthful and beautiful. These possibilities which seem so foreign to our current thought are actually the natural way of life. Only our conviction that we are separate from the divine within us could cause the experience of aging and death. Only separation thoughts could cause the body to be unhealthy.

So let us accept the fact that we have created any symptoms of unhealth we may have, but not judge ourselves for it. We are returning to the Godhead and our experience of oneness. We've been doing our best and we will continue to, until we know oneness once again.

Causes of Illness

Not all health problems stem from mental-emotional cause. (I realize I am reversing earlier writing to the contrary—that's what happens when you grow as you write books!) A man who unknowingly eats contaminated food usually gets sick. Why he gave himself that experience often has an inner cause; but sometimes he is purely innocent of the dangers of the third dimension.

There may be a profound reason for choosing illness which has nothing to do with mental/emotional cause. I have a friend who was called by his spirit at dawn to come down to the river running through town. He arrived there, and waded in, just as a screeching freight train overturned on the bridge and a ripped tank car began spilling weed killer into the river. The fish tried to escape their watery home which had turned to death by leaping out of it, only to fall back. My friend's spirit reached out and helped the spirits of the dying fish and plants. He received a potent dose of the poison; it took him years to recover. But it was a mission his spirit chose, and he accepted the illness that resulted from it. He held no bitterness about it. Illness resulting from service is obviously in a category of its own.

These exceptions being noted, we turn to the other ninety-seven percent of illness—which is from mental/emotional cause. The one basic thought of separation from God splits into an infinitude of specific thoughts and feelings. Any one of these, if strong enough long enough, can cause illness. Here are common possibilities:

1. If you are overly subjective to people around you, you may "catch" their feelings and thoughts—and the illness accompanying them.

   All of us are subjective to the beliefs and patterns of our upbringing. If your family has an inherited or frequently occurring disease, the original mental/emotional cause is from the person in your family tree who first got the disease. If you believe in the disease and expect it, then you may get it too. But your only mental cause may be your belief in it. You can clear this and remain or become healthy.

It should be added that as you chose the family you were born into, within your own psyche may dwell the same mental cause your ancestor had. If so, you will need to clear that as well.

Only if you are subject to the idea of illness may your body contract illness. Only if you are subject to the idea of accident, may you be involved in one. These two ideas exist in virtually everyone; it is wise to protect ourselves with thoughts of health and safety.

Except in children, this over-subjectivity is something to correct (see Genetic Chain Busting below).

2. You're not willing to forgive. You may be punishing your father or mother, for example, for how you were treated as a child. See, you hurt me so badly that I'm sick and can't get well. (Another common reaction to childhood hurt: long after you've left home, frequently getting your parents to bail you out of trouble.) Your inner child may feel this is its only way to get even.

   You may unconsciously feel that forgiving means laying yourself open to past traumas happening again. You need to feel protected; you need to feel loved; and you probably need, within yourself, to come up even to others. Consider a wise and loving counselor, and see the "Clear!" and "Contact!" chapters.

3. You're keeping yourself in intense, difficult emotion such as grief, fear, anger or guilt.

4. You fear the release of the condition. You may lack confidence that you can take care of yourself and make your own way in life. You may believe that the only way you can be loved is to be ill, so that others must take care of you. You may fear that with a healthy body you will have to do what you long to do, but you fear doing it or failing at it.

   This kind of fear is often very deeply hidden and may be impossible to get to. Begin to love yourself as deeply as you can, unconditionally. This will open up your emotions. You may start to feel what is buried and come to terms with it.

5. If your life is unbearable—you're in a miserable mar-
    riage or job, or other life condition from which there
    seems no escape—you may choose to be ill. My friend
    Norman felt trapped in a job he hated, and gave himself
    muscular dystrophy. He is now healing himself. (Norman
    has generously agreed to share his healing process with
    others: see References.)

    A major trap is fearing to leave a job that earns well
    because you're convinced you'll be in lack. This is espe-
    cially tough if you're supporting a family. A similar trap is
    fear to leave an unworkable marriage which supports you.

    There are always, always other options for your life!
    Become aware of your feelings and admit them to your-
    self. Learn how to communicate them to others. Take
    steps to change your life. If your body is already ill, know
    that you can choose a new life upon your return to health.
    For suggestions, see the chapter "Fulfill Your Purposes."

6. You don't enjoy an aspect of your life, such as your job,
    and you develop an ongoing complaint such as chronic
    fatigue syndrome. Chronic conditions—or one trouble
    after another—may also arise from a general belief that
    one is a victim in life, that nothing ever goes right, that
    there is always something to complain about. Have you
    ever heard a group of friends competing with each other
    for the worst problem? "Well, that's nothing, let me tell
    you about me!" Same idea.

7. You are stuck in a rut, fearing to follow your heart and your
    spirit into new avenues. Getting sick is a wake-up call.

    What have you been resisting? What wants to come
    to you? What do you long to express that you haven't
    allowed? What new life wants to be born within you?
    Accept! Follow! Do it!

8. You have chosen this condition on a deep soul level, for
    soul's purpose. That purpose will be fulfilled quickly or
    slowly. You may quicken its fulfillment by asking your
    spirit why you chose it. Learn what you have given your-
    self to learn.

In the Pink

Color is more and more recognized as a viable healing force. Pink is a color of health and vitality, and this initiation puts pink to work!

Call your spirit. Envision a pink flame or light, and infuse your entire body with it. Include each organ, gland, bone, muscle, and all the systems of your body. Pay attention to each part, feeling deeply into it. If you feel difficult emotion anywhere, dissolve it in the flame. Really let it go!

Feel each part "in the pink" of perfect health, especially any part that's been having trouble.

Let the flame/light increase until you envision your whole body shining like a brilliant pink sun. Feel the light radiate from every atom and cell! Be there for a time, and enjoy!

If you prefer, use lavender or another color instead of pink.

To Fast, or Not to Fast?

To fast: my personal definition is to take just juices or water, with supplements, for some days. Fasting is an effective way to clean your intestines and thus purify your body. A clear body has more energy. Fasting also quickens the frequencies of body, mind and heart.

Fasting isn't right for everyone. It isn't even right for everyone who has fasted periodically to continue. My body became allergic to psyllium seed, with which I began each fast, and I realized fasting wasn't right for me then. So if you're wondering about fasting, see how you feel about it or ask in meditation. If there's a question of health, consult your doctor or health practitioner.

Given how often we eat, and the energy digestion requires, our system hasn't had time to deal with the toxins we ingest. These toxins become stored in the body. During fasting, they are released into the blood stream on their way out and can make you feel weak and irritable. So it's easiest to fast when you have time to rest during the day. It's also helpful to take a vigorous daily walk.

Before you begin, cut out all meat for a few days and go to vegetables, and the last two days to salads and fruit.

A good fasting liquid (delicious, too!) is the "master fast:"

> 1 gallon of spring or distilled water (different experts swear by one or the other)
>
> 8-12 lemons
>
> as much cayenne pepper as you can stand (at least ½ tsp)
>
> 1½ cups (more or less, to taste) maple syrup (grade C if possible, the less refined the better) or barley malt syrup

You may use this as the basic drink (careful, you can actually gain weight on it!). You can include other liquids as well—I like a vegetable juice or broth (see broth recipe below).

Follow your knowing about how long to fast; three to five days is suggested as a beginning, and seven to ten days or longer when you have some experience.

It's important to include enemas or colonics as you fast, because liquids do not have the bulk necessary to move the bowels. For a do-it-yourself home colonic that is safe, pleasant, effective and saves much expense in the long run, contact Colema Boards of California (see References).

Certain products seem universal to any cleansing system. Psyllium seed, apple pectin and other products coat your intestines and encourage old material to detach from the intestinal walls and wash out with colonics or enemas. Bentonite is a liquid of very fine clay particles which absorb toxins and make your fast more pleasant. And a green product of some kind like chlorophyll, blue-green algae, or spirulina will help purify and vitalize your system during the fast. Ask for all of these at your health food store.

Here is a whole program for liquid fasting that includes both fruit and vegetable juices, raw and cooked. I don't know where it comes from; it seems to be passed from person to person.

Morning

Mix prune, concord grape juice and water in equal parts. Drink 4 ounces warm.

After ½ hour, drink 1 cup of ginger tea.

Ginger Tea

Grate 2" of ginger root in 16 ounces of water. Simmer, and add lemon and honey to taste.

This tea is not only delicious, especially in winter, it's also great for colds and bronchitis.

Lunch through Dinner

Drink as you will a cup of vegetable broth, or 4 ounces of carrot juice.

Vegetable Broth

1 gallon distilled water

green cabbage (few quantities are given on the vegetables)

red potato

celery

parsley

3 white onions

1 can lima beans

1 can hominy

1 can beets

Simmer 15 minutes and let stand for 2 hours until beets turn white. Strain. (I like to add liquid aminos, like Bragg's.)

Carrot Juice

Juice together raw:

2 lbs. carrots

3 stalks celery

1 cucumber

1 Granny Smith apple, if available

1 handful sprouts

6-8 spinach leaves

Drink the complete batch each day, 4 ounces at a time.

Coming off the fast

Day 1: same but add fruit.

Day 2: fruit in the morning, steamed veggies at lunch and dinner.

Day 3: add salads (no wheat).

Day 4: back to normal.

You and Weight

Ah, weight—the nemesis of so many! "Ideal weight" is a social phenomenon that varies with time and culture. But of the immortals I know about—Babaji, St. Germain, and a few Taoist immortals—none of them is fat! A lean body requires less energy to maintain, so more is available for happier uses. For now, we will ride with the assumption that a slender body is a healthier, happier, more energetic body.

Being underweight is a problem for some, of course. The major mental-emotional cause seems to be lack of self esteem, coupled with the belief that the skinnier one is, the more one is admired and accepted. I believe it was Wallis Simpson who said "You can't be too rich or too thin." This can lead to bulemia and similar patterns.

As overweight is the much more common condition, let's take a deeper look at that. Here are major causes I've discovered in my work with people:

1. Lack of self esteem, often based on feeling unloved within the family. One overeats for comfort, and/or to create an "unworthy image" in a society that idolizes skinny bodies.

2. A need to feel protected. This need can come from very deep levels. Physical or psychic abuse can trigger extra weight at any time of life. I have a friend who gained weight immediately after she was raped, and it was hard for her to let the new pounds go. And I've seen women who fear attracting men use extra weight to make their body, in their own eyes, unattractive.

3. Closely linked with #2 is that sex in our society still suffers from a tarnished image, leading to odd thought forms: beautiful equals dumb; spirituality and sexuality don't go together; and to have a desirable form means one will not be fully respected. Thus in the mind, extra weight can equal respect.

4. Subjectivity to people in one's life who weigh a lot. This can be a hard one to conquer. "This is our family, or group of friends, and this is our body size" can be an unspoken dictum which must be followed to keep the love of others.

5. The genes of an overweight parent passed on to the child. We have assumed we have no control over heredity; but this is not the highest truth. It's one of those things that has been all-powerful by our belief. It is possible to change anything in spirit.

6. "If you eat fat or starchy foods, you're going to gain weight." Food does not need to be connected with weight or loss of it, because our body always follows our belief (our command). I have a friend who gained weight while she was on a diet of air (prana, life force, taken in through the skin cells as well as the breath). Another fasted completely for two weeks and lost not an ounce. A third, with a weight "problem," mastered being able to eat anything and keep her body slender. As masters who enjoy huge feasts have been known to say, "We don't actually *eat*."

7. Conditioning from past lives. I gained some unwanted pounds and found it difficult to shake them off. It took me a while to receive the information that in former lives, at a certain age I gained weight in exactly the same way. My body felt quite proud and happy about this accomplishment! Looking deeper, I found the thought that extra weight equaled being respected.

If we were always hungry in a past life, or starved to death, holding extra weight can feel like a buffer against such dangers. Also, if in a past life the body wasted away before death, a slender body can bring up that fear.

Any of these or other mental-emotional causes can trigger a response in the body such as a hypo-thyroid condition, which is then blamed for the weight. The cure may—but doesn't often—heal the real cause.

Weight Away!

Here are ideas to try out:

☆ Do your very best to discover and clear the mental-emotional cause of overweight.

☆ Love your body exactly as it is, whatever its weight. The importance of this can hardly be over-emphasized. Love for your body nourishes self esteem and self love. It is a force for having the weight you want. (See Love Your Body! in the rejuvenation chapter.)

☆ Remember that *you* are the power, and your power backs up all your present beliefs. You may change any belief. Redefine food and eating as having *no power* to make your body weigh more than you choose. Be aware of this as you eat.

☆ If you don't feel ready to change old beliefs, diet and exercise *because* you acknowledge the power of your belief. Bless your food. Be conscious as you eat, enjoying tastes and textures to the full. Then you are more satisfied with eating, and likely to eat less.

☆ Attend your body closely as you eat, and stop the moment it wants no more. You will probably eat less; this will kick in the belief that you will weigh less.

☆ The word "lose" may have unhappy connotations. Rather than "losing" weight, call it "gaining" the joy of being slender or lean.

☆ Include in your definition of "slender" robust health, strength and vigor.

☆ Think thin! Envision your body as you have a passion for it to be. Continuously ignore the mirror, and don't get on the scales. Declare you are your perfect weight *now,* and stick to it. Feel happy about it, grateful for it. If you are determined enough for long enough, you will succeed.

☆ If you discover that past life conditioning is the cause for present weight, talk to your DNA. Thank it and praise it for following your unconscious command so perfectly. Communicate that you have changed your mind, and now choose your body to weigh such and such. Get the agreement of your DNA; its joy is to assist.

Here are statements for creating or holding your ideal weight:

Whatever its weight, I love my body and see it as beautiful. I am not subject to social conditioning. I rejoice in the magic and life of my body as it is. Whatever the appearance of my body, I am lovable and loved as the divine being I Am.

I am the power that determines the weight of this body.

My body weight is ruled by my belief. I am at choice to change any belief I recognize.

Food has no power to make my body take on weight or keep weight. What I eat, and the amount I eat, has no undesired effect upon my weight.

Everything I eat turns to health, youth and beauty.

My body is divine body.

Move!

Here are movements I often do that bring joy to my body. Some are based on hatha yoga, an ancient and highly recommended practice, and others come from miscellaneous sources. I thank my friends Edel and Sola for some of these.

Wear loose clothing, and don't push yourself; just stretch as much as you can comfortably manage. Do them in any order.

1.   **Spine.** Stretch your arms straight up above your head and stand on tiptoe, stretching your whole body. Come back down onto your flat feet, and very slowly bring your straight arms downward to the front, bending your head forward with your arms. Continue downward very slowly, bending your spine vertebra by vertebra. If there is discomfort anywhere, stop there and breathe right into it, slowly in and slowly out, and then move on. You will wind up with your arms and head hanging. Gently swing back and forth a little. Take some deep breaths in, and on the outbreath see if your spine will bend still further.

     Slowly, very slowly return to a standing position, letting your arms hang by your side. Think of your vertebrae as golden coins one on top of the other, with some space in between. Your neck and head are last to come up. Repeat if desired.

2.   **Neck.** Let your head fall first forward and then back, a few times; then to each side, ear toward your shoulder. Your shoulders are relaxed and down. Slowly turn your head a few times to each side.

     Very gently circle your head around, first one direction and then the other, letting it fall as low as it does. If there are places of discomfort, stop there and breathe into them.

3.   **Eyes.** If my eyes begin to go south on me, I practice these exercises for one week and my vision snaps back again.

     Hold up a finger a few inches in front of your eyes, or as close as you can clearly see it. Look back and forth from the finger to at least twenty feet away, several times. Blink your eyes a few times and close them briefly, to relax them.

Next hold up a finger of each hand, each a few inches to the side and slightly forward of your eyes. Keeping your head still, look back and forth between the two fingers. Blink as above.

Now look as far as you can up to the right, and down to the left, back and forth a few times; then vice versa up left, down right. Blink to relax your eyes.

With your head still and your eyes looking at the floor, very slowly take your eyes in a circle, first one direction and then the other. Focus as far as you can in every direction for the 360 degrees. If you notice your eyes jumping from one spot to the next, go back and make a smooth eye movement. Do these only once. Blink.

Finally, rub your hands briskly together and "palm" your eyes. Cover an eye with each palm, and overlap the top of your fingers on your forehead. Keep your eyes open, and feel how they begin to relax. Palming is most beneficial; it has been known to heal blindness.

4. **Shoulders.** Bring your shoulders forward and up to ear height, then back and down, a few times. Lift your shoulders straight to your ears a few times, letting them fall. Shrug off burden!

5. **Arms and wrists.** Hold your arms straight out to the side, and circle them in tight circles several times one way, and then the other. Tense your muscles with the movement, and then relax.

    Do the same, except in great wide circles.

    Rotate your wrists around several times, first one way and then the other. Shake out your hands.

6. **Side.** Place your feet wide apart, legs straight. Stretch one arm straight up beside your head, palm facing outward to the same side, and keep your eyes on this hand. Meanwhile, slowly slide your other hand as far down the same-side leg as you can. Breathe deeply in this position. Come up slowly, and repeat for the other side.

7. **Pelvis.** With your spine straight and still from your waist up, tilt your pelvis as far forward (gently!) as you can, and then swing as far back, several times. Do the same to each side. Then rotate your pelvis outward as far as you can in a full circle, first one way and then the other.

8. **Knees.** Bend your knees slightly, and place your hands upon them. Swing your knees together around in a circle several times, to the right and then to the left.

9. **Ankles.** Tip up one foot (no shoes) so that foot is vertical above its toes, a couple of times. Then keeping your toes on the floor, rotate your ankle around several times in each direction. Repeat with the other foot.

10. **Spine** (cobra). Lie down on your stomach, and place one hand, palm to the floor, on each side of your head. Breathing in, gently raise your head and shoulders back as far as you can. Your hands will be pushing from the floor, and your arms will still be bent in the furthest reach of the position. Hold your breath a bit; then slowly return, breathing out. Do a few times.

11. **Abdomen.** Lie on your back with your hands behind your head and knees bent, feet flat on the floor. Bring your head up with your hands, tensing the muscles of your abdomen, just until it begins to pooch out, and return. Do a number of times.

12. **Combo.** Lying on your back, your arms resting on the floor out to the side, bring your knees together to your chest. Keeping them bent, swing them all the way over to one side, that side knee touching the floor briefly. Bring your knees back to your chest and then over to the other side, back and forth. Keep as much of your spine as you can flat on the floor. Your head faces the ceiling.

Enjoy!

Genetic Chain Busting

I know the idea of clearing genetics through intention is not yet accepted by the medical community. Nevertheless, if we acknowledge our oneness with the infinite power of the divine, we must know this is possible.

This initiation helps free you from the limitations adopted by your ancestry. Also, in the reality that time is an illusion—all time is actually here now—your declaration can help those in your family tree, both in the time they lived as your ancestors, and now.

Whether or not your ancestors accept this help, you are able to free yourself from inherited limiting patterns both physical and psychic. Disease tendency and inherited disease, addiction, abuse, co-dependence, and other dysfunctional patterns can be broken. You can also break the patterns of aging and death.

This is not a mental exercise, but an initiation which takes genuine will power and passion. Are you ready to welcome the unlimited? Are you ready to have a different outlook from almost everyone else? Are you ready to speak the truth, silently or aloud as appropriate, when another speaks of limitations? Are you ready to declare health in the face of any family disease, even if you have it already? Are you ready to declare yourself ageless? This is what we are talking about! If you feel ready to address only one or two issues, like freeing yourself from co-dependence or illness, that is wonderful! You can do more later if you choose.

Name the limitations of your family you choose to free yourself from. Find your desire and intention to be truly free.

Go into the basic meditation ("Contact!" chapter). Call your divine master self and ask it to provide you with a sword of light. If you like, bring in Archangel Michael with his dazzling, all-powerful sword.

Wield this sword as a powerful cutting tool, dissolving one pattern after another. Lift the sword above your head, and bring it down in a powerful stroke all the way to the floor, with a great loud outbreath through your mouth and plenty of pure intention!

Here are statements to empower your process:

In the name, and by the power, of the lord god of my being, I now free myself from _____ *! I break that genetic chain! I will never* _____ *! My choice is to* _____ *! That is the way it is! And so be it! I am free!*

Take time to feel and bless the new!

If you find after a time that something didn't "take," it means it was so deep that you haven't yet gotten it all. You got the layer that was perfect for that time. Do the process again, specific to that one issue.

Blessings to you in your new freedom!

Clear Accident Karma

A healthy body is all in one piece—obviously!—and everything works. It is wise to clear all karma you are ready to release that would specifically harm your body. I would not have been injured in an auto accident if I had known I could do this. It is also wise to ask your spirit to remove any "instant" karma that would do the same. Christopher Reeve, the American actor who became a paraplegic in a riding accident, said that a couple of weeks beforehand he was studying paraplegics, and wondered how it would be to be one. Isn't that interesting?

Go into a quiet space and call your spirit. Find your desire and intention to be safe from all "accident." Let this desire burn brightly in your mind and heart. Say with conviction and power:

In the name, and by the power, of the lord god of my being, I now ask and affirm that all karma that would harm my body in any way, that I am ready to release, now leaves me! I call the flame of my divinity to blaze through my subconscious mind, my body, my feeling, my conscious mind, and my aura now, to clear and cleanse all that no longer serves me! (Breathe! Let it go on your out-breath.)

I also ask that any instant karma I create from thought, that would harm my body, be lifted from me immediately upon its creation. It is my full choice and intention to **always** *have a healthy, strong, protected body that functions perfectly in the world. So be it.*

Allow this now and feel it, strongly, clearly, passionately! Really mean it. Really do it.

Sports such as skiing seem to invite the occasional wrenched knee or broken limb. Even here, you can bring your conviction to your ongoing safety. Oneness with all is the key. For instance, you would never choose to be skiing under a mountain when an avalanche breaks loose. Here are statements for the prevention injury from any kind of activity:

I _____ (name your activity) *safely. I am one with the land, air, water or snow, my equipment, the trees and animals, all other people and their equipment—everything. When I am in a car, I am one with the car, the road, all other people and vehicles on the road, animals, the weather—everything. My deep mind knows all there is to know. I am clear and wise in all my decisions both large and small. All works in perfect harmony and perfect timing for my continued safety, and the safety of all around me. I accept my safety. So be it.*

Let Go of "Incurable" Illness

The plague-type diseases that have ravaged the human population throughout history have literally frightened many to death. Fear of a horrible disease with the reputaton of invincibility is easy to understand; but that fear is evidence that we are facing the wrong way. It is belief in appearances, real and horrific as those appearances may be.

When we turn around to face God and the reality of perfection here and now, we are the ones who become invincible. In *Living Mastery* I describe friends with the HIV virus for 10 years or more who will *never* come down with AIDS because they simply give it no power. God is in all things, and God is love, not destruction of anything so miraculous and tender as a human body.

Confidence in the face of fearsome disease is a great learning, an awesome wisdom. Any of us may develop such wisdom, as it is all within us. Whatever the state of our health, we need not fear *any* disease. If we are feeling afraid, we may embrace our fear and rise above it. We are the power that prevents disease or heals it.

A woman's doctor told her she had breast cancer and her breast must be removed. "I don't think so, doctor," she replied and walked out. She healed herself.

If you have an "incurable" illness, first do your best to discover and clear the mental/emotional cause, below.

Here are statements to bring you back to health:

I love that in me which chose this illness. I love myself for feeling fear and other difficult emotions about it. I am good, exactly as I am.

As I chose illness on some level, I have the power to now choose health.

I choose now to give no power to appearances. I do not look at illness, I look only to God. In God/Goddess is only perfection, perfect health and vitality. I am part of God, so perfection is my only truth. I choose to see and know only this perfection. I concentrate upon it, rejoice in it and give thanks for it! Perfect health is my truth, now and forever. So be it.

See also the section "I Return to Health," below. Use any other method that appeals to you, such as visualization (also below). Blessings to you in your return to health!

See the last two sections of this chapter for affirmations.

Clear the Cause

The cause of most physical difficulty comes from our reaction to something present or past. When reactive energy gets stuck in the psyche, it may manifest as a physical difficulty.

If you are experiencing such difficulty, here are possibilities of things you may be reacting to:

1. Abuse, or an attack upon you
2. A difficult relationship
3. People in your family getting cancer or another disease
4. Someone you love is injured or ill, or has passed on
5. Any difficult event or series of events
6. A difficult environment

7. A similar condition now to one in a past life in which you were injured or killed

Common reactions are fear, resentment, anger or rage, sorrow, guilt, confusion, feeling powerless, and infinite combinations of these feelings. If these are not expressed or cleared they fester, and can cause illness, injury or death.

To heal the cause of an illness:

1. Call your divine spirit, which includes your ability to know anything. Focus upon the body difficulty. Ask *What is the cause of this?* and then listen. That may be all you need do to discover the cause. You may also ask your body itself for the cause. It may help to draw a picture of the illness, or of your ill or injured body.

   Feelings may arise. If they do, go deeply into them. Let them speak to you or show you things. A picture may come, or a knowing or words. A past life may show itself.

   Again with the help of spirit, release this old cause. Use the violet flame if you choose ("Clear!" chapter). When you are ready to acknowledge the cause, it means its service to you is completing. Use more initiations from "Clear!" if appropriate.

   Healing *can* take place without knowing the cause.

2. Forgive yourself for creating this cause through thought and feeling. Remember forgiveness is not a mental exercise, but an emotional release. Take time to feel this forgiveness, and breathe with it.

   Whether or not you feel forgiveness is complete, finish the process. You may do more later.

3. If a person is involved in the cause, do you feel the need for protection from him or her? If so, do the Invincible Protection initiation in "Clear!" Then you may more easily forgive.

   Forgive any others involved. Take all the time you need. If you feel it's not yet complete, plan a time to return to it. You may want to do a Relationship Healing with someone.

4. Declare your freedom from the old ways. Here are suggested words:

   In the name and by the power of the lord god of my being, I, _____, now declare my freedom from _____! I am no longer subject to this way of being. I put it behind me. I have learned from it, and I expand beyond it! I Am free!

5. Declare what is true for you now, what you choose:
   In the name and by the power of the lord god of my being, I, _____, now choose perfect health! My spirit is whole and perfect, therefore my body is whole and perfect. New, unlimited thoughts I choose are _____, and _____ .

   Feel and see your new condition, deeply deeply. Accept it, be happy and grateful about it.

6. If needed for completion, repeat the initiation as frequently as you feel guided.

7. Daily empower yourself in your new way for at least six weeks. (See the 40-Day Process in "Empower Yourself.")

If you find that no matter what you have done, your body is not well, be patient and loving with yourself. Be patient with your condition. Recognize that some causes of illness are extremely deep in the psyche. When you are willing to face whatever may be inside, and love yourself, you will move toward health.

Heal with Visualization

On public television there was a true account of healing through visualization. An elderly woman had a large, inoperable tumor which the doctors labeled "terminal."

This woman got hold of some information about visualizing herself back to health. She began to work two or three times a day, seeing in her mind's eye the little faces with big mouths, from the video game "Pacman," gobble up her tumor.

After a few months, she visited her doctor. He was quite surprised to find that the tumor had not grown. But neither had it diminished.

This courageous woman determined to do more. She withdrew to her room and visualized five times a day.

Again after a few months, the doctor examined her. The tumor was gone, and she was in perfect health.

Her doctor came on and said that because of this one healing, his hospital had formed a new policy. Doctors would never again label anything "terminal."

You'll notice that this woman did not address the cause of her illness. Perhaps she prayed, but she didn't mention it. And the tumor disappeared. Let us always leave the door open for things to happen the way they happen. They don't need to fit our expectations.

Carl Simonton, who worked with cancer patients, is a breakthrough pioneer on visualization. His book, *Getting Well Again,* is a hallmark for this work.

Visualization

Call in your spirit, if you choose, to inspire and assist the healing. Of course you may work to clear cause or do anything else that benefits you along with your visualization.

Form a picture of your illness in any way that works for you.

Next, form an idea of how best you may visualize it going, going, gone! Get busy on it. Experiment with how often you do it; our friend above needed five times a day.

If you have trouble visualizing, ask your spirit to improve your ability to visualize. Or melatonin, available at the pharmacy, is said to help visualization.

Some ideas:

1.   See your white blood cells, those that fight disease, multiplying tremendously. You may give them faces, like Pacman or sharks, or not. See them attacking and destroying every bit of the illness. If you like, declare often: *My immune system is totally strong and completely destroying the* _____ .

2.   See garbage collectors drive up, load all or part of the illness, and cart it off to the dump.

3.   Use a laser light, a ray gun or other weapon to dissolve it.

4.   If it's a tumor, see it shrinking more every day.

5.   Visualize an affected part of your body the way it looks in perfect health.

6.   Fill your body with a light so bright, no illness can withstand it!

7.   See an angel or a master you love come and lift it from you.

Use your imagination!

Hands-On Healing

For yourself or another:

Call in the energy and knowing of perfection from your spirit. Say a little prayer, silently or aloud, for the greatest possible blessing to come through your hands.

Rub your hands together to get the energy flowing. Place your hands lovingly upon the affected part. Again call in the energy of the divine or a favorite master. Direct your loving intention to the part, and see it perfect. An energy force may begin to pour through; you may feel it or not. There may be heat or light, or both. You will know when the treatment is complete.

Have no attachment to the results. If you are doing this for another person, help them be open to healing or not healing. Not everyone is ready to accept healing, even though they may feel they are. Also, their karma may not permit it. Trust the working of the divine to be perfect for that moment.

I regard Reiki as a most powerful tool for hands-on or distant healing.

See Perfection

For you or another:

With any health problem, turn from viewing it as a problem. Steep yourself in spirit, where there is never a problem, only perfection. Call in a favorite master if you like. *God Is!* See, feel and know only *perfection*. Envision *perfection*. See nothing else! Claim it, ask or pray for it from Mother/Father God.

Again, have no concern about results. Those on the planet who heal as Jesus healed do not heal everyone. Even if healing doesn't happen, the vision of perfection will lodge upon the aura and be there when it can be of use. Simply do your best.

I Return to Health

Use the statements that serve you:

In my return to health, I easily hear and follow my inner voice of perfect wisdom.

I am not a victim. I have created this experience to learn something I wanted and needed to learn. My learning transforms my life into a better one.

I am able to discover the cause behind any illness or injury of my body. I am able to clear this cause in the time and way best for me.

I accept no illness as terminal. My choice and word, on both surface and deeper levels of my being, determine the course of my health.

I am open to all that can benefit me. I draw to myself, and spirit brings, all helpful information now. I invite the wholeness and healing forces of earth and all of nature to assist me. I put to work, as guided, the initiations in this book and/or other sources.

I give myself all the rest my body needs to return to perfect health.

I know my body is formed and re-formed every moment by thought. I make good use of this knowledge!

As my body's cells are almost completely replaced every eleven months, I command now that any sick cells be replaced with perfect, healthy ones.

My interest and involvement in my return to health is scientifically proven to be a great healing force.

I choose people around me who truly empower me in my return to health.

My spirit is perfectly whole and divine, and this is who I truly am. My divinity naturally expresses as a healthy body.

To increase my health, I choose to feel peace, love, joy, and gratitude, and to think joyful unlimited thoughts.

If my efforts to heal my body are not bearing fruit, I choose to understand that unconscious levels of myself are holding on to difficulty. I take my guided next steps to have patience, take passionate action or anything in between.

I do not allow any health difficulty to reduce my happiness, or my positive effect upon the world.

As I know my oneness with the divine, I may clear any health problem quickly. I may help others do the same. So be it.

I Am Perfect Health!

I honor this body, holy temple of the divine. I love it and I take care of it. As part of the divine, it is perfect.

My body is in vibrant health, strength and vitality! All the cells of my body are strong and perfect. They are daily bathed in the perfection of my divine being.

My spine and my whole body are flexible, strong and comfortable. I can do whatever I choose with my body, in wisdom.

All my organs function perfectly in joy, love, life, light, and ease: my heart, lungs, liver, kidneys, sexual organs, stomach, brain, and all the rest.

My eyes see clearly at all distances.

My ears hear perfectly.

My blood is clear and pure, light-filled and freely flowing through every proper pathway.

My nerves are strong and calm.

My bones are optimally dense and flexible.

My muscles are strong, with the potential infinite strength of the divine.

My skin is clear and firm.

My weight is what I choose it to be.

The ductless glands associated with my chakras: my sexual glands, pancreas, adrenals, thymus, thyroid, pineal and pituitary, are giving out their life, light, love and joy hormones in optimum amounts and perfect balance for my entire body now.

My seven energy centers (chakras) are open, vitally alive, light, and spinning in optimum speed and direction. They are a clear link from my lighter bodies: astral, etheric, and higher.

My meridians and acu-points are all clear, and life force flows freely throughout my body.

The three channels along my spine—the pingala, ida and shushumna—are clear and perfect.

To keep my health perfect, I choose to feel peace, love, joy, and gratitude, and to think the joyful unlimited thoughts of my divinity.

(If you feel to add:) As long as I choose to remain in physical form, this beloved divine body will function perfectly and in ever-greater strength, vitality, joy, and beauty. So be it.

Health Initiations in Other Chapters

"Rejuvenation and Immortality!" chapter:
- ☆ Love Your Body!
- ☆ Tibetan Rites

5

Empower Yourself

Power, love, and light are one.
Part of the divine, you are all-powerful.
Embrace your power!

"You are all-powerful." How can such a thing be said? What does it mean? We certainly don't appear all-powerful. Each of us can do many things, but much we cannot do.

What do you believe about yourself? What do you know you can do? Your *knowing* is all-powerful. What you know you cannot do is also all-powerful. Our knowing is all-powerful *because* we are divine.

Social conditioning is for the most part a disempowering set of rules and regulations for being human. We have absorbed these rules since before birth. We've learned that yes, if we work hard enough and with determination, we can accomplish certain things. We can become skilled and honored in any number of fields including business, artistry, human interaction, medicine, athletics, science.

As a race, we do not yet know that we can fix our own teeth or grow back a limb. We don't yet know we can heal any injury or illness; indeed, that we may be immune to any injury or illness. We don't yet know we can rejuvenate, shape-shift, manifest something from nothing, travel by thought, and become immortals. The divine we are can do anything that is chosen.

Feeling more and more one with our divinity causes limiting beliefs to gradually fall away. We are able to more and more fully express our divinity. We will come to know that any accomplishment—from the mundane to the miraculous—is natural for each of us.

Social Conditioning about Power

Common as leaves of grass are limiting beliefs about power. These are based in separation fears, victimhood and guilt. Some of these beliefs and their antidotes:

1. I am not a powerful person.

   This belief is nearly universal. Even people who appear powerful in the eyes of the world have fears and misgivings about themselves, their abilities and their lives.

   Antidote: *I am an absolutely powerful person. My strongest beliefs, both conscious and unconscious, create my life. I am able to discover and change limiting beliefs so that my power creates my life as I choose it.*

2. I am at the effect of life.

   This usually includes a belief that things happen at random: accidents, turns of fortune, acts of God that may devastate life with no reason or purpose.

   Antidote: *Life flows in accordance with thought and emotion. Things do not happen by accident. When something difficult occurs, I learn from it and benefit from my learning. I forgive, forget and move on.* "Every dark cloud has a silver lining" is a true statement. To see it may take some looking, but it's there.

3. I can't.

   An unfortunate belief!

   Antidote: *I can. Within the framework of my knowing that I can create and my acceptance of good, I can do anything I choose. I can be anything I choose. I may have anything I choose. I choose all in harmony with life.*

   So many people have proved that even with a difficult start in life—poverty, disability, being unwanted or unloved—they have done what they chose to do. They are no different from you or me.

4. Something is to blame for the fact that I can't.

   We usually blame something—a person, a relationship, an event, a condition, a situation, our health, or ourselves—for not creating what we choose.

Antidote: *As the divine is innocence, all is innocence. Nothing and no one is to blame for anything. Any stopping aspects are within myself, and I have the ability to change these. If I don't change them, I love myself and have patience with myself and my life.*

In my town, there's a fellow with a spastic, disabled body. How easy it would have been for him to be unhappy and blame his condition! But he rides all over the place in his motorized three-wheeled bicycle, goes into stores to shop—whatever he wants to do. There's no mistaking when he's around because when he speaks, he yells. He has the sunniest, kindest disposition imaginable. He awes all of us. He is greatly loved.

5. It's wrong to have all I want.
It's wrong to be powerful. I don't deserve it. These stem from the guilt we feel in choosing to deny our oneness with God, and also from scenarios from all our lives.

Antidote: *It is right and good, in God, to be powerful and to have what I choose in harmony with life. It is spiritual. It is one with love. I use my power wisely and lovingly, for the good of all. I am part of the divine, and as such deserve to be powerful.*

6. If you're powerful, you hurt other people.
For a long time we have separated power and love; the villain in many a story is a powerful man or woman. Most of us have misused power in one life or another.

Antidote: *If I have misused power in the past, I forgive myself. Power and love are one. I am able to be both powerful and kind, and I choose this path. (Did you ever see "A Christmas Carol"?) Who expresses both kindness and power? There's a good person to emulate!*

7. Powerful people are to blame for bad conditions of my life.
Here is victim consciousness.

Antidote: *I take full responsibility as the chooser and creator of my life. People of power are doing the best they can. I honor each as part of the divine. I am equal with them. And, if people are abusing others with their power, they should be stopped. Not in hatred, disdain* or unnecessary violence, but stopped (as when Gandhi ousted the British from India).

8. Power is for others, not me.
   Such a common self-limitation! Here we lack imagination and also research, wherein we would discover that many a powerful person had humble beginnings.

   Antidote: *People in power are not different from me. What others have done, I may also do. If I have not yet chosen to be powerful, I will make that choice when I am ready. I will learn to "take the seat" of power. Mighty oaks from little acorns grow.*

9. I'm not safe to be powerful.
   This one often comes from past lives of being powerful and losing our power—and often our lives—for it. In one of my past lives I was murdered for being the *son* of a powerful lord.

   Antidote: *I am completely safe to be powerful. If past experiences are blocking my present power, I discover and clear them.*

10. I'm not loved if I'm powerful.
    Family and peer group boundaries often exclude power; by intimation one who chooses to be powerful steps outside the warmth and love of his group.

    Antidote: *I am completely loved to be powerful. If my family or peers do not support my choice to be powerful, I attract to myself people who do.*

Most people who become powerful have to buck the tide of resistance from family and friends. But they do!

Creator I Am

Taking responsibility for what we have created up to now, without self-blame, is a most empowering step. Here are statements to that end:

I give myself the honor of knowing that from my most strongly held thoughts, both conscious and unconscious, I have created (or accepted the creation of others I was subject to) every relationship, every circumstance and every event that has ever happened to me, without exception. I chose my parents and family as the perfect ones for me at the time. I see my thoughts reflected back to me perfectly in everything that happens to me and every word that is spoken to me, because we are all a oneness. I am my surroundings. Every experience I have chosen has served me in the best possible way.

I give myself the freedom to heal all causes of unhappy situations. I begin now or continue to re-create my life as I choose it to be. I give myself all the help I need, from my inner self and other people, to accomplish this. I choose my life to be the most wonderful life I can imagine, and more! As I choose, the whole universe completely supports my choice. So be it.

Release Fear of Power

To have a fulfilling life and give our gifts, it is vital to accept our base of power. Many of us fear power, however, both in ourselves and others. Here are fears about being powerful:

1. We've expressed our power in the past and have known loss because of it.
2. We've been an abuser at some time, and fear we will be again.
3. We feel unworthy of having power; and having it would make us wrong.
4. We would lose the love of others.
5. I would be angry in my power, and my anger would destroy.

If any of these ring a bell for you, here is an initiation:

Go into a quiet space and call your spirit. Become deeply grounded and relaxed. Breathe deeply.

Now imagine yourself as fully powerful in a particular situation, project or relationship. Really place yourself there. How do you feel? Enter into the feeling. Allow thoughts or pictures to arise. What are they? Do you fear you'll be harmed? Do you fear others will be upset or angry? Do you fear your own anger? Pinpoint the fear as precisely as you can.

You may choose to go to the "Clear!" chapter for deep work. In the following two sections are statements to usher in a new consciousness.

I Am Safe and Loved in My Power

To make the following words your truth, you may want to work with initiations from the "Clear!" chapter such as Trauma or Past Life Clearing:

I recognize that in being powerful or speaking my truth in this or other lives, I have created difficult situations. I choose to now change this experience.

I forgive all others who have misused power toward me, in this or any lifetime. They were all doing their best. (This may be a big one for you. Breathe, forgive, release from your heart.) I love all who express their power.

I choose to learn that I am safe and protected. I choose to know that I am loved in being powerful.

I accept my own power. I am comfortable with it and harmonious with others. My power and my love are one. Everyone in my presence also accepts my power, and their own, all of us in harmony with each other. As I accept more and more my full and true power, one with the divine, I am able to overcome any difficulty in my life.

My family, my friends and others love me in my power as best they can. I now welcome only those daily relationships and situations that support my power. If something in my life does not support it, I change it or move on.

All power is divine power. I now accept that I am an all-powerful being because I am one with God/Goddess. I am an unlimited, free, divine being.

I create from my heart. I express myself fully and joyously. Anything I want to be, I can be. Anything I want to do, I can do. Anything I want to have, I can have! I give all the gifts that are mine to give. I now embrace this new way. So be it.

All Are Safe With Me

I understand that I have always done my best with what I have known. In gaining wisdom through my lifetimes, sometimes I have misused power. I forgive myself for anything I've done which harmed the body, feeling or mind of another person. I forgive myself for misuse of power. (Again, this may be a big one for you! Take time, call your spirit, get in touch, release from your heart—breathe! You may complete this over time.)

I choose to learn whatever remains to be learned from these experiences. I choose to know that power and love are one. I am not superior to others. We are every one equally divine, valuable, loved and honored by life and by God. I do not need to misuse power in order to express myself, be loved, touch others, be abundant, or get things done. (Again, give time to any of these that ring for you, and take truth into your heart. Breathe!)

I recognize that power is one with love, and all power is divine power. I honor the divinity within all people and all of life. I use my divine power wisely and lovingly. My heart is open. I love everyone. I am kind. I am honest; I speak truly and act in integrity. I use my power to serve. People are safe with me, always. Expressing my power, I am in harmony with life.

I love myself as a powerful being. I express power fully, to the benefit of all life. So be it.

Stand Up for Yourself!

Sometimes we need to be tough. All of us have strong points, but as a race we are too sheepish. And life is liable to tweak a weakness so we may turn it into strength.

When our passions in life are refused expression; when someone habitually puts us down; when we or our group are taken advantage of; when a situation cries out for truth, and no one dares speak; when strong action is hard but is called for; when someone else is being abused in our presence; when defense is necessary to protect life, then we must spring loose the awesome power within us to speak, to act.

If someone intentionally puts us down, it mirrors a fear we have. It is a blessing in disguise, an opportunity to overcome fear.

Breaking through fear requires passion and fire, and one never knows just how it will come out. It's likely to be messy. Nevertheless, it works for the good of all.

Here are varying responses to being put down, repressed, and the like:

☆ Guidance. Tune to spirit, get your guidance and follow it. Or go from your knowing of what is right.

☆ Calm, firm action. My friend Jonna invited a man in need to stay with her family until he could find a place to live. She helped him look, but he turned down one apartment after another. Weeks went by. Finally, Jonna gave him one week to be out. "But what if I can't find a place by then?" he asked. "It doesn't matter," Jonna replied calmly. "Your bags will be on the sidewalk." He found a place the next day.

☆ Action with your heart in your throat. While President Bill Clinton was growing up, his stepfather often abused his mother. One night, when Bill was fourteen, his stepfather came home drunk and began to abuse his wife. Bill stepped between them. He told his stepfather he could never again harm his mother. Bill was prepared to fight. The older man backed down; but young Bill didn't know he would.

☆ Anger. Anger rising may exactly fit the moment. There can be great and beneficial power in anger. If you have kept yourself oppressed in a situation, anger is often the first step out of it. It can clear the decks for a new beginning. (And if anger/rage is suppressed and denied, it will work itself out upon the body.)

Even masters get angry. A Zen master blasted a man abusing a child. A furious Jesus cleared the temple of money changers. Anger can be clean and laser-like. The key is not to hold on to it—let it sweep in and sweep out.

☆ Step-by-step, determined action. When I lived in Memphis, engineers planned a freeway right through the middle of Overton Park, including the only remaining old growth forest. This stupidity enjoyed the blessing of the good old boy system in power.

To save the park, *one woman* sparked a group into action, whom freeway advocates disdainfully labeled "little old ladies in tennis shoes." They put in months and months of dedicated effort (I did some too), and finally accomplished what few believed could happen. If you're in Memphis, take a look. Interstate 40 stops dead—right at Overton Park.

A friend of mine single-handedly caused the complete restructuring of a church that had become politicized and corrupt, simply by telling the truth at every board meeting. Determined action from a passionate heart is irresistible.

☆ Bite the bullet in relationship. A friend, mate, child may awaken an unfaced fear of long standing. A woman habitually put down by her father repeats the dynamic now with her husband. A person is abused early in life, and now someone similar to the abuser awakens a primal fear. It can be most difficult to break through something like this, because the fear is often rooted in helpless infancy when we could neither speak nor act.

Often a time of building courage is required here. Premature words or action can be damaging. You may want to seek professional help to build this courage, or run your ideas by a wise friend. Or rehearse what you're going to do, and plan for any response. This is not a little thing to do; it is huge. Give yourself the respect you deserve in confronting your fear.

Now speak you can, act you must! Claim your worth in the teeth of put-down. Claim your essential safety. Face your fear, and go through it. See the present person for the fallible person he is, not a ghost from the past. No one has power over you. These acts are vital if you are to have a life.

However it turns out, however the other responds, know you did your best and it is good. Keep your courage. Get support. Feel from your heart what to do next. Do it.

☆ If it is possible that standing up for yourself would put you or those you love in mortal danger, then it is not cowardly to leave; it is brave and wise. Find a way to get out and go.

If you find yourself in a situation of extreme disharmony such as war, your spirit will probably lead you out of it unless it is your soul's purpose to stay. You may be guided to speak or act, whatever the cost. If there are there people whose well-being depends upon your actions, shall you move them first out of harm's way?

☆ Last but surely not least, forgive. Heal the relationship with all involved, either together or on your own. Remember all are doing their best, and they are here to learn as you are.

Choose Rightly

Ah, the infinite choices of life! In the great oneness we are, our choices impact all of creation. Right choice for us is also best for the rest of creation.

Wisdom to make the right choices rests in our soul or higher self. Right choice is not primarily a mind-guided process; indeed, sometimes what we are given defies rationality. My father was considering moving to be near me, but he knew if I received clear guidance to move to Timbuctu, I would do it.

Choosing rightly isn't even a desire-guided process, given that most of our desires come from a shallow level of being. But it is surely connected with the deep, true desires of our heart.

The fulfillment of these true desires is an unfolding, organic process which may also defy logic. The timing is not decided by mind. It emerges from what is best for our entire being, including the body, unconscious mind and emotions.

A common pitfall of spiritual aspiration is the head deciding to take a spiritually ambitious path that is premature for the rest of the being. A man in India went all out to raise his kundalini (life force energy curled at the base of the spine which, when raised to the seventh chakra, results in enlightenment). After two years of great concentration, he succeeded—and fried his brain. He died not long after.

Learning to be open and attentive to our entire being is a key to right choice. A friend chose a spiritually advanced program, but felt blocked at every turn. He eventually discovered that his little boy inside, his inner child, feared and resisted the program. He worked with his child to communicate, comfort and heal old conceptions. Finally, it accepted the program and he was able to move forward.

If a clear connection with spirit can be developed, that is a wonderful way to discover what is best. Even then—so we don't fool ourselves—caution must be maintained.

It can certainly feel frustrating to *know* something is your true heart's desire, your destiny, and have it take a long time to manifest. But when you consider the lifetime upon lifetime of limited belief and piled-up karma that we are clearing—often in only *one* lifetime—you are more easily patient.

These cautionary statements behind us, we arrive at a simpler way: follow what rises spontaneously from the heart. Follow a clear and simple knowing.

If you are making a choice important to you now, call your spirit and go into a quiet inner space. Breathe deeply and gently for awhile, relaxing on all levels. Feel your grounding connection with mother earth.

Present yourself with each option open to you, and watch very carefully. How do you feel? How does your body feel? If you have a clear enough connection with your spirit, ask for a message in words, feelings or pictures.

If you don't feel a clear difference between options, it may not matter which you choose. But usually, one will stand out by a response from within.

Clear, Present, and Grounded

When it comes to creating powerfully, it's great to hitch your wagon to a star; but your feet must be on the earth. Here are questions to feel out your situation.

1. Is your choice wise and good for you? Does it feel right to your heart? It is aligned with your soul's path?

2. Are you creating from a clear space? Are there unresolved issues in your life that will slow or block your movement? If so, clear these.

3. Are you choosing something you can actually accept, in the day to day reality of life? Is "all of you" behind this creation?

4. On a practical basis, are you willing to do all that's required to bring this about?

5. Are you able to rise above discouragement or setback? Are you willing to be patient, to persevere?

6. Are you willing to be in harmony with all life throughout the process? This includes interacting as lovingly as possible with other people and the environment.

7. Are you in the company of those who support your creation? If not, are you strong enough to succeed without the approval of others? Will you find the support you need?

8. Have you prepared the ground for your new creation both physically and psychically, so it will fit perfectly into your life? Will others be affected by your success? Are they prepared for it?

These things you may check out; but don't give them too much weight or allow them to confuse you. If your heart longs for a particular thing, just go for it!

Power Thinking

So many of us think of ourselves as somehow less than others, incapable of truly doing or having what we choose. It's so important to change such thoughts! Researchers have discovered that about seventy percent of human thought is negative. Also, ninety-five percent of the thoughts we have one day we repeat the next.

God/Goddess in pure expression as Itself, no distortions, is an absolute force for good. Aligning ourselves with this force means letting go of negative thought and feeling.

If you choose to empower yourself through your thinking, realizing what you presently think is the first step. We all experience "monkey mind," running on and on without recognition.

In meditation, or during the day, jot down thoughts you notice. Carry a little pocket recorder and record your conversations. What are you saying?

Strong emotion offers a fine opportunity to discover thinking: what is the thought within this emotion? I'm not loved? Ah!

One way to promote positive thought is to image success for a particular endeavor, and weed out contrary images. Another is to imagine a beautiful, peaceful scene in nature often throughout the day. Positive thought and feeling allows—and attracts—greater good and happiness.

Excellent training for thinking truth is *A Course In Miracles*. It gives a new thought for each day of the year. It also suggests an interval, such as every fifteen minutes, to reinforce the thought during the day. Repeating truth to yourself in short intervals is most valuable, and can be used with any chosen thought. Many watches beep on the hour—an opportunity!

A positive thought over a layer of buried "stuff" will bring that stuff to light. This is a great gift; then you can work to clear it. So don't force yourself to think positively if something else is happening; don't ride roughshod over deep, contrary feeling. Respect your process.

Below are some ways of thinking to nourish a life of happiness and fulfillment for you. Add your own thoughts, and use them!

I Am That I Am

Whenever your experience does not fit one of these statements, remember that truth is timeless. Divine good is everywhere present, here and now. When you know this, you attract every wonderful thing into your life. So, without denying contrary feeling, do your best to accept these statements as true *now.*

I am part of the divine, perfect and whole. I am the love, the light, the wisdom, the knowing and the power of Goddess/God. I am my divine master self.

I am totally loved and provided for by All That Is, Mother/Father God, and my divine master self.

I am my own best friend. I encourage myself. I'm good! I am worthy, as worthy as anyone. I am equal with everyone.

I am happy. I am abundant in every good. I am healthy and strong. I take care of my body's well-being. I have plenty of money. I am vitally alive, full of energy and courage. I am clear and free. I am intelligent and capable.

I am not an island. I choose loving and supportive friendships and relationships, amd nurture them. My friends encourage me. They empower me to follow my heart and fulfill my dreams. Whenever I need it I get help, both from within and from others.

I am a creative force; I create my life. I express myself, and give my unique gifts. I do what I love, and prosper. I welcome the new, my next steps in expansion and good. I leave behind what is no longer mine. I flow with change.

I fulfill my purposes for being here, the goals and dreams of my heart. Whatever it takes to accomplish a goal, I can do it. Anything is possible in God. The divine within me opens doors, shows the way and brings whatever is needed. I don't let setbacks get me down; I trust life, the universe, and myself as always flowing toward good. I see with new eyes. I know what to do. I keep focused on my goals, and upon the happiness of their fulfillment. I am grateful. I know they will come.

My entire life is an expansion into my wholeness, my divinity. So be it.

Holding to these and similar thoughts can be a challenge, especially when something really does look like a setback. But you will heal what is necessary. You'll become quick to recognize reactive feeling and thinking. You will get yourself back on the powerful, positive track.

Master, I Await Your Word

A young boy polishes an old brass lantern—and a genie appears! He grants three spoken wishes. This old tale, and similar ones, reflect a deep truth: the power of our spoken word.

The universe absolutely serves the word of the master we are. Words hold such power! They are a creative force, resonating with the creative energy of the universe. God *said*, Let there be light!

The divine master you are is never tired, sick, stuck, or broke. It is always abounding in energy, totally whole, strong and alive, moving easily forward, abundant in every good thing, and in charge of its own experience. This is the real you! To speak the truth about yourself is an invigorating tonic.

Disempowering phrases are spoken by the dozen in our society. We are so used to them, we aren't conscious of what they do. Even commiserating with another—"poor you," said one way or another—disempowers both people. The universe is always listening!—and obeying what it hears.

It is particularly important to follow the words "I am" with empowering statements.

Become aware of your words, and consciously and continuously change them around. Form new habits.

Some ideas for change:

I don't know.

> *I'm not aware of my knowing on this. I can access it.*

I desire. I want

> *I have a passion to, I choose ...*

I'm sick, I'm tired.

> *My body doesn't feel well; divine perfection expresses as my body.*

He's just a (derogatory something).

> *He's a beloved part of the divine, doing his best.*

I can't afford that.

> *I won't buy this now, and I am the abundance of the universe!*

I don't have _____.

> *What I choose to have is here! I am so grateful!*

I/you can't do that, it's not possible.

I/you can do anything we choose, within our framework of accepted good. We can completely expand the framework.

I hate this job, but I'm stuck here.

I chose this job. It's supporting my life. It is perfect for me at this moment, and I give thanks for it. I will create being supported by doing what I love.

I'm sorry.

I apologize.

I've got to make this deadline!

I easily make this timeline.

Nothing is certain but death and taxes.

Nothing is certain but divine love and truth.

How can I begin again after this happened?

Today is the first day of the rest of my life.

I'm just no good at this.

The divine in me can do anything.

It's my fault.

It's your fault. (Just kidding!) I am the eternal innocence of the divine. I am doing my best.

I can't stand this relationship!

I called this relationship to me. It is my perfect learning right now. I am seeing from my love and wisdom what to do next.

He/she did this terrible thing to me.

I am powerful. I choose my experience. I am never a victim. I learn from this, take appropriate action, forgive, forget, and move on. This experience makes me wiser and more powerful than ever before.

I have so many flaws.

My human personality has flaws. My true self is flawless.

I'm confused, afraid.

I feel confused, and that's okay. I am the perfect clarity of the divine within me. It's okay to feel frightened. I am the full courage of my divinity.

I love you to bits, to pieces, to death.

I love you so much! I love you completely!

I'm alone.

I am never alone. I am part of the divine, all that is. I am one with all.

Some power statements regarding a situation:

I created this. I love and forgive myself. I love and forgive others. There is no loss in God. I take whatever action is appropriate for the moment and this action is love-oriented, the highest and best I can see for all concerned. My God-given power is a creative force, and I use that power to create something new here. (For a blockbuster on this, see Troubleshoot a Situation in "Clear!")

Take a tape recorder with you, or a note pad, and record disempowering phrases you hear yourself say. Change them to empowering ones. Record empowering statements of your own and others that you want to remember and use.

In private, say these empowering statements aloud to yourself. Stand or walk tall as you say them.

In conversations with another, correct yourself aloud when you say something disempowering. This also assists your friend.

These are a few suggestions—create your own. We talk a lot! See how much life, love, power, and light you can put into your words. How much can you empower not only yourself, but everyone around you?

Act!

Action includes getting the groceries and doing the dishes, but here let's define it as "right action:" acts which purposefully advance life in alignment with spirit.

Action stems from consciousness—it is the end product of consciousness. Right action comes from spirit, through our heart and out into the world. For this to happen, we must be able to feel what our spirit suggests, or feel our heart's truth; these two are really the same. Right action is the most powerful, at least in the long run, because it is aligned with the universe.

Right action is available in every arena of life. How can this relationship move forward? How does spirit move me in this job? How can I help this situation? How do I choose to create? How does my heart call me to serve?

Acting alone is fine; many of us on a spiritual path seem to think of ourselves as lone rangers. But we have seen the vital power of people acting together for a cause. Can you imagine that unions once did not exist? Action with others is being part of the human family.

A group's purpose does not need to be complicated. My family lived for some years in Memphis, Tennessee when it was still segregated. "Colored" and white people could not eat in the same restaurant, stay in the same hotel, ride the same roller coaster, drink from the same water fountain. Hard to believe now. My mother and a good friend formed a loose group of women, both black and white, as a lunch club. They met once a month. They had no officers.

On a typical month, mother called a good restaurant in town to schedule a luncheon for thirty women—an excellent money-maker for that restaurant. When it was scheduled, she said "Oh, of course you do accept colored women?" There was a long pause. Then the employee consulted the manager. The manager consulted the owner.

In this peaceful way, Memphis became integrated. It was a simple, ingenious idea that worked.

Group action may be complex. Then come such questions as, "Who leads? Who follows? Who does what? What needs delegating? What shall we do next? And how can we do it all in harmony and joy, nourishing and empowering everyone involved?" Group right action is an art!

Right Action in a Group

First of all, what is your own heart's desire for action through a group? How does your spirit direct you? Are there others who have or may discover the same desire within themselves? Talk about your desire in a welcoming environment. Or welcome another's idea, and see if your spirit calls you to join the action.

Gather the group together for an opening session. Begin by calling in spirit to overlight everyone, guide all interaction and bless the meeting.

Now is the opportunity for each to share your heart's vision. How do you desire to serve? What do you want to accomplish? How do you see this group working together to that end? When all have shared, is there enough of a consensus on the group's purpose to actually bond together? If there is, celebrate!

Do you choose to create a name? Some others and I once co-created a group we called the Mt. Shasta Transformational Network. It took us quite a while to arrive at that name, but it served beautifully once we got it.

Do you want to elect officers, or be a free-form group? The group purpose will determine if officers are needed.

It is helpful to recognize at the outset something vital to your group dynamic. You are individuals passionate about the action you have chosen. There are going to be strong differences between you. There should be an effort to keep any one person or faction from pushing through what is not right for others. By common agreement—and a loving watchdog vigilance—keep group discussion continually overlit by spirit. This means first and foremost love for each person and respect for their ideas. It means really listening to others, and seeing from their point of view. It means a spirit of compromise. Most difficult, it means compromise when your own passionate conviction is not accepted *in toto.*

When there is non-agreement after everyone has been heard, meditate or pray together for a harmonious decision. The importance of this single step cannot be overestimated.

The Mt. Shasta Network lost its ardor, its love orientation, and group meetings began to focus on one hair-splitting detail after another. It stopped being fun. The Network disbanded. A resolution to keep things fun—not overly serious or heavy about anything—will do wonders to keep your group together. Plan relaxing times together too, just for the fun of it.

For inspiration on group process, read about the Findhorn years in Peter Caddy's book, *In Perfect Timing.*

You, Be There

Wherever you are, take a look around. Pick any object, man-made or natural, and say, *You, be there.* Look at a person you're with and say silently, *You, be exactly the way you are.* Look at your home from the outside and say, *You, be just where you are and look just as you do.* Say this to trees in the forest. Say it to anything.

The point is, you *have* chosen everything in your life exactly as it is. You can re-choose; this exercise gets you into your power to do that.

Walk the Walk

What is your vision of yourself as a master? How do you walk? Masters seem to hold themselves high and straight, but relaxed, full of grace and poise. They don't rush around, but remain centered in who they are. The attitude is one of uncon-ditional love and acceptance of themselves and all around them, and the knowing that all is well.

Walk as the ascended master you are. Experiment around the house, and then take it out in public. I know of nothing that can give such an immediate sense of being a master as this exercise.

Laugh!

When you are laughing, you are in power. Really, you are in enlightenment. There is a meditation that is just laughter, for three or five minutes or more—*genuine* laughter, not just ho-hoing.

Laughter is enormously beneficial. Norman Cousins, former editor of the Saturday Review magazine, healed himself of a "terminal" illness by laughing at a bunch of funny old movies. Try laughing—at nothing or something in particular—for a few minutes a day.

The 40-Day Process

It seems to take about six weeks, or forty days, to instill a major change or take a large step in it. This process is recommended by a number of teachers.

Choose your goal, one you will commit to and feel you can accomplish within the time frame. A goal will involve a change in consciousness, which will produce changes in your life. A goal could be "to feel my divinity more strongly," or "to love _____ unconditionally," or "to speak the truth in this situation," or "to accomplish _____."

In a notebook set down your beginning date, and ending date forty days later. Write out your goal.

Sit down with your inner self each day, and feel/see/hear your next inner and outer steps to your goal. Spirit is immensely practical. Follow what you are given. Set your experiences down; this helps you stay focused and realize what really has been accomplished at the end of the time.

On the fortieth day, look back over your notebook. Congratulate yourself and celebrate!

You may even want to set your next goal and do this again.

Wild You!

Run alone or with a wild friend through the fields at night—be naked to the wind—dance around a fire—drum and chant—howl at the moon—skinnydip—be outrageous! Go all out in a sport, or any harmonious activity where wildness can find a home. The wild you needs expression! Something vital is lost without it.

Women, read *Women Who Run With the Wolves* by Clarissa Estés. Men, read *Fire in the Belly* by Sam Keen, or *Iron John* by Robert Bly.

Sing and Drum!

From the beginning of time, drumming and singing—often accompanied with dancing—have transported human consciousness into more of a divine state. Here something powerful can be done, something wanted can be created. Think of the native American war dance and rain dance.

Gather a group. Bring drums and other wildish instruments. Go out into nature where you will be left alone. Go at night.

What's your purpose? Be wild woman? Wild man? End a drought? Create something? Strengthen a passionate cause? Make up your own songs, and drum and sing!

Let it be spontaneous, let it rise and fall and rise again, as it will.

Here's to infinitely powerful you!—in wisdom and love.

Empowering initiations in other chapters

"Clear!" chapter:
- ☆ Innocence I Am
- ☆ A New Social Agenda
- ☆ Troubleshoot a Situation

"Fulfill Your Purposes" chapter:
- ☆ Follow Your Own Star!

"Live Abundantly!" chapter:
- ☆ Intent, Focus and Power
- ☆ The Power of the Passionate Word

6
Lighten Relationships

Relationships! Infinite realities! Perfect mirrors!
The great mystery of self relating to
the great mystery of other.
Why did God create?
To relate!

Relationships are a crucible, a purifier. They offer torture from the deepest hell, rapture from the highest heaven, and everything in between. They reflect—for both people—our conscious and unconscious thoughts about ourselves and about life.

A good relationship with another draws from a good relationship with oneself. Do we have a strong connection, one way or another, with our spirit? Are we centered in that? Without vanity or arrogance, do we honor ourselves? Do we recognize both our strengths and our foibles? Do we accept ourselves—body, mind, and heart—as we are? Are we kind to ourselves? Do we encourage ourselves?

Many of us, through past difficulties, do not yet have a positive relationship with ourselves. If so, we need to chase away old demons and get on a happy track.

This is a particularly intense time for relationships, as we are moving from a limited vision of life to an expanded one. We do this one at a time; two people in relationship may do it at different times, causing imbalance and strain. It is also a time to clear up karmic relationships from this and past lives, and that in itself is not an easy task! Patience and understanding are required for relationships at any time, and now more than ever.

Let us leap right in!

I Love Myself

Take a cup, an empty cup, and hand it to another to drink from. Or, try to love another when you do not love yourself. Both are equally impossible!

Few of us have drunk the nectar of an ideal childhood. So we must learn to love ourselves; learn that we are worthy of love and worthy of loving. Learn that we are loved.

Here are statements to explore, change, subtract from and add to as you will. Love for ourselves, for our spirit, our uniqueness, must sing in our blood. Only then may we fulfill our lives. Only then may we truly love another, and accept their love.

I love myself! I am a most beautiful, wonderful being. I recognize myself as part of the divine. I am the love of the divine; I am the light, the joy and freedom, the wisdom and knowing, the power of the divine.

My greatest relationship is with divine-I-Am. This is the only relationship which is absolutely vital to my well-being. I follow my divine knowing, my heart, as best I can. I receive the divine's infinite love for me as deeply as I can. This is the happiness and fulfillment at the center of my being.

I am unique in all the universe; I fill a niche no one else can fill. As I discover my gifts, I give them.

I honor myself. I bless myself. I stand up for myself. I am honest with myself. I take care of myself and take care of my life. I take care of my body. I encourage myself and praise myself. I am my own best friend.

I am totally known and perfectly, eternally loved. I have always done my best. I forgive myself for my mistakes. As part of the divine I am completely worthy of all good. Abundance is my natural state.

I am on my perfect path. I have not strayed from it, as all has helped me become wise and led me to this place. All is well!

As I love myself, I love others. As I honor myself, I honor others. I am all that is required to have loving, supportive, honest and happy relationships.

I am love. I am lover. I am beloved. So be it.

Marriage of Your Inner Female and Male

Here is a process that unites aspects of your inner female and male. Both sides have many aspects; every time you do this process, you'll learn something new. The person we were in each lifetime is present within us. And every person important to us in every lifetime is present within us. The mind is so vast, the different aspects may never have met.

(I wish to credit Rev. Matt Garrigan for most of this process—see References).

Go into meditation, or simply into a quiet space. Ask your spirit to bring together appropriate aspects of your feminine and masculine sides.

Mentally place yourself in a beautiful natural setting. You feel safe and peaceful here. Listen—do you hear birds singing, wind soughing through the pines, waves rolling in? A gentle warm breeze caresses you.

You hear a voice calling you, a feminine aspect of yourself. You begin walking toward this voice, which grows louder. Finally, you round a bend or a boulder—here she is!

What is her appearance? Old or young, ugly or beautiful, rags or royalty—accept her. Give her your greeting in love. What would she like to tell you? Listen. Is there anything she would like from you? Have you been ignoring her knowing, her feeling? Give her what you can in the moment. Tell her you will return.

Now you hear the voice of a masculine aspect calling you. Again you walk toward the call, and finally, here he is! Greet him in love. How does he appear to you? What does he want to tell you? What does he want from you? Give him what you can for now.

Together, you and he travel back to the feminine. Witness their greeting. Do they already know one another, or are they strangers? After awhile, ask them if they would like to be friends, or even to marry?

If they choose marriage, invite them to go separately to prepare while you create the space for it. Create what you wish—a lovely outdoor setting, a cathedral. Do you want flowers? Arches, angels, a heavenly choir, a solo flute? Friends in attendance? A facilitator (you?), or none? When you are done, also create a honeymoon setting for them.

When the space is ready, go to the groom. Does he look the same, or has he changed? How has he chosen to appear for the wedding? He has a gift for his lady, the thing she most wants. What is it? A quality, an immortal rose, a necklace, a secret formula, a ship, a sword, a healing, a horse? Bring him to the wedding site.

Now go to the bride. How does she appear? She may be changed! What gift does she have for her groom, the thing he wants most? Escort her to her man.

Let the wedding unfold as you desire, in great love. They present their gifts to one another, and receive them with joy and wonder. Listen to what they vow to each other, what they will each give to this union.

Give them the gift now of their honeymoon setting. Witness their merging as they desire, sexually—or perhaps as light!

Finally, look them up five years later, to discover that they are truly happy, happier than when they wed, and opening up more to one another every day.

Merge Your Right and Left Brain

We know that the right side of the brain and the left side of the body are the feminine side, and vice-versa. As with humanity and our inner male and female, these two brain-universes need some loving help to get more together. This process is an expansion of one from Brain Gym (Edukinesthetics).

Place your hands a couple of feet out on either side of your head. Take the right side of your brain energetically into your right hand, and the left side in your left hand. See if you can feel, one after the other, the quality of each side. With deeper union as the goal, begin to move your hands slowly together, trying to keep in touch with both sides and letting them do their own dance.

Gradually bring your hands together, feeling all the way, until they finally are clasped in front of your forehead. Imagine doorways opening, energy flowing, love abounding! Greater communication and understanding. One wholeness.

Brain Gym gives many movements for getting the right and left brain together. One is simply to place both hands in front of you, in prayer position, and move them in a large sideways figure eight, beginning down to up and around to the left. Follow the movement with your eyes, but keep your head still.

Life in the twenty-first century invites separation between the right and left brain. You may want to do these exercises frequently.

Declaration of Divine Friendship

The core of every good adult relationship is a genuine, loving friendship between peers. We're all divinely equal; peers are people of the same *evolvement,* so we may truly give and receive with each other, learn from and teach each other. We all need peers.

The most passionate or romantic involvement ends more likely sooner than later without true kindness and caring. The foundation of friendship encourages inter-dependence. This is not the games of co-dependence—expectation, role playing, dominance-submission, possession, or leaning so hard on each other that we fall without the other's support. Neither is it over-independence, where each tries to be an island of self-sustenance. In inter-dependence we each stand centered and strong in our own relationship with spirit, and from that space we love, encourage and support one another.

Here are thoughts you may share together, adding your own as you choose.

It is a privilege for me to be in divine friendship with you! I recognize you as a beautiful being of divinity, wisdom, love, light, and strength. I focus upon this truth. We are equals.

The primary relationship for each of us is with the divine. Our purpose together is to share our divinity as fully as we may.

I follow my heart into fulfillment of my purposes, including oneness with the divine. I support you in doing the same. I love to see you grow and express as you desire and are guided. I encourage you, and am grateful for your encouragement. I delight in purposes we share together!

I do need you; we need each other. We have an inter-dependent relationship.

I enjoy our differences, our similarities, and our oneness. We both understand the principle that our love is like a bright beam shining into all corners of our psyches, bringing to light what remains to be forgiven and released. I share difficult things quickly, openly and honestly, taking responsibility for my own feelings. I help you heal and grow, and accept your help. I forgive you instantly or as quickly as I can, keeping the energy clear between us. I give thanks for all I am learning.

I give one hundred percent to our friendship. I give you my gifts. I honor and gratefully receive your gifts to me. I release expectations. I am trustworthy and honest with you. I accept the highest thought between us.

I create and share adventures with you that keep our friendship alive and expanding. I have fun! I am new today, you are new, and our friendship is new. I nourish it with my spirit, my truth, my love and support. I bless this divine friendship.

I give our friendship to the divine within us which guides us every day. As long as it remains the highest good for both of us to be in close exchange with each other, I commit to it. If it becomes no longer our highest good, I will recognize it, as will you, and we will change the form of our relating. And I am your friend, in deepest love, forever.

Intimacy? Oh, God!

A truly intimate loving relationship between mates is the scariest of all. We may become masters of friendship; we may know mate relationship that is actually friendship, or a mutually pleasant (or unpleasant) arrangement with little heart openness, or is a forum to loose one's troubles upon the other. But to really open our heart to the joys and pains of deep, mutual love is a mastery few of us have. It is fraught with the perils of facing unresolved issues from childhood and past lives—because love brings up anything unlike itself.

If you have desired a mutually loving relationship, deep and intimate, but have not allowed it to come to you, take a look at relationships where you've opened your heart. (Your last one may have been in early childhood.) Take a look at romantic involvements. What were your experiences? Ask yourself: what needs to change in order for me to love? What are my deepest relationship beliefs, my personal laws?

Some of the most common—and painful—of these:

☆ I need to be perfect to be loved, and I'm not perfect, so I'm not loveable or loved.

☆ If I love, I'll be abandoned: my partner will leave me for someone else, through death or for another reason.

☆ If I love, I'll be rejected. My love will not be returned.

☆ Spirituality and closeness with others do not go together. I hold to past life patterns as nuns, monks or yogis.

☆ Only as long as I can appear perfect and wonderful, and my partner can appear perfect and wonderful to me, can we be together. But since I'm not all perfectly wonderful, I will be discovered (and so will he/she). At the first sign that we are showing our "true" (bad!) colors, it's downhill from there. We're outta here!

Are any of these yours? What others do you have? Write them down if that serves you.

Now, get to work. Make up the opposite affirmations and say and feel them often. (You will find many below in Affirmations for Relationship). Allow the old pains to come up; explore them, release them as you are ready and let them fall away. Replace them with your chosen truth.

This may take time, even years. But when you become ready, look out! Your partner is on his/her way to you! It's *still* scary, but you can handle it!

Pair Up—Or?

People in intimate relationship that is both happy and fulfilling know a great blessing. Most of us are developing this skill by trial and error.

Wherever we are on our relationship path, there may be times—even years—for being single; perhaps too to be celibate. We may need a time to discover our spirit more deeply, or make a life-turning transition or journey.

On the other hand, if we've lived many a life in a monastery or nunnery or an Eastern equivalent, denying sex or intimacy as part of the divine, we could just be repeating the same old pattern. It may be time for a change!

Both the rightness of relationship and the rightness of solitude need to be honored, in their time. Look with your deep eyes and see where you are on this question.

Communicate!

Open, honest sharing blesses a relationship—if it is given and received responsibly. Most of us fear being honest, but where does dishonesty leave us? We must empower ourselves to communicate.

The person in our presence is doing his or her best. We are looking through lenses forged by our own history, and reacting to things we haven't resolved within ourselves. When we understand that, we can more easily take responsibility for our own experience. It is good to heal within ourselves as many difficulties as we can, so they don't even need to be brought up. When we must speak about a problem, we learn how to do it responsibly: *I feel,* rather than *You did this to me.* An attitude of humility, and willingness to learn, is a big help.

Here is a structured process that can strengthen honest communication between you and your friend. Some couples like to do this once a week. The ground rule is to take responsibility and speak in "I" terms. The sharing does not need to be difficult things only; it beneficially includes acknowledgments you hadn't gotten around to giving, and "I love you."

Set a time that works for both of you. If one or both of you can't find the time or don't want to do it, that may be something to look at.

Sit and face one another. Decide who'll go first, or flip a coin.

1. The first speaker shares from the heart until complete. An example: *When you did this, I felt _____ .* The listener does not answer, but acknowledges that he or she has understood what's being said.

2. The listener keeps in mind that the speaker is sharing feelings birthed in the past. He or she doesn't take offense.
3. When one is finished, the other shares. You may answer each other in your shares, but don't get into defending yourselves.
4. Go back and forth as long as it is fruitful.
5. Forgive one another.
6. Share your desires with one another. Share what you would like to receive from each other. Be honest about what you feel you can or cannot give.
7. Reaffirm the love between you. Carry out the desires of your heart. If you choose, do the Declaration of Divine Friendship above.

Name the Game

A game is a dishonest dynamic between two people, both of whom are being dishonest with themselves. Both have an investment in playing—usually an avoidance based on fear. A gamey relationship is not a happy one. (The old book by Eric Berne, *Games People Play,* is a classic on the subject.)

A game can only exist if:

1. Both people are playing it, and
2. It isn't acknowledged. It withers in the light of open communication. It is an act of power to name the game.

I once had a client (I'm changing the facts—only the game is the same) whose husband continually did the things that infuriated her most, like spend money needed for bills. She asked him over and over not to do it; he listened carefully and solemnly agreed. Then woop! he did it again. Furious and frustrated, she complained to her friends.

What she didn't realize was that she was telling him exactly what *to* do. She carried a deep belief that men dishonored her. Her husband "heard" her inner command as "Spend this money to reflect my belief about men." Rather than realizing what was going on, he just did it. He could only have done it if he carried a corresponding thought that he held another—and thus him-self—in disrespect.

When she discovered the cause of both their behaviors, she was able to stop her part of the game. Their relationship benefited.

This is an example of how every difficult pattern in a rela-tionship—when we learn from it—nurtures both people. All "garbage," in this case the game, can be used to fertilize a better relationship. So there is no judgment of games; they can be a doorway to a happier relationship.

Look at one of your relationships. Is there a game going on? If yes, what exactly is the game? Why are you playing it? What are you gaining from it? What do you think your friend is gaining from it? Be honest with yourself.

Are you willing to have an open, clear relationship? If yes, is speaking to your friend an option? If speaking is not an option, you might ask yourself: *What am I doing here?*

If you feel speaking—no matter how frightening it may be—can work, gather your courage and speak! See if you can do it as suggested in the Communicate! section above:

> *This is my experience. (It is helpful to pinpoint exactly what you see happening) I say this, then you do that, and then … And I feel … I realize why I've been doing this, which is … How do you feel about what I'm saying?*

Your choice to bring things which were comfortably hidden out into the light of scrutiny will probably shock your friend. You are leading the way, and they may need time to catch up. Allow that they probably have an entirely different experience than you. Try to discover what that is, and honor it.

At some point, communicate how you would like things to change. Be very careful to speak for the benefit of *both* of you. You've been co-creating the game together; there is no victim. As you see it, what would most benefit your relationship?

If your friend is not able to see the game right away, or at all, or remains in denial of it, be patient and feel from your spirit how to proceed. Next time it happens, you may catch it on the spot and talk about it.

Games can be quite convoluted and based upon deep and painful issues. Look at the game the couple plays in Albee's "Who's Afraid of Virginia Wolff?" Clarity may not come quickly, and you may choose to get outside help. You may find that your friend is unable to give up a game you have moved beyond; in this case, a new form for your relationship may be the best step. But if you can both see the game and change it, what a breakthrough for you both! What a blessing!

Here's to the replacement of all destructive games between people with clarity, honesty and love.

Come Even

When you want to forgive someone, sometimes anger or hate is so strong that you can't begin. Pent-up feelings from a hard relationship, especially where we were dominated, become a poison that may be buried so deep we aren't aware of them. Even if we are, we may feel unable to release them.

A master once gave me a vision of a pile of garbage—suppressed anger—lying in the sun. A black plastic cover was put over the garbage, which became putrid in the heat. The message was that the longer such feelings are suppressed, the more trouble they cause. As well as messing up present relationships, they can cause illness or accident. Someone I know with muscular degeneration is carrying her anger to her grave.

This process is a step toward forgiveness. It's really for the child in you that feels victimized or dominated, less than the other person, to *come even*. Then relaxation, forgiveness and forgetting can follow. It's meant to be done alone.

Who is hard for you to forgive? Choose someone. Say:

I call in my spirit (or whoever you wish). I ask that any emotions or words I release about _____ be immediately dissolved in love and light, so they are rendered harmless. This is a step in forgiveness.

In your mind's eye, if you like, place this person in front of you. Get in touch with your feelings about him or her. Say the things you never could say. Feel free to yell, throw a tantrum, scream and holler. Use your body and breath to punch the person out, run over him with a tank, stab him, beat him up with a baseball bat. If this seems too violent, just imagine what these feelings were doing to you as you held them in! And you have rendered them harmless to the other. Let yourself come to completion.

Remember that you are *releasing,* not simply feeling old victim stuff and holding on to it.

When you are complete with anger release, other feelings are likely to come up. Tears or laughter, whatever they are, let yourself have them. Follow wherever you go.

Finally, check yourself out. Are you ready to forgive now? If so, do! If you are not, let it rest and repeat the Come Even in a few days or so, and more if needed until it feels done. Then do a big forgiveness and relationship healing (below), and congratulate yourself! You have released yourself from an old prison and you are free! You have also benefited the person you are forgiving.

Dissolve Psychic Cords

A vital part of a divinely guided relationship is freedom: freedom to be yourself, to follow your heart, to speak your truth. Freedom and love are one.

Nearly all relationships suffer from psychic cords. These are made of emotional energy which is not love, but rather attachment, fear, dependency, expectation, guilt, anger, jealousy, dominance, kow-towing. They have nothing to do with the bonding of genuine love as between a mother and her newborn, or a husband and wife. "Smother love," however, involves psychic cords.

You may be corded to a person who's in your life or not, either living or departed.

One person may initiate cording, and if the other unconsciously agrees, then both are corded. It's possible for only one person to have cords, such as to a lost love.

You may need to give special attention to a long-standing relationship like a parent or child. A common dynamic is feeling that you must take care of someone else energetically, be taken care of, or both. Worrying about someone is part of the same dynamic. You are setting up one of you to take the place of divine care and love. Perhaps the dynamic was set up long ago, has kept on keeping on, and you aren't even aware of it.

When this happens, energy drains from the one trying to give care to the other. And it is denying the divinity of the one perceived as needful.

Psychic cording can also be with places, objects, and events. Thinking lovingly and happily of someone or something is harmonious; feeling an emptiness, an unfulfilled longing, may be cording or not, depending on where you are coming from.

Freedom and love are one! Freedom means being fully present with our energy field intact; in this state, our choices are open. Dissolving cords is an act of love. It requires passion and determination, and it will change your relationship. It is a large, powerful thing to do. If your relationship is a deep one, once you dissolve the cords it will take will power to keep them dissolved and keep freedom between you.

The cords you will see are your own cords to the other, but your clearing will help her or him to clear as well.

Choose a person with whom you feel you are psychically not clear or free. Sit in a quiet place and close your eyes. Picture your friend sitting in front of you. Can see, or feel, the cords? They usually go between the chakras (especially the lower three), and clairvoyantly may appear as rubbery, and gray or grayish-green in color. They may look like single cords or may be a tangled mass. You may think you are imagining them, but probably you are doing some accurate clairvoyant seeing. You may also feel them as emotions.

When you have seen or felt them clearly, say gently to your friend:

I am going to dissolve my psychic cords with you now so that we may more truly love each other, in freedom.

If you realize you've been draining your own energy trying to take care of them energetically, add:

I recognize you as fully divine, fully loved. You don't need me to send you energy, and I don't need to be needed. I release that mistaken idea of love; my real love for you is too precious. And I do not worry about you. Your own divinity is your infinite source of energy and goodness. It is here with you now. I will continue to see you as the divine you are, and keep my own energy with me. So be it.

If you are longing for a person, object, event you're not experiencing now, say to yourself:

I am whole, a fully divine person, right here and right now. I am complete. I do not need you to be fulfilled in life. I am fulfilled. I choose to feel this truth more and more, beginning now! So be it.

Now take a sword of light, as in the "Star Wars" movies. Locate your willingness to be free, your desire and passion to be really free! Call Archangel Michael if you choose, with his sword, and ask him to join you in cutting the cords. He's an expert!

When you feel ready, take a deep breath in, and on a strong "Whoosh!" of out-breath, bring the sword down all the way to your feet. Give the breath resistance and noise; blow through your lips until the very end, when you open your lips for a final, forceful puff of air.

Another way to dissolve the cords is to go gently back and forth between the two of you with the sword.

Now, check things out. Did you get all the cords? Did you get any of them? There may be quite a resistance to this! See where you are. You may be able to dissolve them all today, or it may take repetition.

If you don't feel ready to dissolve psychic cords, love and forgive yourself for that. The time will come.

When the cords are dissolved, feel your new freedom! It may not be comfortable, like something is missing (true!). You've created a vacuum, and you'll want to fill it with new choices. What are they? How does freedom change you? How does it change your relationship? Decide upon ways of being/doing with your friend that support both of you as free beings.

Check your "freedom quotient" and re-dissolve cords frequently (even one or more times a day) for awhile, at least several weeks. Cording was an established habit, and attention needs to be given to hold and expand your freedom.

Relationship Healing

You can heal relationship with someone living or departed. It is equally valuable for a relationship you are with, one you are ending, or one that is ended but not resolved in your heart.

It may be helpful, before the healing, to do the Come Even and/or the Communicate! process, both above.

Ask your spirit to lead you in the healing. Get together with your friend or partner, or call him or her to you in a lighter body. If you do it alone, the healing will benefit both of you.

Call in your divinity, and that of your friend, and take the time to feel connected with your spirit. Here are statements for you or both of you to say. Change or add to them as you choose:

Beloved _____! We chose to come together before we met. I love you so much that I invited you to be part of my life. And I know you love me so much, you invited me to be part of yours. We have come together for perfect purposes.

I know I have done my very best with you, each moment, with what I have truly known. I have never harmed the essence of your being, which is eternally divine and whole. But I know you have felt hurt at times, or angry with me, and this I have held against myself. I have given you all the love I knew how to give; and I have received from you all the love I knew how to receive. I forgive myself for anything I have felt toward you, said to you or about you, done, or seemingly failed to do. I forgive myself now as deeply as I can, for everything I have held against myself regarding you.

(Take time to do this now. Breathe! Release yourself emotionally! Really do it! If you need more work with this, see the forgiveness work in "Clear!")

I know you have done your very best with me, each moment, with what you truly knew. You have given me all the love you knew how to give, and received from me all the love you knew how to receive. I forgive you for anything you have thought or felt about me, anything you have said to me or about me, and anything you have done or seemingly failed to do. I forgive you now, as completely as I can.

(Do this now. Breathe! If there is something in particular that needs your forgiveness, give special attention to that. Release your friend *emotionally.*) Dissolve psychic cords between you (see above).

Call the violet flame of forgiveness and purification to blaze through the entire past of your relationship. Let it burn up and transmute, into light and love, any difficulties that were between you. See the flame blazing up from the center of the earth, through every aspect of both of you. Feel it! Let everything go!

I give thanks for this relationship! I choose now to learn anything I have wanted to learn from it, but hadn't yet allowed. (Ask your spirit, now or later, to show you what this might be.)

I now create a new relationship with you. I see you as the divine spirit you are in human form. I see myself the same way. We are both the love, the joy, the wisdom, and the light of the divine.

If you choose, do the Declaration of Divine Friendship above.

What is your new relationship? If you are physically together, see and feel your love, honesty, laughter, joy, cooperation, and support. If not, feel the harmony and peace between you. See and feel it all clearly.

If you're together now, will you each nourish your new relationship? You may repeat this process to help positive changes blossom into fruition.

From this moment, you have a new relationship. Congratulations!

Tantric Sex

Sex is meant to be a holy act. The more love there is, the more it resonates with the love of God/Goddess. The male and female polarities of God, in ecstatic union, created the universe and every ongoing moment of it. Sex is the embodiment of this dynamic.

Of course, celibacy is just as fine a path—*if* it comes from your heart.

Women, usually more connected with the love aspect of divine nature than men, are natural teachers for their partners in sex. In the East, women called *tantricas* used to initiate men into sex. This was part of the practice of tantra, an ancient philosophy which includes sex as a catalyst for enlightenment.

In making love, try some of these tantric principles.

☆　Prepare your surroundings to be sensually pleasing in every way—clean, beautiful, fragrant, and softly lit.

☆　Envision yourselves as god and goddess, and treat each other so. Focus upon the expression of love between you, moment to moment, rather than heading for a goal. This allows each moment to be all—complete in itself. Remember how wondrous a kiss could be when loving stopped there?

☆　Rather than moving toward orgasm, try integrating your energies so that you move to higher and higher levels of intensity and pleasure. If you were to draw the energy path, it would go up gently, plateau off; travel up to a higher level and plateau off; and keep on going! A few ways to try this:

☆　Sit facing one another, looking deeply into each other's eyes. Breathe long, slow breaths together.

☆　In the same position, as one partner breathes in, the other breathes out, and vice-versa. Picture a circle of energy coming up the spine of the woman as she breathes in, arching from her crown chakra over to his, and moving down his spine as he breathes in.

☆　With the woman on the man's lap, enter into sexual union almost imperceptibly, little by little. After joining, allow stillness to be a large part of the experience. Include the two kinds of breathing above.

☆　If the energy of one of you is about to go over the top, the other begins to breathe rapidly. Both breathe together, gradually slowing the rhythm and integrating the energy.

☆　Take breaks; rest and talk. When you come back together, the energy can build to a higher level.

☆　Sexual energy is part of your life force, called kundalini, coiled at the base of your spine. As your first and second chakras are activated in lovemaking, visualize this energy as golden. Intend that it travel up your spine to your crown chakra. Breathe it up. But be gentle; kundalini power is nothing to play around with. Don't force anything, just flow with love.

There are many more suggestions in tantric manuals. See Margo Anand's book *The Art of Sexual Ecstasy,* for one. There are also many workshops on tantra now; clear discernment is advised!

Within the framework of mutual desire, love, and pleasure, honor your sexual expression. Honor sex itself. Honor yourself in desiring it and having it. Sex is innocent.

A Sexual Blessing

In the following, if you choose, change "I" to "we."

I accept conscious sexuality. I recognize both myself and my partner as the god/goddess we are. I treat us both as such. I give our love a beautiful space: a gift to our senses and worthy of the presence of the divine. I choose a time for loving when we are both fresh and full of energy.

I choose to give each moment of our loving the attention, love, honor, spontaneity, and rich variety it deserves.

I release the goal of orgasm, and any formula of foreplay. I allow love to always be the focus and the expression, to flow however it does over an abundance of time, in natural surges, ebbs, and re-surges. I allow more and more energy to be integrated, without needing to be thrown off in orgasm. Orgasm is fine too, and there need be no weakening effect; my partner and I nourish and strengthen each other on all levels through love.

I am open to the tantric practice of my sexual expression quickening my enlightenment, including raising the energy through my spine to my crown chakra.

I also have the freedom to choose celibacy for a short or long time, understanding that it is no closer to God than is sexual expression. I honor whatever is most joyous and right for me.

I bless, honor and love my sexual expression as the expression of God's love through myself. So be it.

The Parent-Child Relationship

Principles of relationship based upon the divinity of both people hold true between parent and child. The child is equally divine with the parents, equally powerful, and her soul may be older and wiser than her parents'. The relationship is based upon mutual love, honor and respect.

The parent-child relationship is different from others in that the parent invites a person not consciously known to him into his life. But the agreement to come together was made before the child was born, and no matter how the two relate, this agreement should be given the honor and commitment it deserves.

Wonderful friends of mine are a couple and their seven children. Both parents are committed to the marriage and to the complete well-being of each child—a commitment that arises naturally out of who they are. The children are treated with a loving kindness which nurtures their confidence and creativity, and calls forth in each the same love and nurturing of each other. Some of the usual dynamics happen here and there, jealousy or upsetness or the like, but it blows over quickly and is forgotten. This whole scenario will become commonplace in the approaching golden age; but at the moment whenever I visit, my heart aches with yearning for all children to be so loved. We would live in a healed world.

For parents, here are ideas for relating with your child.

☆ Your relationship with your divinity is the single most important example you can set for your child. As you follow your heart and fulfill your purposes, you give her an invaluable gift.

☆ Part of your purpose in raising a child is to express your own divinity more deeply with the help of the mirrors and interactions between you.

☆ This child is not yours, but God's. She has her own reasons for coming to earth and her own purposes to fulfill. Your job is to support her in this. Any attachment for her to follow in family footsteps, or do things you want for her, needs to be released.

☆ Respect and love create a milieu where physical punishment is not necessary. Your child needs encouragement and praise. Putdown and violence of any kind, emotional or physical, are out of the question. When mistakes happen, amends are in order. Forgive yourself as quickly as you can for any hurt you bring to her heart, mind or body. If you are unable to be gentle, get help! Clear the pain out of your own being. It should be totally clear to your child that she is completely safe, loved, and valued by you. You can only give this to her if you are giving it to yourself.

☆ Respect, love and honor all others in her presence. Express your honesty and integrity.

☆ Play and laugh with her! Bring out your own creativity. Go on adventures and have fun—these require only imagination, not travel. Be together with nature. Horizons unlimited!

Affirmations for Relationship

Here are strong, positive statements to help turn relationships to the light. You may recognize "antidote" statements from *Living Mastery,* though often with different headers and wording. Most are for any close relationship, some are for intimate relationship, and some for people you don't know:

☆ **Divine we are.** *I Am a whole, strong, divine person. I accept and love myself as I am. I am loveable and loved, just as I am. I do not need you in particular to be happy and fulfilled. You are equally divine and strong, and do not need me in particular. God is the primary relationship for each of us. (For a relationship of deep love and long standing, these statements may not feel true. Try them out and see where they lead you.)*

☆ **Interdependence.** *All of life is interdependent and one. Separation is an illusion. We all need each others' love. I do need close relationships, and I know you do, too.*

☆ **Appreciation and honor.** *I am so honored that you are in my life! I am so grateful and appreciative that we are together! I honor myself and honor you. I accept your honoring of me.*

We are both worthy of love. We are both *divine beings, worthy of love exactly as we are. We cannot be lessened.* I am not concerned about what anyone thinks of either of us.

☆ **Dedication.** I am dedicated to your well-being as to my own. I love you!

☆ **Mutual love.** Ours is a deep, lasting, mutual love. I open my heart to you and love you fully, and you fully return my love. You open your heart to me and love me fully, and I fully return your love.

☆ **Fulfillment.** I know who I am and what I choose for my life. I follow only the divine within me, my true heart. I am here to grow into my full expression of divinity in your presence and with your support. I do all that is truly important to me. I support you in doing the same.

☆ **Responsibility.** You and I together create what happens between us, and we are each responsible for our experience of it. Both of us do our best with what we know. I love and forgive myself, and you. If you feel hurt, I have compassion, and learn how to be more loving; I also make amends whenever appropriate.

☆ **Self-authority.** I do not presume to tell you how you are feeling or what is best for you. Only you know that. I communicate what I perceive, which I see through my own filters. If I perceive you are being destructive toward yourself or others, from my love for you I speak! And I completely honor your self authority, your free will, and your life choices.

☆ **Communication.** I take responsibility for what I think, feel and do. You are an innocent, faultless being, and any judgment I feel is my own misperception. I release as much as possible through my divine connection. I know you can hear anything I feel the need to say, and I share responsibly—I do not dump on you. I encourage you to do the same. Communication is a great power for good in our relationship, and frees us to feel our love for each other. I am dedicated to truth between us.

☆ **I am happy and free!** I am already happy and free inside, and I don't need you or circumstances to be any particular way. I alone am responsible for feeling my happiness and freedom.

☆ **Forgiveness.** I know you always do your best with what you know. There is never a reason to blame. I am whole and fulfilled, whatever you do. I forgive you and forget it. I do communicate clearly *what I would enjoy creating together.*

☆ **Acceptance.** *I accept and love you the way you are. I honor your pattern of growth; you are exactly in your right place. I use neither criticism nor conditional approval toward you; only unconditional approval. If I have some knowledge I think may benefit you, I give it freely and in love. I have no attachment about whether you use it.*

☆ **I am good.** *Any criticism toward me is a service that shows me a thought I am holding about myself. I am glad to see it so I can let it go. Nothing can reduce the perfect wholeness and goodness of the divine I Am, so I never need defend myself. I do choose to be in the presence of people who support and encourage me.*

These next two are especially for caregivers and those who need to be taken care of.

☆ **You are divine and cared for.** *You are a whole, divine being. God takes care of your life. I am with you as long as I am guided to be, following my heart. If I am guided to do something else, God will provide for you in a new way, and I will do my best to help that happen.*

☆ **I free you!** *I do not desire you to do for me out of obligation. I free you! If it is best for you to leave, do that; I am always taken care of. I do not choose to manipulate you in any way.*

☆ **No martyr me!** *My giving is joyful, and it fulfills me. It increases my aliveness in all ways. I do not need to do things for you in order to receive in return. I do not hold you in guilt to give to me. I deserve and receive love just for being. You are free!*

☆ **No domination.** *The role of dominator is not stronger than the role of being dominated. With equal power we have both chosen our roles in this relationship, in order to learn that we can be both equal and loving. We were both leaning on each other. We can now drop the pretense of either kind of weakness and be the strong, loving, equal people we are.*

☆ **Sexual fulfillment.** *I am a fulfilled person. I feel and know this. I communicate freely to you what I enjoy and invite you to do the same. In our sexual sharing, I share my love with you without expectation. We express perfectly for now, and expand from here!*

☆ **If it's over, let's go!** *If our relationship is past rejuvenation, it is* best for both of us to leave it. We are never alone; God is with us each moment, as our primary relationship. Letting each other go creates a vacuum that draws my expanded good to me, and yours to you.

☆ **I trust myself, therefore I trust life and you.** I trust my love and your own. I know that the more deeply I am known, the more wonderful I am known to be (as are you). My trust draws only trustworthy people to me; therefore I can safely be intimate with you.

☆ **Up and down we go!** Our relationship ebbs and flows. Our passion wanes and waxes; closeness follows times of solitude. Together we trust the ups and downs of our relating, because a down always leads to a new up.

☆ **Free of the past.** I heal my relationships with my parents and forgive them and myself. I heal my relationships with all others. I affirm my full, free and independent adulthood! I am free to have the kind of relationship with you that I really want, and to see you as yourself rather than as a projection from my past.

☆ **Joy!** We are here to be happy. We deserve and need joy! If we are not creating it together, let us learn how to do it.

☆ **Changeless, eternal love.** I loved you infinitely before we met, and I always will; as you love me. I do my best to clear any limited perspective that clouds my love for you. If it is time for us to change the form of our relationship, our love continues forever.

☆ **I cannot be abandoned.** I do not have to leave first for fear you will abandon me. I am part of God, and God cannot leave Itself. I am forever safe and loved in my oneness with God. I can stay with you without fear.

☆ **We'd rather be happy than right.** We choose peace and understanding, not right/wrong conflicts. We are each right from our point of view, and we stretch to accept each other's. We find the highest thought in each situation and follow it.

☆ **We plan forays into the unknown!** Ruts are not for us. Physically and spiritually, through our hearts and minds, we continue to expand our love and our life together.

☆ **Perfect equality in God.** Equality is the bottom line between us. If one of us is more wealthy or in a more prestigious position, or of a certain race or religion, or younger and more beautiful, our equal-

ity is the same as ever. I honor that through whatever our differ-ences seem to be.

☆ **Love beyond boundaries.** *We are free to express beyond roles, beyond gender or position, however we are moved; that is the way of the divine. We love one another.*

☆ **Only friends in the world.** *Though we have not known each other before, you are the love of God as I am. We are one, brothers and sisters. You want and need my love as I do yours. You mean to me all that I mean to myself, and I give you the love I am.*

On the Death of A Loved One

Help a Loved One To Pass On

A major premise of this work is that a human body does not have to die. But the great part of humanity is not yet ready for this message. We must honor where we are as whole and good; if we do not choose to embrace immortality, or if we do but aren't experiencing it, that is perfectly all right. Death is a new birth, a well-traveled path to continue life.

There is still so much ignorance in the world about the tran-sition called death, and so much unnecessary sorrow! It's pos-sible for a soul to be complete with earth life at age three or younger; that isn't a wasted life. When a person is ready to depart, any means will do including disease or accidental death.

It is natural to mourn, but the death of a loved one is much easier to accept when we know she or he is still alive, doing different things in a different place—almost always a happier place. We forget about the higher worlds from which we come, and to which we return.

If someone you love is facing the death transition, greater knowledge may be of great comfort to them—or to yourself, if you are looking at that possibility.

First, know that *you can create your passing as you choose.* If you want to go quickly and painlessly, you most definitely can. There is no need to bow to any old belief about cancer or what-not in your family. My mother's family has a history of cancer; both her parents and one brother died of it, and two of her sisters had mastectomies. I spoke with her several times about being able to go as she chose. When she left, her heart took her out quickly and painlessly.

Know your own power to choose. Affirm it. If the time has passed for this affirmation, do your best with what is happening. God is here with you.

If you have a belief in hell, and especially if you fear going there, it is strongly suggested that you choose a new belief. God has never, ever judged you. You have done your best. You are forgiven. God sees you only as the beautiful, divine, innocent light-being you are. Help yourself come to *know* these truths.

If you find yourself passing, stay focused on love. Look for the light, and *head for the brightest light you can see.* This will be your higher self, waiting for you in total love. You may also see loved ones who passed over before you. It is a wonderful help to focus upon love, your love for God, yourself, your higher self, and all you see.

Confusion can enter because it's an intense transition; stay focused on love and light. It is good to plan for the possibility that you might become confused or frightened in the transition, or feel lost. Decide that you will call your own higher self, God/Goddess, or a loving master or personal guide. Whether or not you have a relationship with a master, he or she will love to serve you. Jesus or Mary, any archangel, Babaji or Buddha, your guru if you have one, or any ascended master you call upon will be immediately by your side. Ask to be joined with your higher self.

You'll probably experience something like this: with your higher self, you'll look lovingly upon your life, see what you wanted to accomplish, what you did well and what you'd like to do better. You'll quickly throw off any age you've known and become youthful and beautiful in body again, a body that may feel pretty much like your young physical body. You'll feel your divinity much more clearly. You'll stay on the lighter plane, peacefully learning and expanding in wisdom. Then you will probably choose a new earthly life, perhaps into your own family.

Whatever takes place, know that *all is well.* You are loved! You are taken care of.

Help a Loved One Who Has Passed On

Most people leave the body when it is their highest good and greatest joy, though their choice to leave is usually unconscious. There is no accidental death, but anyone—especially children—subject to the creation of their parents or to their surroundings may pass on when it is not their own desire.

Most often when people leave, they are able to join their higher self—the dazzling light and love reported in so many near death experiences—and go to the place that serves them best. But it is all too common for people to get stuck on the earth plane after passing, where they no longer belong. Often, they are attached to their beloveds on earth and choose, inappropriately, to stay. Those who die suddenly or in pain or violence may get confused in the transition and not join their higher self. It is also possible for different levels of consciousness to be in different places: the mental body may remain where death took place, for instance, and the emotional body with loved ones.

You can connect with loved ones who have passed. They are now in the mental/emotional realm and are able to pick up your thoughts. You can call them to you, and communicate easily. Whether or not you are able to feel their response, they can hear you.

You may understand that they have joined their higher presence by getting a sense of light, joy, or love. Or they may appear to you in a dream or vision—even in a tangible body—to show you they are in the light. If there is any doubt, say the words below. For these I thank the Teaching of the Inner Christ.

Call your loved one to you. Call with your heart and with your words. Wait until you feel he or she is present with you.

Speak from your heart. Put to rest anything unfinished between you. When you are complete, ask if he or she would like to communicate, and feel deeply for his or her words.

Finally, tell him or her you are going to speak words that will help him or her join the light and love of his or her divine presence, if he or she has not already done that. Then say:

Dear _____, your I Am Presence now makes certain that all your levels of consciousness are present for this healing. (There may be a pause here.) You are welcome in love. You are surrounded and

*filled with the Christ (or God) love and light. You are healed and for-
given. You are lifted free of Earth's vibration, and free of all pain and
suffering. You are now joined (or your favorite master now joins you)
with your own true higher self of love and light. (Add anything further
you'd like to say, and tell her good-bye.) Your higher self will take you
now to your next right place. I bid you farewell—go in peace!*

See if you can sense their departure, or the light—anything
that tells you it is accomplished. If you feel it hasn't worked,
you may speak lovingly to them of God's love for them. They
are forgiven, they deserve a happy place, and it is better for
them to relate to their new realm now and not try to stay with
the physical plane. Say anything you feel inspired to say. Then
repeat the healing words.

Some people are just not ready to go on. If this is true for
your loved ones, let that be all right. You may check on them at
intervals to see if they are ready to join their higher self and go
to their next experience.

After loved ones have gone into the light, they may move to a
level so different from earth that you feel unable to contact them.
You may call, and they don't come. Understand that life is glori-
ously diverse and infinite, on many dimensions, and a realm lighter
than earth is just as real and involving as life here. If there is a
truly urgent matter and you call passionately and consistently,
they will probably come. Otherwise, let your loved ones go.

Companion and Wild Animals

Sai Baba once said that everything, even the lowliest little
fly enjoying lunch on a pile of horse dung, would one day realize itself as part of God. Every consciousness would succeed
in this ultimate goal.

Animals are like our younger brothers and sisters; they're
on the same trail we're following. Except for some dolphins
and whales, they just have further to go.

The more complex the nervous system of an animal's body,
the more likely it is to have an individual soul. Lower orders of
animals, birds, and insects usually have "group souls."

Because animals are part of nature and are innocent and loving, they have much to teach us. Animals who become human companions may develop highly individualized souls, and have special gifts to give. They may do extraordinary things to help their humans, and even people they don't know.

There can be such love between an animal and its human that it reincarnates over and over to be with that person. Once my beloved cat Oscar died unbeknownst to me while I was traveling. When I went to bed each night, I would hear the pit-pat-pat of little cat feet on the floor, and then feel thump! at the foot of my bed. For a time, I thought nothing of it—but it repeated every night. Finally, I realized it was Oscar.

Ten years later, with a new female cat, my spirit said one day out of the blue, "You have known this cat before." I hadn't asked the question, and the possibility had not even occurred to me. When I searched my past, I finally realized—Oscar had "reincarnicatted!"

Our relationship with a beloved dog or cat or other animal, as with our close human souls, can span not only years, but lifetimes. It deserves our nurturing love and respect.

Wild animals generally mistrust humans because most are not emanating the pure love that is our deep reality, and mankind's violence toward animals is known. But in the presence of a master, one who is this love, the wildest of animals becomes gentle.

Even if we are not fully realized, when we come upon a "dangerous" wild animal we may remember truth and say silently to it, *You and I are both part of God. We cannot harm one another. I love you.* There's a beautiful story in *Unveiled Mysteries,* by Godfré Ray King, about his encounter with a huge wild panther on Mt. Shasta.

Initiation

Most desired by animal companions from their humans is love. Communication and understanding run a close second. Animals so want and need these. When we learn how to listen, they are ready to let us know how they feel and what they want.

Observe your animal friend closely, looking with eyes and heart that desire to know and understand more deeply. Animals have clear body language, eyes that show emotion, facial and vocal expression just as we do. What is he or she saying?

Sitting with your friend, tune in to him or her. *Here I am, ready to listen to you. I love you. What would you like to tell me?* You'll probably get feelings and pictures, and their meaning can be quite precise. This may come easily to you. If it doesn't, do your best and don't be discouraged. Your desire to communicate will bear fruit.

Certain people have developed the art of communication with animals to a high degree. One of these is my friend Sharon Callahan, whose work I highly recommend (see References). With a little research, you can find others.

Nature

Nature is such a vast, wild mystery! Her physical diversity and grandeur alone make Earth one of the most spectacular of planets. And what most of us can't see—the tree and mountain spirits, plant devas, fairies and elves, the under-earth gnomes, the playful dancers among the waves, the wind devas, angels of place, the nature god Pan—is even more amazing. *The Real World of the Fairies* by Dora Van Gelder, and *In Perfect Timing* by Peter Caddy, reveal secrets of nature.

Before you come to see nature spirits by looking directly, you may see them from the corner of your eye or with your third eye. I've seen elves this way. You can also hear them through clairaudience. In an old forest I once heard piping, as if it came from within me.

You can connect with Pan just as with another master. Depictions of Pan as drunk and promiscuous miss his essence entirely. For a clearer vision, read the chapter "The Piper at the Gates of Dawn" from *The Wind in the Willows* by Kenneth Grahame, or listen to Robert Crombie's tapes on meeting Pan from the Findhorn library (see References).

Every nature spirit is different. Two of the same kind of bush may have entirely different personas. Some trees don't enjoy human contact and friendship, and others do—you can have a tree best friend. Mountains have great huge spirits that can be communicated with. There is an infinity of potential relationship with nature.

When you are deep in woods, desert, river canyon—or in your back yard or city park—put out your feelers to discover what you're not seeing. Give your love to all around you. Make friends with the flowers, bushes and trees. Go barefoot and feel the earth. Listen with your heart. Focus lightly, and watch the corners of your vision. Open your third eye. Invite connection!

Be naked in the wind. Give it your love and honoring. Request it to blow more gently or intensely. Ask it to caress your body. It is a phenomenal experience to feel the conscious, loving caress of the wind.

Be with a tumbling stream or river. It can see you and feel you. Form a relationship with it.

Give a loving greeting, blessing and thanks to Helios and Vesta, the sun, when she rises and sets or any time. Blow a kiss to land on her surface.

Place

Every area of nature, and every part of a city or town—even down to small pockets like a particular property—has its own "feel," its own frequency. If people live there, of course that affects it; but they were likely drawn there because that place felt best to them.

These frequencies can differ vastly. After Peter Caddy made a tremendous success of one Scottish hotel, the company transferred him to another. There, he could get nothing going at all! The very walls—and the surrounding countryside as well—seemed steeped in darkness. It was a learning to him about the importance of place.

Where we are affects us on deep levels. Heidi thrived in the mountains, but the city crushed her spirit. Most of us have experienced that one place feels much better to us than another.

If you're interested in a particular area or city or home, go there and just be for awhile. How do you feel there? Do you feel alive? Happy? Does it nourish you? In choosing a new place, feeling is the key.

Your New Home

Someone moves into a home, and things suddenly break. Someone else buys a car, and quickly wrecks it. Have you heard of such?

Things have consciousness. A home or car has an "elemental," a rudimentary consciousness which is formed by the relationship between itself, its environment and its people.

My parents once owned a '63 Chevrolet that they drove down to Mexico on vacation. As they pulled into a gas station, a whole section of pipe broke off and hit the pavement. As it turned out, they were in the only station within three hundred miles that could fix the problem! We had that faithful car for many years, and my sister was the last of our family to drive it. Three days after she sold it, it broke down completely.

The principle seems to be: the physicality of things is literally sustained by its love with its people.

If others have used something before you, not only are their energies imbued in its physical substance, but the elemental which was formed is still present. When you become the new user, it is extremely wise to initiate a loving relationship with it. This helps the elemental quickly adjust to you and feel good with you. And the car or whatever will work better! When the home or car is new, it still contains the energies of its builders; a loving relationship wants to be established.

Here is a way to do this for a home or apartment; change it for other things:

To begin, let in fresh air and light. You can "smudge" the home with a smoking bundle of sage, a ritual sacred to native Americans. Or diffuse aromatherapy fragrances throughout, light candles, or follow your own ritual or creativity. Say:

I/we love you, beautiful home! I welcome you into my life! I am so grateful for the gifts of shelter and warmth, light and water you give me. I am grateful for this home.

I now ask my divine presence (or St. Germain) to blaze through with the violet flame, cleansing and purifying all energies here, lifting and dissolving all that is not harmonious.

Take time to see and feel this happening. If it's a large home, you may want to do this in every section or room. If it's an apartment, blaze the flame through the whole building to release all energies that no longer serve the other residents, according to their free will.

I'll be staying here now, and I want a happy relationship with you. I so appreciate (name the things you love best about it. Praise it sincerely!) I bless this space. (Include the yard, if any, or the whole apartment building.) I ask that everything work well, and that I am safe and harmonious with you. I ask my divine presence, my guides and angels to fill you with love and harmony and keep all safe, now and always. So be it.

Some old buildings come with their own entities, or ghosts. If you sense such, do an entity healing if you feel comfortable with that (see "Serve the One"). Or ask a skilled person to take care of it.

Things love to be appreciated and cared for, and in their own way they return the love. Keeping your home or car beautiful, orderly and clean—both physically and psychically—nourishes you, it, and your relationship.

When you leave a building, sell your car—let go of anything which has served you —thank and bless it in its new experience.

Great blessings to every one of your relationships!

Relationship initiations in other chapters

"Contact! Your Spirit" chapter:
☆   How's Your Relationship with God?

"Clear!" chapter:
☆   Co-Creators We Are
☆   Troubleshoot a Situation

"Empower Yourself" chapter:
☆   Stand Up for Yourself!

"Goddess, Awake!" chapter:
☆   Conscious Motherhood

7

Fulfill Your Purposes

My unique self is beyond price.
I am here to discover and express it.

An apple tree grows into itself. If it is well nourished, it grows into the largest and most beautiful tree it can be. It is unique, different from any other. (Imagine the divine love, intelligence and creativity that stores a unique pattern within every apple seed!) The apple tree interacts with its world—sun, rain, earth, air and the nature spirits—and fulfills the unique blueprint stored within its seed.

And so it is with us. In a nourishing environment we are not only fed and sheltered, but loved, recognized, understood and encouraged. We are given tools to feel our deep divinity and follow it. We are encouraged to know we can do or be anything we choose. And we are given the freedom to grow into ourselves.

Like the apple tree, we may not have optimum conditions when we're growing up. But unlike our stationary friends, we are able to create the conditions in which we thrive. These include connecting deeply with our own spirit. They include being with people with whom we feel at home, who invite us to give our unique gifts. Each of us has the potential to become the greatest self we can be.

Your purposes are unique, like the apple tree's unique pattern of growth. But they are likely to include these:

☆ Remember oneness with your divinity. Experience this oneness and express divinity as much as you can. This includes being happy!

☆ Forgive everyone—parents, siblings, mates, close friends, co-workers and all others from this life and previous lives.

147

☆ Clear everything else from your past that is unresolved.

☆ Serve: love the world through whatever you do.

In the often difficult conditions of the world today, many of us have not fulfilled our purposes. But an unfulfilled purpose of one lifetime carries over to the next. There is always—*always*—a new day, a new chance, a new life. Every one of us, in our own right time, will fulfill every one of our purposes in joyous completion.

Statement of Purpose

☆ *I came to fulfill the purposes chosen by my soul. My central purpose is to connect and merge with my divine essence and express divinity where I am.*

☆ *I am here to fulfill myself and be happy. I'm here to give my gifts to people and to life, as I am guided. Love is my most important gift; the forms it takes are secondary.*

☆ *My gifts are unique—only I can give them. The universe would be incomplete without me and my gifts. Up to this moment, what I am doing is right; new activities emerge as I expand. I live a divinely guided life of joyful, ever-new creativity.*

☆ *Being myself, giving as I am guided, all of life supports me perfectly. I do only what I love, and am completely supported in doing it. I accept and create this truth in my experience. I am here to receive as well as give, to receive all the goodness I possibly can from the divine, through people and through life. I fulfill, in the ways and times right for me, all of my purposes. So be it.*

Follow Your Own Star

Your path is no other's—and no other's business. Mate, father, mother, friend—*no one* has the right of dominion over you. It is not of spirit for anyone to tell you what to do or not do, or pressure you into a traditional path through guilt. Each child comes to break the mold of what has gone before. If you are walking in your family's footsteps, or those of your community, this may be right for you or it may not. Look inside, *deep* inside. Touch your spirit. Are you following the passion of your heart? What *is* your passion? Heart's passion unfulfilled is a life not lived. It benefits no one, including your family, to follow a path that isn't yours. And it benefits *everyone* when you follow your own star.

You are here to *live!* "To make manifest the glory of God within you," as spoke Nelson Mandela, in a way no one else can. Without your unique expression, your piece of the puzzle expressing divine life on earth is but the palest pattern of what it could be. It takes courage to forge your own path, but it is infinitely worthwhile.

There is always opportunity to make a new life decision—a decision *for* new life. In the movie *Unhook the Stars,* Gena Rowlands plays a widow with grown children who changes her life entirely.

If you're a mother whose kids have left the nest; a retired person; if you have a life or a job that doesn't light up your heart, look up! Look around! There is more! You're needed in a way that gives your heart joy, and fulfills your true purposes.

Love Made Manifest

When I was little, my mother told me a story about an artist who poured his love and passion into his creation. People were drawn to his intensity, and marveled at the beauty of his work. They gathered around him. He looked up. He felt good that his creation was appreciated. He engaged with people.

He became less focused upon his work. Its beauty dimmed. After a time people lost interest in him and his creation, and turned to new things. The artist felt sad. But he returned all his focus to his work, and it grew shining and vibrant once again. This time when people gathered around, he honored them but kept his focus where it belonged—on his work.

I have always remembered this. It seems to have many layers of meaning. Our work is between ourselves, God, and the canvas of life we are creating upon. Even when we are part of a group effort, this is true.

Also our creation is not ours—at least, it does not belong to the ego. How anyone responds is not relevant: praise adds nothing, and criticism takes nothing away.

Anything we do gathers luminosity and magic when our love, which is spirit, flows into it. To pour ourselves into activity or art or work for *its* own sake is to be a creator, an artist in the highest sense of the word. We love the work in ourselves rather than ourselves in the work. Then we are fully alive. Both our being and our creation are an effortless service to others.

It is a rare person who loses herself in her creation. We love the magic of this so much that many who do it are famous. Think of Judy Garland. A bag of neuroses in her personal life, when she got up to sing we were transported. *She* was transported.

What do these ideas mean in more concrete terms? Here are some thoughts:

☆ Throw your whole self into what you are doing, leaving your ego behind. If you are part of a group work, think in terms of "we."

☆ Do not imitate; you deprive the world of your own gifts. Maybe you're like Janis Joplin and your gift is easily tapped into. But if you have to dig all the way to China, find your own voice and honor it.

☆ Allow your work or art its own life, its flow. At certain points, one activity will be finished and another ready to begin. It may come time to leave an entire profession for a new one. Don't hold to something that is done with! Follow your heart—follow your joy—into the unknown!

☆ If your work connects you directly with people, as on the phone, do your best to be present with yourself and present with them. Again, think "we." Have as your intention that everyone you touch is benefited. Forgive yourself immediately if you slip.

☆ If you are a spiritual teacher, being fully present with others means being fully present with yourself. Do your best to not hide behind the teacher role, or hide relevant things about yourself. Being fully oneself is dynamic and unpredictable—often uncomfortable for us teachers!

☆ If your gifts are appreciated and "gotten," that does feel good. Still, wisdom takes lightly both praise and blame. Is there a learning in it for you? If not, let it roll off.

If You Don't Know What You Want to Do ...

If you don't know what you want to do; if you feel a desire to serve but don't know how, here are some ideas:

☆   Connect up with your inner self as deeply as you can. Meditate regularly.

☆   Keep a journal that says "My heart's desire is _____" and write in it each day.

☆   Ask your spirit how you can best give to yourself and to life.

☆   On a day without pressure, give yourself a fantasy. Leave out reference to money, family, health, or any other condition. Ask yourself: *If my life were precisely as I would love it, what would I be doing? What is my heart's passion?* If the answer isn't immediately clear, take some time. Keep asking questions, and let one thing lead to another. Come to the place where you feel *Aha! This is it!*

When that feels complete, ask yourself: *What aspects of my life do I want to keep?* Jot them down if you wish. Finally, ask yourself: *What aspects of my life do I choose to release?*

How can you best fulfill this dream of your heart? Can it be integrated into your present life? Would it mean changing your life entirely? Will you do it *now?* Or *begin* it now? Everyone is different. My friend Patricia takes a couple of days off each week for her own purposes. The great artist Gaugin left his life in England to settle on a South Sea island, where he created the paintings he is loved for. What is *your* path?

If when you do this fantasy, you get *Fly to the Bahamas and lie on the beach for the rest of my life!* it means you need rest. There is probably activity on the other side of that. Get as much rest as possible for the next few weeks or months, and then do the fantasy again.

☆   Make a list of your ten most enjoyable activities. When this is done, brainstorm with a friend or two to see how you could earn a living with one of them. Find out anything you need to know. Form a plan and go for it!

One fellow who most loved bicycling through wild country realized he could lead others on his journeys. He began to earn a happy living this way.

☆ If you've been asking what to do and still have little or no sense of it, just *start* something! If it isn't the right thing, you'll soon discover that and move to something better. But just starting may be right on.

Do What You Love, and Prosper!

Though we are meant to do only what we love in life *and* be fully abundant, rare is the person who can claim this reality! We need to transcend society's limiting thoughts, and our own. The statements below are meant to strengthen this possibility for you.

Read each statement, and call upon your divine being or the violet flame (see "Clear!") to release whatever is contrary to your intention. Then declare the statement, and feel it deeply. It is suggested that you stand for each declaration and speak powerfully. Remember to have patience and perseverance with these thoughts, as you may be clearing in layers and embracing the truths bit by bit:

My life is meant to be totally fulfilling, in ease and joy. I choose to do what I love! I know everything will work out. So be it!

Many of us have taken vows of poverty in past lives, or have otherwise come to believe that to be spiritual we must be poor. This is even called God's will! Call in your divinity!

In the name and by the power of my divine presence I Am, I now dissolve all agreements I have ever made in any lifetime, which would limit my acceptance of full abundance in life, including abundance of divine energy money! (Take time, breathe, do it!)

It is completely of spirit, right and good, for me to accept divine abundance in every area of my life. This includes divine abundance of money. I choose this now. So be it!

Another great clearing for most of us is knowing we really have gifts to give, and these gifts are worthy and *recognized* as worthy. And, that we are safe and loved to give them. The statement below, as any of them, could be a huge shift for you. Breathe!

Any blocks to giving my gifts I now ask to be dissolved in the light, love and healing power of my divinity. As part of the divine, my gifts are infinitely worthy. In giving them, I am safe and loved at all times.

The world recognizes the worth of my gifts. I attract only appreciation and love from others. So be it.

How do you choose to change your life and manifest the new? Become clear on this.

Now watch yourself closely through the day. Notice where you still assume or speak the old conditions. They may take time and patience to truly clear away. Meanwhile, change your language: *I am not stuck in this job. I am free, through my divinity, to follow my heart and be abundant.* Follow your guidance and take the steps into your new reality!

If you feel you should be a spiritual teacher, or you are one but feel blocked in giving your gifts, see Spiritual Teacher's Special in the "Clear!" chapter.

From Old Work to New

Like many, you may have a job you don't want but need its income. If you know what you do want, you can successfully move from the old to the new. Moving gradually works best for most people: you put more and more attention and energy into the new, until finally the switch is complete.

If you want the same kind of work but with a different company, meet the people there. Find out what's needed and how you may best serve. Build a bridge. (I once volunteered at a job I wanted, and they hired me.) If you choose a different kind of work, learn what you need to know. Ask people who are doing it. Read books on the subject. Take courses.

If you choose to have your own business, become clear on exactly what you want to do. How do you choose to serve and bless the world through your activity? Does it meet the criterion of right livelihood: is it in harmony with life? It doesn't much matter what the work is, as long as your heart is in it and it doesn't harm others. This part of your process is vital because it creates the overlighting spirit that will guide your entire activity.

Unless you are a single person, how will this change affect your family? Talk with your nearest and dearest, and get their support if they can give it. Are there financial considerations to be worked out? Would any of them love to participate with you? How? Does this work for you?

Do you choose a retail store? A mail order business? Selling to stores? Or is yours a direct person-to-person service such as body work?

When you are clear, begin devoting a couple of intervals or more each week to your new activity. If you need to get training or prepare a product for sale, do that. Produce a brochure or at least a business card. If something requires money you don't have, find out how to draw up a financial plan; there is plenty of information on this. If the activity is ready to go but requires advertising, decide where you will place ads and design them. Et cetera. Be practical, grounded, real. Get it done, step by step.

If you come to a stop in your thought, such as *I can't do this,* or *I can't go any further because* ..., or any stopping thought at all, do not give it power. Brainstorm your way around or through it. "Where there's a will, there's a way" is not an idle saying! Remember the power of your oneness with spirit! Call it in! Put it to work!

Your unique circumstance will determine how you make the shift. Can you begin receiving income from your new work? Are you able to cut your days at your old job? Do you have to begin your new work all at once? If so, you will probably want savings to support you for awhile. If this change is really important to you, you can cope with all the details.

One fine day, you will leave your old work entirely and embrace your new life: doing what you love!

Here's a list for moving from old work to new:

1.   As always, connect with your inner self. Get clear on where your heart is, what you really want and how you

choose to serve. See the whole picture. Form your intention. Pray about it. *Commit* to it.

2. Know that your talents and gifts are worthy, unique, a wonderful gift to the world, and totally deserving of generous remuneration.

3. Form a plan. How can this that you love be done? Call for inspiration. Brainstorm with your friends.

4. Focus on the new. Begin giving it your time and energy.

5. If you have a job you want to release, go to part-time if that serves you and devote more energy to what you love.

6. As soon as possible, begin your new activity and begin receiving income from it.

7. If possible, give away samples or energy in your new activity to get the ball rolling. Come from the spirit of abundance, joy, and giving. This opens doors and magnetizes people to you.

8. Get the word out about your gifts.

9. Give generously and joyfully to those whose gifts you receive. Giving and receiving each other's gifts is what makes life worthwhile. It completes life.

10. Stay attuned, daily, to your inner truth. Does this your new work want to change yet again? To expand? To transform? Life flows on as ever, never stagnant! Always follow your heart and your joy.

Blessings to your changes!

Mission Statement

A mission statement is a declaration, usually within a page in length, of your own specific purposes in life as you see them. It is your soul's purposes for this life, as well as any other purposes you have chosen from your heart. It includes your commitment to those close to you. It includes what is best for you, those around you (like your family, friends and co-workers), all of humanity and Earth. A life built upon these principles is fully aligned with divinity.

You are invited to create a Mission Statement. Draw upon your own wisdom and knowing, from the Statement of Purpose above, and any principles from here and other sources you choose to adopt.

Give yourself a few hours or longer in private. Meditate deeply with your spirit. Ask with all your heart what your purposes are. Allow a clear picture to form, clear knowing to fill you.

Write things down, and work with them until a statement emerges that feels exactly right. Then keep it close, refer to it. Change or add to it as you are guided.

If you have understood yourself correctly, your Mission Statement will be from your soul, and from the deeper divinity within you. A wonderful tool to guide your life!

My Purposes Fulfilled!

My life is about joy. I am here to be happy!

I am here to be myself and express my uniqueness.

I am part of the divine.

I Am divine love and light; joy and peace; knowing and wisdom; power, one with love, to create my life as I choose; and unlimited abundance.

I follow my spirit and my heart.

I fulfill myself and my life.

My father and mother have their purposes and I have mine. The greatest gift I can give to life, to myself and to them, is to follow my own calling.

It doesn't matter my sex, my race, my tradition, my "class," I can do whatever I want to do.

I do whatever I want to do.

I am infinitely creative!

I let go of feeling burdened, yet take care of things.

My life is joy and freedom!

My life is easy!

I create space in a busy life to give myself rest and recreation.

I am a wonderful and worthy person.

Just being who I am, my honest self, is a wonderful gift.

As part of the divine I have worthy gifts to give to life.

My spirit shows me all my knowledge, wisdom and gifts from other lifetimes that I desire to experience, expand and share now.

Others recognize the worth of my gifts.

I do not compare my gifts with those of others. Each is unique.

There is no competition in God.

I am safe and loved to speak my truth.

I am safe and loved in giving my gifts.

If I have misused power in a former life, I forgive myself now. As I express myself, everyone is safe with me.

I give generously and freely, happily and easily. I receive others' gifts joyfully.

I give my best.

I give to equals. I receive from equals. I teach equals. I learn from equals.

I deserve to live abundantly in giving my gifts, whatever they are.

I now cancel any mistaken vow of poverty from any lifetime.

Having abundant money is good and right in spirit!

It is right and good in spirit for me to earn my living giving spiritual gifts. God approves!

I do only what I love to do, and am supported perfectly in my life.

May you fill every one of your purposes in joyful ease!

Purpose initiations in other chapters

"Clear!" chapter:

☆   Spiritual Teacher's Special

"Ascend!" chapter:

☆   My Last Life On Earth

"Fulfill Your Purposes" chapter:

☆   Action as a Goddess/God

8

Live Abundantly!

God's will for every one of Her/His creatures
is infinite abundance of all good.

Abundance is our natural state. Then why is abundance elusive
for so many? It seems we have been in an unnatural state! One
of the results of feeling separate from the divine is lack. Separation is really the single cause of lack, because in the divine
there is only fullness, wholeness, and infinite abundance.

Remembering—knowing and feeling—that we are part of
the divine is the only real, the only lasting cause of our return to
abundance. Some metaphysical truths to speak:

☆　*I am one with the divine. The divine is abundant, so I am abundant. When there is no distortion from human limited thought,
there is complete abundance of every good.*

☆　*God/Goddess/the universe knows me completely, loves me completely, and effortlessly moves so that I, and all of Itself, am whole
and abundant.*

Separation consciousness breeds lack of self worth; doubt
that abundance is possible, let alone easy; doubt that abundance is good and right; and doubt that we are safe and loved
to be abundant.

So on a psychological level, being abundant rests upon several convictions:

☆　*It is not only possible, but easy to be abundant. This is a friendly
universe which supplies all my needs and wants.*

☆　*I am worthy to receive my heart's desires, and I can handle having what I choose.*

☆　*It is right and good, spiritual and Godly, to be abundant in all
ways including money.*

☆   *I am forever safe to be abundant; I will not lose abundance or be punished for it. If I lose one form of abundance, it returns in another form.*

☆   *I am forever loved by others when I'm abundant. I am in harmony with all.*

Abundance naturally includes all heart's desires fulfilled, including the deepest: our return to divinity. But one category deserves special mention: money! For so many of us, what a headache! And unnecessarily! There's been such weirdness around money.

Let me share a story with you. Since my journey to India in 1996, I have followed my guidance to increase the number of beautiful master pictures I carry and make them available to more of the world. (I offer these through my company name, Ascension Mastery International, or AMI. A sampling of the pictures is shown in black and white at the end of the book.)

There was another activity like mine. Its owner offered pictures I didn't have. These pictures are so exquisite, I wished sometimes that I could be their custodian.

In 1998, I learned that this business was for sale. I called the owner, and he told me how much he wanted to receive. It was a good and fair price, but totally beyond my capacity to pay. We had known each other professionally for a number of years, and I expected he would feel he could trust me. So I sat down immediately and wrote him a letter, asking if he would consider my operating the business and reimbursing him most of the profits over a few years.

Just about then, an old friend I'd lost track of came into town. He had a hard time reaching me, but finally we connected. I showed him with great excitement the pictures I hoped to inherit.

The next day, there were two messages on my answering machine. One was from the business owner saying he was sorry, but he chose to be bought out quickly and fully. The other was from my friend, saying if I needed help procuring the business, let him know.

I had no idea my friend was in a position to help. When we talked about it, he told me he had received some inheritance, and had been praying about how to serve the world with what he didn't need. This felt like the answer to his prayer.

The three of us connected by phone the following day, and spirit's light came flooding over us. We all felt the transaction to be supremely guided and right. The other people who were planning to buy the business seemed to melt away. My friend bought the business for me, and I am reimbursing him.

The timing of all this was awe-inspiring to the three of us. We could scarcely believe how it happened. But the true learning is that when we are fully ready for something, heaven and earth move to bring it our way. It is the natural activity of spirit to manifest full abundance.

We have an infinite supply, but because we haven't known it, we haven't called upon it. Time for a change!

On a different note, a psychiatrist once wrote that people usually believe if they just had enough money, everything would be great. So having plenty of money is a blessing because you realize it doesn't make you happy. There's another reason for monetary abundance!

Abundance Yes!

Here are common anti-abundant thoughts, along with a cure for each—an "antidote"—to change our perspective. You may find it beneficial to concentrate for periods of time on some or all of them, to anchor them in your mind and heart. Change a statement as you like, if it empowers you.

As with all inner work, truth brings up anything unlike itself, to be transmuted. Expect this. Use initiations in the "Clear!" chapter for deep release. Persist, but at the intensity that works for you:

1. I'm not worthy to have it. I don't deserve it.
    Antidote: *I am a divine, holy being. I am the eternal innocence and worth of the divine. My innocence has never been and can never be changed. Nothing and no*

one could be more worthy than I. Only through human error could I think differently. In spite of my beliefs to the contrary, I have always done my best each moment with what I have known, and I always will do my best.

I am worthy of good. I deserve only good. I deserve all the abundant good that life yearns to pour out to me! I accept this, more and more fully!

2.   It is not good, not spiritual, to be wealthy.
Antidote: *I hereby sever any vow I have ever made to be in poverty, or to believe that poverty is spiritual or Godly, good or right. It is absolutely spiritual and good—Godly— to be abundant, in money as in all good. It is God's will that everyone be abundant. I choose abundance!*

3.   Money is the root of all evil; it's bad.
Antidote: *Money is simply energy, and the basis of all energy is divine light and love. Used wisely and lovingly, enjoyed without attachment, money is a powerful tool for good not only for me, but for everyone. Money makes it easy for us to exchange our gifts with each other. It allows ease and comfort in life, time to rest and re-charge, and abundance to share with others.*

4.   It isn't possible for me to have what I choose.
Antidote: *I recognize that I may have anything I choose. As part of all that is, I already include everything I could possibly desire. Whether quickly or over time, with my persistent knowing, what I choose must come to me. It is the law of the universe.*

5.   There is not enough to go around. Lack is inherent in my life.
Antidote: *My experiences of lack come solely from my belief in lack. There is an absolute plenty for me and for everyone. The universe, God/Goddess of which I am part, is infinite abundance. It is natural that I be the same. When I believe and know abundance, I experi-ence abundance! I magnetize it.*

6.   I am not safe to have abundance. If I receive this, it will be taken away, or I will be punished. I will know loss.
Antidote: *I have experienced loss in the past: the shock*

of leaving my mother's womb, loss of someone I loved, loss of wealth, and more. But I experienced loss from limited consciousness; it is not truth. There is no loss in God, because all good is ever-present, manifest or ready to be manifest. I need not withhold good from myself for fear it will lead to loss.

I am safe to accept whatever I choose to have. I now accept all abundance of good, because there is no loss for me. Only safety and joy, peace and harmony come with my good, and expand forever.

7.   Did you read about the lottery winner, now a millionaire, who kept the same old job he never liked in the first place? His thoughts probably went something like this:

I have to fit in with my surroundings. Who do I think I am, to have more than other folks? This is wrong! If I used my winnings people would be jealous of me and might even hate me. And it would be disloyal to my parents and friends to be rich, like saying their way isn't good enough. They might not love me any more. I would be uncomfortable and embarrassed. I wouldn't know myself any more.

Most of us fear rising above the norm. Those who do are usually idolized and lionized by some, and judged and criticized by others. Not a very safe space! It takes courage to deal with this.

Antidote: *I do not define myself by, or box myself within, any human construct. I am beyond social class. I can give a great gift to my family and friends by demonstrating that we can all change and accept the abundance of good that is here for each of us. I am loved and safe in having all I choose to have.*

8.   I'm not clear about what I want.
Antidote: *As I connect more deeply with my inner presence, I become clear about the direction of my life, and my heart's needs and desires, in spiritual growth, relationships, work, money, creativity—everything. I open my heart and feeling nature to see what my true desires are. I follow my heart and my joy! So be it.*

9. My life goes along as it goes. It doesn't change much.
Antidote: *The past is over. It holds no power except my attachment to it and my belief that things will stay the same. This is the first day of the rest of my life. I may change any pattern I am not happy with. So be it!*

10. Ever see anyone on vacation break a leg or get too sick to enjoy it? Ever see anybody total a new car? Receive a windfall and blow it? The thought: I can't and won't accept anything better than my usual norm.
Antidote: *I can and do accept everything better than normal! Not only that, but I invite it into my life! I dare to be abundant!*

11. Wealthy people are selfish and arrogant, with no care for others. Everybody I know criticizes them (so who would want to be one?!). If I became wealthy, I would be the same.
Antidote: *Wealthy folks are folks just like me, no better and no worse. Famous folks too. Some are greedy and some are generous. Some are arrogant and some are humble. They have sorrows and difficulties as I do. I do not generalize about them. I honor and embrace each person's path in experiencing wealth, and honor and am equal with each wealthy man and woman. In receiving my own wealth, I use it wisely and lovingly.*

12. I resent others having more than I do. Wealth is for other people. I am powerless.
Antidote: *Whatever I resent others having, I deny myself. What I bless for others, I allow myself. I don't waste my time and energy on resentment. Instead I honor and bless wealth for others, and know that what anyone has, I may also have. I am all-powerful in choosing and creating wealth in my life.*

13. You gotta work hard and long for a living, and that will be just enough or not even enough to get by. (Dad?)
Antidote: *My life as part of God/Goddess is meant to be easy and fun, doing what I love to do and being fully supported. That's the natural way! I accept this for myself and others.*

14. I'm not aware of the power of my thought and feeling creating my life.
    Antidote: *I am creating every instant of my life. Every thought and feeling I have is creative, and the universe works to manifest them in my life. The strongest of these have created my life exactly as it is. As I know myself more deeply, I am changing my thoughts and feelings to create my life as I choose it.*

15. I know my thought creates, but my mind wanders around a lot and I don't stick with a desire until it's fulfilled.
    Antidote: *As I learn focus, intention and persistence, I give the universe time to fulfill all my heart's passions.*

16. I'm not aware that I am totally known and totally loved.
    Antidote: *In a self-aware universe of love, I am part of everything and everything is part of me. I am totally known and infinitely, eternally loved. Every one of my needs is known, and when I accept it, every one of them is filled. The universe—the divine—is trustworthy. I am cared for and provided for by an all-loving Father/Mother God, an all-loving universe.*

17. Have you seen the bumper sticker, "Live simply that others may simply live"? Part and parcel of this erroneous thought: If I accept desired abundance, someone will do without. Also, I'll dishonor those who have less.
    Antidote: *Abundance increases in the world in direct proportion to each one's positive creativity. There is plenty for all of us; and we take care of our planet. As I accept my own abundance, I assist everyone else to do the same. Also, I have plenty to share with others as my heart and wisdom guide me. And if living simply is my desire, my abundance, then so be it!*

18. Money is power. If I have money, I will misuse my power as I have in a past circumstance. So I won't allow it.
    Antidote: *As I am already all that is, I am not changed or unbalanced by having what is chosen. I am completely grounded and stable in accepting my abundance. If I have misused power in the past, I have learned from that and I forgive myself for it. I know that I am love. I*

am wisdom. I am giving. I am wise, loving and gener-
ous with my abundance, always. I am now trustworthy
to have power. I trust myself to use it wisely and lov-
ingly, and I will.

19. My sexual expression affects my money. If I do not accept or express my sexuality, I do not allow my creative
energies to flow out, or money to flow in. Or if I'm in a
sexual relationship, that means (most often for women)
I can't have abundant money. (Do you have another belief concerning sexuality and money?)
Antidote: *Whatever the state of my sexual energy or*
expression, my creative energies flow easily from me,
giving to the world and receiving in turn. When I am in
a sexual relationship, I am continuously abundant in
money.

20. Life just isn't this good, and can't be this good!
Antidote: *God, the principle of life, is an outrageous*
giver, totally loving, who wants me—as part of Itself—
to receive the infinite abundance of the universe. I only
need to claim and accept my desired good. I choose
to understand this truth in the depths of my being, and
thus to live a transformed life.

21. Because I don't now have what I want, I see lack in my
life and believe it's real. (This is a huge one.)
Antidote: *I choose to know, see, feel and rejoice in the*
truth of my unlimited abundance, which is right here,
right now, in the timelessness of God. I do not give
power to appearances of lack. I stick with the truth,
patiently and persistently, and know my greater abun-
dance manifests!

Abundance Meditation

I thank my friend Shalomar for ideas in this meditation:

Go into meditation and call your spirit. Begin to feel, deep within
you, that peace and stillness which is your truth. Focus on your solar
plexus, and see there a glowing sphere of light, emerald green tinged
with gold, representing your abundance. As you breathe in and out,

brighten this sphere. Finally, take in a deep breath, purse your lips, and sharply blow out through them, exploding the sphere to surround your aura.

Again with your breath, brighten this larger sphere, and again take in a deep breath. This time, blowing out your exhale in the same way, explode the sphere to touch the golden "grid of abundance" surrounding you. Feel and see how this grid is in constant giving and receiving with the whole universe.

Follow the lines of energy, expanding the golden sphere with your breath until *you* are the whole universe, giving and receiving unlimited abundance with yourself. You are everything. You see that when you give, you give to yourself, and when you receive, you receive from yourself.

Let now this golden sphere that is you-as-everything, touch and bless each person with unlimited abundance.

Still feeling the allness you are, gradually get in touch with the individual you once again. Before you fully return, look to see how you can be of service to others.

Come out of meditation, and carry the spirit of it into your life.

Forces for Abundance

Here are attitudes and actions, both inner and outer, that open us to abundance and bring it into our lives.

Leap From Solid Ground

So a choice has been made to leave something behind—a job, a relationship, a home—and create something new. We know this choice is our true heart desire. Are we ready for it?

I once rented a home with a woman friend. Some of our sharing was enjoyable and some wasn't. After three years, it felt like time to move on but wherever I looked, I could find nothing suitable. I was puzzled; once I make up my mind, things usually move quickly. Finally I found a home I loved, and was accepted. Less than two weeks later, it was sold to someone else.

"Wow," I thought. "I'm not in alignment. This isn't working!"

When I looked deeply, I acknowledged that my friend pushed old fear buttons in me, and I did the same for her. But instead of dealing with it, we had both danced around it all that time. Hidden fear had grown enormous.

On an evening soon after I said—and it took *all* my courage—"There's a big rhinocerous with purple polka-dots in this room, and we're both pretending it isn't here! We need to face what's going on between us!"

The rhino thundered into visibility. I was scared and so was she. Anger got out of control. But we got through it. The air cleared and we could breathe once more. Over the next few months we became truly clear with each other.

Then an interesting thing happened. The landlord of the home we were sharing took a sudden early retirement, and wanted to move in yesterday. And of course, we both found lovely new homes quickly and easily.

Check to see that you are truly clear and ready to leave something behind and move to something better. Is there solid ground under your feet to leap from, or is there the soggy swamp of unresolved stuff? If so, clear it up. Then you will manifest your new good.

Giving

One day I drove way out of my way just to donate warm clothing to a store's giveaway box. That done, I decided to buy some cheese. When I took it to the counter, the clerk said "This is past date. Please take it free."

On my way back home, I was mesmerized by a sight in the sky: the formation that has become known as one of Mt. Shasta's most famous "ship clouds." A multi-layered, crescent-shaped cloud with a long tail, it retained this exact shape and stayed in place for twelve hours while ordinary clouds blew on by. Where I had been in town, I hadn't seen it because it was just overhead. My impetus to give gave me yet another gift.

There is nothing like giving to attract abundance: giving for the joy of it, expecting nothing in return. A smile is a gift; a flower is a gift. A caring act is a gift. Tithing to a church or organization which inspires us; giving to those less fortunate; bringing a spontaneous gift we know a friend will love—these are but a few possibilities.

The crux of giving seems to be a giving *spirit;* otherwise where is the gift? Giving is joy! We are expressing our joyous divinity.

In an airport, I was feeling great love for everything. To myself I repeated "Love, love, love," and blessed everyone I saw. At the check-in counter, I asked the clerk if she had a seat closer to the front. "Yes, here's one," she answered.

On the plane, I walked as usual into the coach section, but couldn't find my seat. Confused, I backed up—into business class. I realized that the universe responded to my gift of love by making a "mistake." I enjoyed that abundance!

Here's to giving!

Gratitude

To attract abundance, one attitude works best: gratitude. To be thankful for what we have may sound hokey—we've heard it a thousand times—but it goes deeper than that. Given our limiting beliefs, spirit has brought us every single thing we would let ourselves have. Something to rejoice about! That very rejoicing—gratitude—opens our receiving doors and invites more in.

Gratitude is a close way to *be* spirit. Spirit rejoices! The fertile ground life springs from is joy. If you get close enough to a tree or a flower, you can feel its joy. Gratitude is an added spiritual spin on joy, and there is no more wonderful feeling.

You can grow gratitude. Start with little things: what am I grateful for this moment? Build upon this beginning. A profound spiritual goal is to feel grateful for every single thing that happens—no matter how it may look—in the knowing that life always expands toward the good.

Intent, Focus and Power

When we think something, or ask for something, the universe goes to work *immediately* to take care of it. But we change our minds so often that it usually doesn't have time to fulfill one thing before the next thought rolls in.

I recognize the importance and power of my intention to have what I choose. I know how to focus my mind, and keep it focused upon my intention. I know how to back up my intention with the power of my emotion. I know all I need to know to create, quickly and easily, what is wanted.

I do not need to waste my time in wishing. I am not afraid to be powerful in creating what I choose; I have the courage to be powerful. I am powerful in accepting what I have chosen. I am loving and wise in my use of power.

The Passionate Word

Words spoken in passion are perhaps the most powerful force in the universe. If your whole being stands behind your words: THEY WILL MANIFEST. Your words should be positive and specific. You may speak for your own life, or for the life of another person with their outer or inner agreement. It is a great service to speak passionately for humanity's enlightenment, for Earth's healing on every level, to bring rain to a parched land—words of pure loving service for all.

What is it you choose? Is your whole being behind it? Bring up your emotion! Speak passionately from your heart that this will be! Speak until you are done. Then let it go.

Ways of Manifestation

There are two major kinds of manifestation.

The first is to picture or outline with perfect clarity exactly what is wanted. If it is a car, for instance, what kind of car is it? What make and model? What color? What extras does it carry? You think in terms of a blueprint, like an architect's plans.

You outline what is vital to you. If you don't care what color the car is, leave that out. If it is a relationship you are creating, you may call for the specific qualities vital to you and be vague regarding his or her appearance. Or vice versa!

The other way of manifestation is to say *God, whatever is best for me, bring that. I welcome it with open arms!* And *be* wide open! In the methods of manifestation below, you may use either of these two kinds of manifestation.

Have What You Choose

I thank the Teaching of the Inner Christ for ideas included in this section.

1. Come from your heart. Be clear about what you want. Choose something you believe you can have, at least reasonably soon. If you want the moon, take it step by step.

2. Recognize the qualities of yourself and the divine, or All that Is:

    I recognize that God/the universe/my divine self is totally abundant and loving and naturally brings to me, as part of Itself, everything I could desire.

    I am one with God/universe, one with my divine self. I am beyond boundaries; I am everything. I already include all I could want. As part of the divine, I naturally and easily receive everything desired.

3. Claim it, ask for it or pray for it:

    I, _____ , now claim _____ .

4. Accept it. Feel yourself having it. What does it feel like? See it, touch it, smell it. Feel your worth, your safety, your goodness and ease in having. Become conscious of anything that comes up against it, and see how to move with it into truth.

    Include the acceptance of what you have asked for, *or better.* And don't tell the universe *how* it is to come. Statement:

    I now accept this full abundance of good from my beloved Father/Mother God, one with me. I am the happy acceptance of this abundance here and now. As there is no time in God, this good is already present! I feel it, I rejoice in it, and I am completely grateful for it! So be it.

5.   Give thanks that it is *done;* feel the joy, fullness, grati-
      tude of having it *now.* A statement:
      *I thank all of spirit, God, the universe, for being the unlimited
      good and givingness that provides my very life and breath, and all
      I could desire. I give great thanks to my beloved divine presence
      for the plenty I now have, and for all that is manifesting to me. I
      give thanks for this I have claimed. So be it!*

6.   If you feel absolutely clear that it is coming, and you find
      your clarity present from day to day, you need do noth-
      ing more. If not, take time to re-focus until it arrives.

A Simple Way

When you feel ready to have a certain thing, sit down in a
basic meditation. Call forth your divine master self and its
power. Get in touch with your absolute intention to have what
is desired. Then *give* it to yourself. Have it, feel it, revel in it,
celebrate it! Feel the joy of having it all the way through your
body. Then, know that it is done. Go your way and know it is
coming to you through the illusion of time. If you begin to doubt,
do it again with equal conviction. *Nothing* can stop your receiving *when your whole being is aligned with the process.*

The Power Committee

Form a committee of anyone you choose: favorite masters, angels, guides, as well as your own divine presence. Gather
a group you can remember easily. Talk to this committee clearly
and passionately about what you want. Ask its members to
bring it to you as quickly as possible. Expect it!

A Letter to the Karmic Board

Twice a year, the first week in January and the first week in
July, the ascended masters of Earth (The Great White Brotherhood) gather at the ascended master retreat in the Grand Teton
Mountains in Wyoming. They look at the whole picture of
humanity's evolution and that of our planet, and see how they
can be of greatest possible service in the coming months. They
form plans, and act upon them.

Part of this gathering is the "Karmic Board," a group of great masters who are able to see deeply into the soul evolution of each being. A most powerful activity is to write to this Board with your choices for the coming year or half year. It is not that the masters decide whether or not your desires will be met. It is that if your choices are in alignment with your soul's evolution— and if you are tuned to your divinity, they are—the Board's masters back them up with all of their love and power. Often quite magical things happen after letters to the Karmic Board.

It's powerful to do this with a group of sincere friends, as well as on your own. You may do it any time of year, but the two weeks are especially recommended.

Write your letter to the Karmic Board in pencil; lead is said to join the physical and lighter dimensions. In the first part of the letter, put your desired choices for the next six months or year for Earth, humanity, nature, or any other body you would like to serve.

When that is complete, write your choices for your own life.

Call in Archangel Michael. In a safe space, set your letter afire and ask Michael to take it up to the Board for you.

Now, go into a meditation and transport yourself, with the help of your divine presence, into the Tetons retreat. (For more on how to do this, see the Bi-Location Process in the chapter "Ascend!") Now in your etheric body, you will be lovingly greeted and given a beautiful robe to wear which is yours to keep.

You will find yourself in a great hall adjoining the Karmic Board's meeting room, waiting your time to go in. Take time to look around you at the masters who are present, the bustle of activity; study the beautiful tapestries and the magnificence of the hall.

Your own master self, or another master, will appear by your side to escort you to the Board. When it is your turn, usually not long, go in together. The Board's masters have received your letter, and are expecting you. They will give their backing to what you have written, or may make suggestions for a change here and there. When you are complete, thank them.

You are invited to explore the retreat further if you wish. You may visit the twelve "flame rooms," each with a huge etheric flame the color of one of the seven major "rays" of esoteric teaching (see the works of Madame Blavatsky and Alice Bailey), and rooms for the five higher rays.

The Sears Catalog Window

My friend Jack Rowe gave me this one. Go up to the catalog window in your mind. The very clerk you want comes to greet you, and asks how she or he may help you. You place your order, and the clerk takes it down, clarifying every detail. She takes the filled order sheet and puts it in the stack with the others to be filled. If you wish, ask "When do you expect this in?" Or you can simply walk away, knowing it is taken care of. Hold this knowing and expectation until it arrives.

Let the Universe Do It!

The universal divine effortlessly handles an infinite number of things at the same time. You may want to use this when you have "too much" to do. Draw a line down the middle of a sheet of paper. On one side, write what you will do. On the other, give the universe *its* jobs. Relax about these. And stick with it!

Ask Once, and Proceed in Faith

In his book *In Perfect Timing,* Peter Caddy tells wonderful tales about how, as the Findhorn community grew, all needs were supplied. For instance, if they needed a larger meeting room, they found out how much it would cost and asked for that amount from God. Then they moved ahead on the project *as if the money were already present.* Invariably, that money arrived on time! And they were guided to go for the best quality, not to compromise.

The key for this method is the *quality of faith.* If doubts persist and undermine faith, it's best to use other methods.

1. What is the need?
2. If there is cost involved, how much is required to supply the highest quality of everything?
3. Ask God for this amount. Ask once only.
4. Move ahead! Act. Expect the money, with no concern about where it comes from.
5. When it arrives, give thanks for its manifestation! Give thanks for the fulfillment of the need.

I Am Divine Abundance

I am the image of God/Goddess, part of God, and. beloved of God. The divine expresses universal abundance through freely giving and receiving. Abundance is God's desire for, through and as me and all of life.

I am a wondrous giver. I am perfect abundance and wholeness. I am freedom, joy, and well-being. Abundance is my natural state. Any reality of lack is impossible, because God-I-Am is the infinite source of good for me and for all, right here and right now. I am abundantly provided for, today and every day.

I accept my prosperity in humility and gratitude. I accept my prosperous abundance of love, joy, freedom, spiritual growth, healing, light, power, and perfection in all areas of my life.

I know that money is loving, good, innocent, light-filled energy of God/Goddess. It flows to me and to all people easily and abundantly. I accept it with joyous gratitude.

I follow the law of circulation by giving lovingly, generously and freely to others. I know that as I freely give, so I freely receive.

I accept good I have not consciously asked for, trusting God/my divine self to bring me all I can accept in every moment.

When I ask for something, I am asking for everyone, and my receiving is benefiting everyone. I keep this in my heart.

As I receive and give abundantly, I assist all of humankind to do the same. My abundance helps all to be abundant.

So be it.

May you know an infinite abundance of all good—and share it!

Abundance Initiations in Other Chapters

"Fulfill Your Purposes" chapter:

☆   Do What You Love, and Prosper!

9

Goddess, Awake!

O Goddess! O Divine Mother! Honor to thee!

Empowering the goddess within: could anything be more important now? Compassion and love for all life; nurturance; protective fierceness; intuitive knowledge; beauty; and the wild, instinctual nature of the goddess—these are a few of her gifts. The compassionate qualities of the feminine will heal the world.

In her brilliant and much needed book, *Women Who Run With the Wolves*, psychiatrist Clarissa Estés writes passionately of the need for women to find the buried instinctual self or wildish self inside and "sing it to life" again. This is the very heart of our life, our passion, our primal urge. It is *la loba:* wolf woman. It is one with spirit.

La loba is the goddess as she expresses on earth. Though she is easily appropriate in any social setting, she does not allow socialization to glaze her over or subdue her.

Once long ago, as I sat in Zen meditation, wolf paws began to appear in place of my hands. At the time I assumed this was an astral invasion. Today I know it was my totem animal, black wolf; and also *la loba*.

I strongly suggest that if you haven't read this book, and used its tools to dive into your own psyche, do it!

Woman of Power

The honoring of one sex over the other, the domination of one by the other, has swung back and forth through the eons. All of us have suffered, and there is no one to blame. We have been doing our best with our foray into density and duality. What is needed is healing and forgiveness, and the welcoming of each other in pure equality, honor, love, and oneness.

177

Healing is catalyzed by knowing you are powerful. Power allows forgiveness. Here are three statements:

I embrace the truth. I am goddess, the divine feminine. I am sacred and my body is sacred. Without me there is no creation of any kind; there is no life. There is no universe. I am the creative womb; I am the matrix from which creation springs.

I honor who I am. I am powerful. I am whole. I am compassion. I am love for all life. Nothing that has ever happened in the world has changed me. I am eternal. I am Isis, Quan Yin, Goddess Tara and Saraswati. I am revered.

I am wild woman, wolf woman—la loba. I am wise woman. I am the cycles of life. I am the sacred blood. I am sensuality, sexuality and beauty. I am instinctual knowledge and movement. I know beyond words. I dare to be myself in every situation and relationship. I am needed as myself. So be it.

Heal the Feminine

I am the powerful co-creator of all that has happened to me throughout time, throughout lives. In deep agreement with others I have been part of events that were difficult for me and difficult for them.

I forgive myself, and all people, for accepting the falsehood that feminine could be less than masculine, or woman less than man. I forgive all experience that has come from this belief: poor respect for women, restricted roles, low pay and glass ceilings in work, and lost opportunities. From earlier times I forgive loss of status or loss of life for women healers, women who didn't produce male children, and women who dared be powerful.

I forgive rape and abuse in this life and other lives, as one who was raped or who raped, or one who abused or was abused. (This may be a profoundly deep process for you, one that needs time. Most of us have these issues, but are often not aware of them because they are so painful to bring up. If you need deeper work here, see the "Clear!" chapter or get help.) *I am protected at all times* (see Invincible Protection, same chapter). *I never again choose rape or abuse. I am safe and loved.*

We have all done our best, we were in error, and we deserve forgiveness.

Forgive here now—or become aware of the need for forgiveness. Open your heart. Forgive yourself. Forgive any man you have feared or resented or hated; men in general; anyone. Call a rose-gold flame from the goddess you are to cleanse every level of being. What no longer serves you, now let go. Intend! Breathe! If you feel unable to forgive now, love yourself and know that it will come.

What Needs to Die? What Wants to Live?

Here is an initiation my spirit gave me, inspired by *Women Who Run with the Wolves.*

Give yourself a day for this, at least, with no commitment to others. Rather than meditating, simply feel moment to moment your instinctual self. Feel your instinctual knowledge: when to sit and be with yourself, when to eat, when to move, when to do something else or something new. If possible, spend some or all of your day in nature.

Dive into your deepest heart. What in your life is *of life,* alive for you, imbued with your heart's passion? Are there ways you choose to nurture any of these more deeply?

What in your life is *not* of your life, your passion: it wants to go. Feel this out. What shall you do with this?

What is *not* in your life—you have been ignoring its knock!— that you choose to let in now? How shall you go about it?

What is your next step, right here today? Take it or set it in motion within you.

As you re-enter social context, practice feeling the deep passion within you, and let it affect everything: your very movement, posture and visage; your words, your action.

The Integrity of Feeling

Women who have become legendary as *women,* transcendent of their role in life, all seem to radiate a—what is it?—a certitude imbued with passionate feeling. Look at movie stars Elizabeth Taylor, Greta Garbo, Ingrid Bergman and others. Look at Jacqueline Kennedy, Eleanor Roosevelt, Golda Meier, Mother Teresa. With vast differences in personality and intent, they have in common this shining core of feeling and an underlying current of strong intelligence. This is the goddess.

The men we love most also radiate strong feeling: James Stewart, Gary Cooper, Clark Gable; Winston Churchill, Franklin Roosevelt, John Kennedy, Martin Luther King. The goddess shining through men.

Trusting feeling, honoring it, shining it, is part of the instinctual nature. It is integral to loving yourself, which in oneness is also loving others. It is integral to your ability to be present and alive. It comes from a deep confidence: you are present with your feeling, present in the world, you are honest, you are *spontaneous*—you are goddess!

Loving yourself as you are is key to shining your goddess self. Self love leads to self knowledge. It nurtures confidence. Here are some statements:

I love myself. I am the goddess! I am beautiful and worthy. I know myself. I have abundant self esteem and self confidence. I honor my appearance. I honor my activity in the world. I honor my home and environment.

I am a passionate being, and I feel deeply. Without undue power to ego, I honor the integrity of my feeling. My feeling is my aliveness! I am present with myself and present with others, and I am honest. I am joyfully spontaneous! So be it.

Goddess Beauty

Ah, if we could see ourselves as spirit sees us!

I am so infinitely beautiful! I am all the aspects of Goddess/God: love, wisdom, knowing, power—and eternal beauty. I am a great being of light, a star being. I do not allow the mirror, or others' perception of me, to diminish my self esteem. I do not allow age or illness to dim my perception of my true self. I remember who I am!

I choose to see myself as the divine sees me. I am an eternal, beloved being, part of the divine. How long I've been in this life, my health, my circumstances—none of this matters. I honor my body and my appearance. I love this beloved, sacred form which is made of divine light energy.

As goddess, I am the very essence of beauty. I remember the truth of my goddesshood. Humbly recognizing my oneness with divinity, I carry myself high and proudly. I am grateful for this truth. So be it.

Conscious Motherhood

Bringing a child into the world—a divine being into form—is a sacred act. When aligned with spirit, a birth may be planned before conception. The whole process is filled with love.

The motivation for having a child is one to be carefully examined. Do you want someone to carry on your family name? Do you want a boy? A girl? Someone to be proud of? Someone who fits into your style of life? Someone to take care of you in your old age? There is nothing wrong with these desires, but if they are not tempered with deeper truth, they will probably create hardship between you and your child.

Here are different ideas. I want to have a child because:

1. It is a relationship to pour my heart into, to give my love for the joy of giving.
2. It is an activity aligned with my soul's purpose, which will assist my expansion into spirit.
3. It is a great adventure to welcome a child into my life! This is God's child, with its own life and destiny. It is my joy to be present as its passion and purpose unfold. I hold no expectations; my only desire is that this life fulfill itself. It is my joy to assist as best I can.

When you are ready to conceive a child, or if you have already conceived, here are suggestions for a joyful, loving experience for you and your baby, and for the father if he is present.

Call the soul that most rightly and joyously comes to be with you and your family. Ask spirit to help with this; there are many, many beings who desire incarnation on Earth at this time.

If you are able, contact the incoming soul directly. It will not feel like a baby! It is a divine being, presently expressing divinity. You may feel awed by its greatness; but it is your greatness as well.

During the pregnancy, you may receive impressions from this soul as words, feelings, knowing, or pictures. You may get a sense of its purpose on earth; whether it is a male or female soul (the gender of the baby is usually the same); its name; and more. You may even find yourself knowing that this is the soul of a parent, grandparent or other family member who has passed, or of a dear departed friend. Sometimes if a child of yours has died early, he or she may come back as a new baby.

If you feel unable to receive this kind of information, do not be concerned. Your love will carry everything. If there is a person of true spirit you can trust, she or he may assist you with this.

Water birth has been the most wonderful for many mothers I know. It often reduces labor pain for a more enjoyable birth. At the birth, the father, loving friends, skilled medical assistance are, of course, with you. Soft lights and beautiful music complete the scene.

Your baby enters blood-temperature water, which is a loving welcome into a familiar environment rather than the shock of cold air upon its wet body. It rests from the birth, umbilical cord still intact, until it is ready to begin breathing—often a half hour or more. Then it may be laid on top of its recent home, your womb, to be dried off, loved and caressed. Only after breath begins is the cord cut.

When the baby is clean, dry, and warm, hold a little ceremony to welcome this divine being to our planet! (I am reminded of the opening scene from the movie, *The Lion King.*) This is such a personal thing; here is a possible scenario.

Have an altar already prepared with representations of divinity, nature, beauty, fragrance, candles, incense—anything desired. If you have divined something of your baby's purpose for coming to Earth, you may place on the altar something to represent that. Someone presents your baby to the altar, or you hold your baby, saying something like this:

> *Beloved Mother/Father God, here is a divine part of Yourself, come to Earth to fulfill soul purpose. We welcome you, beautiful soul! We honor you and love you. We will do our very best to give you the love and nurturing that sustains you, and supports the fulfillment of your unique purposes. We know being with you is part of our own purpose, and we rejoice!*

Perhaps rub a bit of fragrant oil on your baby's third eye, or sprinkle it with a few drops of pure water—again, whatever loving creativity comes up with.

Every blessing to you and your baby! Blessings to your family and all those present through your pregnancy, birth, and life!

Your Sacred Womb: Honor and Control

If you are fertile and it is not right for you to have a child, or not now, it is a wise choice to be master of your womb. This is the natural way.

As mentioned in *Living Mastery,* the belief of a south Pacific indigenous culture prevented conception in girls who were having sex, until they were married. And I myself have conceived three times, yet I have had neither an abortion nor a baby. The souls departed by my command.

The more we love and honor something, the more say we have in its workings. I remember a painful aspect of an aerobics class. The woman leader frequently closed her fist and socked her womb with great force. She wanted it to be flat as a board (which it was anyway). Obviously, she did not love it! Woman's womb is sacred, meant to be honored and loved.

Here is a meditation for women. Men, you have a sacred creative center here as well, your second chakra at your abdomen. If you wish to do the following meditation, place your hands there, and honor your sexual organs as well.

Go into meditation. Call Divine Mother to you if you like, or any of her forms. Place your hands upon your womb. With the assistance of spirit, feel the totality of sacredness here. Your womb can nurture a divine child who is the very image of God/Goddess; one created by divine love, intelligence and will. One who can realize and express its oneness with God.

Your womb is also the birthing place for creative ideas and works.

Forgive yourself, and humanity, for our extremely limited understanding of the sacredness of the feminine, and thus the sacredness of your womb, your vagina or *yoni,* your cervix, your ovaries and tubes.

Send your love into your sacred womb. Feel the love of spirit. Honor it with all your heart. Honor it whether or not it is fertile; and whether or not it is there. (If you have had a hysterectomy, the energy form of your womb remains; this is still the creative center of your being.) Here are some statements:

My beloved womb, I honor you. You represent the divine feminine on Earth. Forgive me that I myself was not aware of how sacred you are. You are infinitely sacred. I love you.

I honor your cycles, my beloved womb, also part of the divine feminine here. I honor the sacred blood that flows (or flowed) from you, the nurturance for a divine child. I honor my moon time; it is a powerful portal for releasing what does not serve me, and for receiving divine inspiration, knowledge and power.

My beloved womb, only when I am guided from my heart, deep and wise, do I choose to conceive a child. I now ask to become completely conscious of you, through love, with the assistance of spirit. I choose to know when I ovulate. I choose to conceive only when it is my conscious choice. I choose to know if I conceive.

As an all-powerful aspect of the divine feminine, I now love, honor, and am in control of my womb. So be it.

This will probably bear a good bit of repetition—these are new ideas for most of us—until it is truly in place. If your womb is not now fertile, it may become so through the love you give it.

If you have conceived and you do not now choose to have a child, say to it:

Beloved soul, there has been a misunderstanding. I have not opened my womb to a child at this time. I command you to leave. You will find a mother to welcome you at the right time. I bid you farewell.

Remember that you are speaking to a mature soul, not a baby. Repeat these words often, with intention and power, until the soul returns to its lighter realm.

Business Goddess

For our planet to be healed, it is vital that old business practices based entirely upon profits be transformed to benefit both humanity and nature. The compassion and wisdom of the goddess, her nurturance and sense of oneness, are greatly needed here.

Women and men both, you who feel compassion and concern for the world, can open up the vision of those you work with—even if you have come to a position of power through following the old ways. You can help others understand that practices destructive to the environment or unfair to people—

any practice not imbued with love, equality, and honoring of all life—is in the long run harmful to the business itself.

There are many examples of the truth of this: Nike Shoes which has lost business because it allegedly pays too little to its Asian workers; tuna canning factories boycotted for refusing to protect dolphins; Procter & Gamble and other companies boycotted because of animal testing, and many more.

On the positive side, look at the Body Shop, started by one woman who has worked diligently to improve the life of every person who supplies her company—and who has enjoyed phenomenal success. There are many, many examples that could be added.

Look at your business deeply. Take it into meditation with your spirit. What is the overall philosophy? If it is less than enlightened, what has to take place in order for it to change? What are practices that support the good of all? What are practices that do not? Who are the people that need to be impacted? What is an initial step you could take, guided by your wisdom?

Plant your feet carefully, plan your steps carefully, speak with care. Talk with individuals first. Speak in a way that can be gotten, from a heart that honors your associates. As much as wisdom allows, keep others informed of what you are doing, and garner their support. You want to do what works.

Below are possible actions:

☆　Is there any person(s) in your company who may join with you? Feel them out. It is a most powerful force to work with others to create changes for your company. Prayer together can work wonders. (Read Catherine Ponder's book, *The Prospering Power of Love.*) Get together frequently.

☆　Volunteer to form a committee for a positive purpose.

☆　Search out consultants who can move your company in a direction beneficial for all. Present your findings to your associates.

☆　Do research on companies that have made positive changes and report how they are working. Come with suggestions.

☆　Draw up a plan, support it with facts, and present it.

☆   Create a new position for yourself for the purpose of creating positive change; outline your duties clearly, have a salary in mind, and knock on the boss's door.

☆   Move things as quickly as they can be moved; don't overstep your speed so that your work is for naught. But when a leap is wanted; when you need to confront the president, do that! Do what *works.*

If you find that your company is not able to move toward more enlightened philosophy and practice, know that your gifts are wanted elsewhere. Create that happening. You are now meant to be a force for good in the world.

Action as a Goddess/God

What single motivator lies behind action for the good of all? Of course, it is love. Wholehearted love for ourself and our life; wholehearted love for everyone else, everything else. When we determine to come from love, our divinity is shining through. Our lives become a blessing.

As goddess, we naturally feel love. We also know when it is missing; and it is the love within us that helps heal such situations. Love is the single most healing element of life.

Spirit is the love from which all human love springs. It is a wonderful thing to be guided in every action from this pure source. Action from love is the goddess and god within, working together. It is most needed upon our planet!

Take a deep look at your life. Is love at the core of your actions, your work? Is what you are doing guided from your spirit? What wants to change? How shall you do it?

Look at your relationships. Is there safe space to open your heart? If so, are you doing it? If not, what needs to be changed? How shall you do it?

Here are some thoughts:

I make the choice to guide my life from my source—spirit—in greatest love for myself and all others. I know this is a huge choice, affecting everything I do and every interaction with others. When I seem to fail, I forgive myself immediately; thus I expand into more love.

My loving action helps heal the world. My life becomes a beacon shining out divine love, bringing hope and encouragement to all. My life becomes a blessing. So be it.

Goddess I Am

I am the goddess!

I am the divine feminine in form.

I am the matrix from which all creation springs.

I am the attractive principle; I am the receptive principle.

I am love, and wisdom.

I am the very essence of eternal beauty.

I am intuitive knowing which needs no words.

I am alive with feeling!

I am spontaneous!

I am power, one with love.

I am the masculine as well as the feminine. They are inseparable.

I love and honor the masculine as much as I do the feminine.

I am oneness.

I am infinitely loved.

I am infinitely loveable, exactly as I am.

I love and honor myself.

I love and honor my feminine body, and my appearance.

I love and honor my sacred womb, my yoni, my ovaries, my tubes, my cervix—or the energy form of these.

I love and honor the sacred blood of woman's womb.

I am equal with every man, and every other woman.

I use my receptivity wisely; I am guided from my spirit.

I know who I am, what I want, and what is right for me.

I follow my heart, my passion! I create!

I am strong and assertive, whenever that is appropriate.

I do not adapt to situations that are not good for me; I find my true family, my creative talents, my true path.

I choose to be among people who see and honor my real self, my abilities and talents.

When it is called for, I honor woman as natural teacher to man in the things that are most important: love, compassion, oneness, and the well-being of all.

My influence heals the world.

Infinite blessings to you in embracing your goddess self!

10
Serve the One

When you go out of your way for another
you take a short cut.

Serve the One

Service is an enigma. Why serve? Who is served? The obvious answer—I serve them because they need help—is too simplistic, and based on the illusion of separation.

When we look deeply enough, suddenly all is simple. We are one—the many as the one. What gives joy to me—this part of the one—benefits you and everyone. What gives you joy benefits me and everyone. If one's joy is to meditate in a cave for twenty-five years, all benefit. If another's is to paint what is in her heart, all benefit. If his joy is writing books on fourteenth century religion, if hers to be a rock musician—the same.

For some, the heart's joy is direct service to life. We feel our oneness with others, and thus arises compassion. In mahayana Buddhism, one takes the bodhisattva vow to see the end of suffering for every being. When direct service is our path, no vow is needed; it simply is our joy to assist as we are moved.

Service comes from being, flowing effortlessly into doing. Meditation is a service from pure being. Prayer is powerful service from being, with a spin on it to send it into the world. If doing comes before being, action may be motivated by anger or ego rather than love. In that case the action is likely to do more harm than good. If we come from the love of our being and look around us, we will know what to do. Our service will be for the good of all.

A trap for many servers is playing a role that separates. Most social workers, doctors, nurses, teachers do this. It's hard not to do. If you notice this dynamic in your own work, it may assist you to work with Lightworker's Syndrome in "Clear!"

Our opportunity is to know, from deep heart feeling, our oneness and equality with everyone else no matter what their present circumstances may be. We not only love, we honor. Then we give the greatest service of all, recognizing it as the one to the one, and that we are served as we serve.

Service doesn't need to be "hands on." If it is not your purpose to serve in person a cause that moves you, donate to it. If you are serving those in drastic need, you may do it from a place removed or from down in the trenches. There is no better way, except as determined by your own heart.

As the ways of active service are infinite, we will concentrate here on service from being.

Prayers for Earth

For our beloved Gaia, Mother Earth, we may harness the power of sincere intent, positive word, passionate prayer. The planet has suffered from a humanity in dominion but lacking in wisdom and love. Now we are in a period of great upheaval, a transition to a new way of life. The prayer of just one person— you!—is powerful and important. The prayer of a group multiplies this power exponentially. Now is a perfect time to gather in groups and focus upon the good of all. Here are possible prayers—add to them from your wisdom.

The Network of Light

In recent decades, a network has formed on Earth from the love and light of those assisting the planet. Viewed etherically, it looks like a glowing, pulsating web of light. At first, the points of connection were far apart. But as more and more of us awaken and contribute our gifts, the connections have become quite close. The more who join, the brighter glow the strands, and everyone—whether or not consciously—is more deeply impacted. A book that describes this process clearly is Peter Caddy's memoirs from the early days of Findhorn, *In Perfect Timing*. The network of light is of great import for Earth.

To become a conscious point in the network of light, and connect with the rest, strengthens the whole.

See and feel the master presence of everyone in your group. From your hearts, send a great beam of light to the center of the group, joining as one blazing sun of light.

We place Earth in our center. We see our point of light upon her.

We connect consciously with: (now, anyone speaks the name of a person or group and where they are located, and everyone visualizes the group's sun of light connected by a powerful, glowing arc of light to this location. When this is complete:)

Now we see the entire network of light, including ourselves and the connections we have acknowledged, completely covering beloved Gaia. (Take time here. It is a breathtaking sight!)

We see this light network becoming stronger day by day. The awakening of every being is quickened with it, and in turn the network is strengthened still more. All of Earth is blessed. All humanity is blessed. So be it!

Healing Prayer

Again create the sun of divine light in the center of your group.

We ask our divine aspects, the ascended master host, the angels and archangels to give your energies to this healing for beloved Earth.

We call the spirits of the natural world: the devas for earth, air, fire and water; the devas and nature spirits for trees and plants and animals, for the oceans and skies; and the spirits of place.

We acknowledge our group mastery and sincerity, and the blazing sun of divine light in our center. We consciously connect with the entire network of light, so that healing resonates throughout the world.

We place Gaia in the center of our group. We call the violet flame of purification and forgiveness, from Archangel Zadkiel and the master St. Germain, to come from the core of Earth and sweep with a great blazing glory through every atom of the planet, every heart and mind, all of life, everything! We affirm that all dark energies of the lower astral plane are lifted. We affirm that all thought forms available for healing are now lifted, healed, and dissolved in divine love and light.

O beloved Mother Earth, Gaia, we so thank you for being our home! We honor and bless you!

Beloved nature spirits and devas, we thank you and honor you for all of the loving service you have given to the natural world. We call for a conscious, loving relationship between humanity and all the devas and spirits of nature. Humanity's uncaring is replaced with conscious, loving care and activity that heals every aspect of Earth.

We send love and healing energies to all of Gaia. We bless your waters—brooks, rivers, seas and oceans. We see them totally cleansed and pure. (Take time to see and feel all these healings. It is especially powerful to visualize brilliant light through each aspect.)

We bless and bring healing to your land, from the core to the surface. We bless your atmosphere, and see all pollution replaced with pure, delightful air. We see the restoration of old-growth forests.

We affirm that every person is awakening to oneness with divinity, to freedom, joy, love, and mastery. We see the network of light becoming stronger each day, ensuring that all of us are coming home.

We each see now our present vision of the ideal for Earth. (Take time. Then if you like, anyone may share this vision aloud, so it is strengthened by the group.)

We affirm that Gaia, and humanity, are completely protected from interference on the path to enlightenment.

We know that Earth's transformation takes place quickly, and she lifts into higher dimensions where only harmony exists. We bless this! So be it!

Go Gently Into the Age of Light

Beloved Mother/Father God, beloved Earth Mother Gaia, and all the spirits of nature, we ask your help in creating a peaceful transition for Earth into the age of light. We ask the divine being of everyone who lives here to join together and create peaceful progress.

We know the enlightenment of humanity is vital to a peaceful transition. We now call upon the healing love, light and power of the divine within each to dissolve every past thought form, belief, prejudice, hatred, fear, ignorance, and limitation of any kind which would keep the beloved people of our world in disharmony within themselves and with each other. These are being dissolved NOW, to the degree of readiness and willingness of each.

We invite every person to become aware of their true heart's desire, through awareness of their inner divinity, to be continually at peace and in love with self and other. We invite every heart to be filled with the love, light and wisdom that is the truth of being.

We bless the political leaders of every town, county, state, and nation; and the leaders of every business, every organization, every church and spiritual group. We see through any appearance of ignorance to the truth within: a wise and loving being with the courage to act in love, for peace.

We bless (a particular upcoming event).

We ask the devic spirits of Earth to cleanse the land, the waters and the air of all difficulty, and fill it with spirit's love and joy.

We see a people and a land in peace, prosperity, equality, respect and understanding, wisdom, and love. We see each person rising into the full god-goddesshood of their being, all limitations gone and joy reigning supreme!

Through these transformations, changes within the body of Earth take place as gently and peacefully as possible for each area. Our entire planet comes through all challenges in shining splendor!

Thank you, God. And so be it.

Prayer for a Person

For anyone—or any group or organization—sick or in trouble, prayer is a mighty force. The sincere prayer of one individual is always heard, and acts for good. Prayer groups have remarkable success, even in distant healings for people no one in the group has met.

If the one we are praying for is not ready to accept healing or to be happier, our prayer is not forced upon them; nor is it wasted. It lodges in their aura, where it may catalyze acceptance of healing or change; and when they are ready, there our prayer is!

We don't know anyone as their divinity knows them; therefore we pray with a humility that accepts whatever happens.

We don't pray, for instance, for a person to live when it may be best for them to pass on—we simply pray for their highest good.

Here is a general prayer that can be changed to meet the needs of a given situation. Of course, the prayer may be adapted for an animal or other living thing. Change "I" to "we" if appropriate:

Dear God, I send your healing love, and that of my divine spirit, to _____ . I ask that, if it be their true desire, they be (completely healed of this illness) (completely relieved of this trouble). (Add anything else you wish.) I ask for their highest good. I see them now, completely expressing their divine love, light, joy, peace, and perfection in the best possible way. I thank you, God, that this is done. Amen.

Now, take a few moments to hold your person in love and pure perfection. See their divinity. Really see and feel all as perfect.

Astral Healing

The astral plane is invisible to most of us, but is quite real and quite close to the physical. Certain darker energies of the "lower astral" can use our healing. It is suggested that you work with this only if you feel comfortable with it.

Thought Forms

Thought forms are the energy forms of thought and emotion that have occurred in a particular spot. They imbue the earth, the rocks, the floors and walls of a building, with those thoughts and emotions. They affect what takes place there afterwards—often hundreds or thousands of years afterwards.

As happy thought forms are not a problem, this is about clearing those that are unhappy or dark. It is usually not difficult to clear a space of thought forms.

Thought forms can also "bump around" from place to place, perhaps because their original physical home is gone. To do a healing for thought forms, say this and mean it:

All thought forms in this space are filled with the light and love of God. They are now dissolved in the truth of light and love! So be it.

When a thought form has been created from strong emotion, it may take more energy to dissolve than the simple healing above. If you feel the healing did not work, call in your divine presence or other masters and go after whatever remains. You may use the same words with more power and passion. Through your love, will and intention, divine energy will disperse the atoms of remaining thought forms.

Entities

An entity is a person who has passed on, but was unable (or unready) to connect with his or her higher self and has remained, inappropriately and usually unhappily (though not always—think of a loving grandmother staying with her grandchildren), with the physical plane. It is quite common for family members or dear friends to remain "behind" for a time after passing.

Often troubled entities (who were troubled people) stay to themselves, but they can influence and rarely even possess a person, with that person's unconscious invitation. People whose auras are open, as with alcohol, drugs, or difficult emotion, are the most frequent targets for influence. Someone being influenced changes noticeably, either steadily or intermittently.

Entities often need our assistance to connect with the light and love of their divinity, and go to a happier realm. Entity healing can be a great service for your loved ones and others who have passed, for anyone being influenced, and for Earth, especially your own area.

If you feel frightened when you think of entities, or uncertain about your protection, *do not attempt general entity healing.* Your service is in a different area. If you feel fine helping a relative or a friend across, that's beautiful; there's a section on that in the "Lighten Relationships" chapter. The work below is less personal.

You can call entities who may need help joining their higher self, and one or more will often show up to receive your help. If you sense entity influence upon a person, you don't need permission to do a healing because you are assisting the entity itself.

The first thing to do when you are about to heal an entity is close your own aura and that of the affected person, if any. Say with pure intent:

My (our) aura is now closed to all but the Christ (or God) Love and Light! (This means the Christ, the Son/Daughter of God each of us is, rather than Jesus. You may however say it to mean Jesus.)

If you are doing a general healing:

I invite all entities who would like assistance to come now for healing. (Give a little time for them to arrive.)

Next, speak the healing words:

Dear one(s), your I Am Presence now makes certain that all of your levels of consciousness are present for this healing. (There may be a pause here.) *You are welcome in love. You are surrounded and filled with the Christ (or God) love and light. You are healed and for-given. You are lifted free of Earth's vibration, and free of all pain and suffering. You are now joined with your own true higher self of love and light. Go into the light, dear one! Your higher self will take you now to your next right place. I bid you farewell, and go in peace.*

With nearly all entities, this healing will be enough. If you are able to check and discover that it did not accept the healing, you may say things like this:

You are good. You have always done your very best with what you've known. God knows and loves you completely, and has never judged you. You will not go to hell, which was not created by God, unless you yourself believe you must. Your higher self of love and light is waiting for you with open arms, to comfort you and help you into your next place of learning—a place that will be happier for you than you are here. I am not trying to fool you, I am speaking truth. As I say the healing words again, just look for the brightest light and go into that.

Then, speak the healing again.

If you realize that the entity is yet present, feel from your spirit what to do next. If you are working with a person being influenced and the entity is still with them, say these words with fire and passion:

In the name and by the power of the lord god of my being (or a master such as Jesus the Christ), I now command you to leave the presence of (the influenced person), and never to return! So be it!

If you are doing a healing for a "free-floating" entity, you may say something like this:

I now command you, in the name of my divine being, to leave my presence. If you become ready to truly join your higher self, you may come again; but not until such time. So be it.

If it is appropriate for the person being influenced, see if you can help him or her discover why he or she attracted the entity. If it seems easily correctable, you may offer your services or refer them to someone else.

If the problem seems deep and immovable, at least for the time being, the person will probably attract another entity very quickly. Your command is good only as long as the person himself doesn't undermine it. You will have to judge whether or not there is more you can do.

As mentioned in *Living Mastery,* there is a pamphlet by the author which gives more information on astral healing. It is available without cost; see AMI's address at the end of the book.

While You Are Sleeping

We naturally give more to life as we expand spiritually. Service is not limited to our waking hours; while we sleep we may leave our body and join ascended masters to help with their projects, or other possibilities. Study at one of many schools of truth scattered about the universe is another common sleep activity.

Tune to your spirit. Ask what is happening while you sleep. If you're serving, how? If you're studying, what? See how your sleep activity fits in with what you're learning and giving while you're awake.

Group Service

Serving through a group is quite an art. Whether it's a neighborhood group or a huge complex like the International Red Cross, certain vital principles apply.

1. Service groups, like most others, tend to get buried in busy work. At least once a month, get together to remind yourselves what you are doing, and why.

    In a large organization, the meeting could be called with a department or a smaller division. It is vital that top leaders meet as well, because their inspiration filters down to the rest of the organization.

    This meeting—call it a re-dedication or inspirational meeting?—is a time to re-open your hearts. It's a time to share accounts of the good your work is doing. A time to honor and thank everyone, and perhaps certain ones; to brainstorm for creative new ideas, or to solve problems; to tune together to spirit, to give thanks, and pray or receive guidance. Setting aside this time pays enormous dividends in keeping everyone inspired, involved, and giving their all.

    In even the largest organizations, a regular gathering of everyone, or as many as feasible, is of great benefit. Each person can then see how important their work is, how it fits into the whole, and the end results.

    Between such gatherings, a bulletin reporting successes and challenges keeps everyone in touch. Input from any person should be welcomed.

2. As much as possible, assign complex processes to a small committee within the group. There is nothing less fun than a large group trying to make multiple, intricate decisions.

3. Ego and desire for power often arise in even small groups. A way around this is to have no leader at all, or rotate leaders. (The Zen Center based in San Francisco, which is quite large, now has rotating leadership.) Where rotation isn't appropriate, the integrity of the leaders determines if true service is given.

4. When differences arise, as they inevitably will, take a break and tune into your heart or spirit. Each one sincerely ask what is best for everyone. Even if differences remain, they will be more easily resolved.

Pure Heart Service I Am

For you, or your group:

I am (we are) one with all.

I am compassion for all.

I am love.

I follow my heart's path, my spirit light, my joy.

I come from love and do as I am guided, in freedom.

I am fully present and fully alive, here and now!

As I serve, I am automatically served.

I serve in pure equality with all.

I see the divine in all I serve.

I give the gift of allowing others to serve me.

So be it!

Thank you for all you are, and all that you do!

Service Initiations in Other Chapters

The "Clear!" chapter:

☆ Lightworker's Syndrome

The "Lighten Relationships" chapter:

☆ Help a Loved One to Pass Over

☆ Help a Loved One Who Has Passed

11
Rejuvenation and Immortality

The spirit which informs your body is immortal.
Your body may also know immortality.

We can literally, permanently rejuvenate. Such a claim would seem on the edge—or over the edge—of insanity! How could one be so deluded? I used to ask this same question.

When we develop certainty about metaphysical truths, the possibility of rejuvenation can turn into a certainty:

1. The divine is absolutely unlimited, totally powerful, and eternal. It expresses naturally as divine order and beauty.
2. The divine is everywhere, as everything, right here and now. This means the eternal divine *is* our physical body. The very substance of our body is divine.
3. We are the image of the divine. Whatever the divine is—such as eternal—may be realized and experienced on every level of our being including the physical.
4. All form is created by thought, and re-created every moment by thought. Thought may be instantly changed; form may be instantly changed.

If these statements are true, the choice to rejuvenate comes with human territory. We have the nervous system capable of realizing and *expressing* our divinity. Our body is made of divine substance: energy, formed into a body by divine thought in our mother's womb.

Being one with the divine, yet believing we were separate, our beliefs have been all-powerful. As we have believed our body must age and die—so it has been.

But now we are remembering our divinity and returning to divine oneness. What a wondrous time! Regarding immortality and rejuvenation, we have wayshowers in ascended masters and other immortals. They encourage us to accomplish as they have accomplished.

Why rejuvenate? Why become immortal? Let us look at some divine attributes:

☆ Eternal life, ever-expanding

☆ Infinite energy

☆ Beauty.

If we fully honor the divine in everything, we will not leave out the body. Rejuvenation and immortality are our *right;* they are our inheritance from Mother/Father God of which we are part. Ancient encodings of unlimited divinity, including immortality of form, lie within our cells. Though these encodings have been rendered temporarily powerless by the limited beliefs or recent milennia, they yet wait for us to re-empower them.

There is a more profound reason for rejuvenation and immortality. This third-dimensional realm is the great trickster. It invites us to believe that solid matter is the most real stuff there is. Even if we recognize our spirit as immortal, to *not* recognize *and experience* our body as the stuff of God is to miss an incredible opportunity for learning and wisdom. The body is an ephemeral conglomeration of divine particles of energy, formed by thought. I am firmly convinced that to experience the body—and all other "solid" matter—as one with divinity is a vital part of the learning we have chosen in taking earthly form.

Of course, life must be happy enough to want to stay—otherwise, what would be the point? As with everything else, rejuvenation/immortality is something we are guided to do or not do. There may be higher priorities.

The divine is here! Present, unlimited in all ways! This is our only truth! This knowing is how others have rejuvenated, and how we may rejuvenate. The processes we use are of little importance, as long as they assist our knowing of this truth.

A deep exploration on the logic of rejuvenation, and reasons for choosing it, may be found in the first book of this set, *Living Mastery.*

Here are initiations from my spirit which have greatly assisted me. With each, call in your spirit and tune to it, relax, ground yourself, and intend that it works. Take time, breathe, and *feel*, making each initiation real for you.

It's likely that with such ingrained, eons-old beliefs around aging and death, these initiations will bear repeating many, many times.

Is Rejuvenation/Immortality for Me?

Let us define rejuvenation more clearly. It can be broken down into two major possibilities. One is rejuvenating in every way including vitality and appearance. The second is to rejuvenate only the vitality of the body and leave the appearance the same or approximately the same. Each possibility may have as much variance as an individual chooses.

Rejuvenating or becoming an immortal is not better than other paths. One or both may be a high priority for you now, or not. Your spirit is guiding you. If you are sure this is your path, skip this process.

Go into a meditation. Invite your divine presence to be clearly with you, and if you wish close master friends and guides. When you feel deeply one, look into rejuvenation as one subject, and immortality as another. What do you feel or hear from your spirit on each?

If you are getting "No," and you wanted to get "Yes," receive what your higher priorities are for this time and align yourself with them. If you get "Yes," go for it!

Clear the Unconscious

It is important to know that we may feel, declare and envision our chosen changes with passion and intention over a long period of time, and unconscious aspects of self *may not hear or be changed in the slightest degree.* The mind is vast! If unconscious levels are in alignment with our chosen path, there will be smooth sailing. If they have a different agenda, we can decree until we're blue in the face and they will not budge. They must be brought into the process. Being buried, unknown, undealt with, beliefs we are not conscious of are somehow the ground of being, our strongest reality. They will prevent the success of any choice which they oppose.

Unless this is your first life on earth, your unconscious contains buried memories, feelings and convictions about your own aging and death from other lives. Your unconscious may also believe that safety lies in keeping the same program. These unconscious beliefs may be accessible to you, or may not be as yet.

Invite your unconscious mind to become open to your communication. Love and respect help bridge the gap. Often you can feel your unconscious as deep emotion underlying surface feeling and thought. You may feel this deep emotion in your solar plexus or abdomen area. Take time with it, breathe, feel.

If you think there has come an open channel between you, speak something like this:

Beloved part of myself I haven't been conscious of: I love you and honor you. Thank you for following the aging and death agenda of the past. By obeying my belief, you have been serving me perfectly.

I want you to know that I have remembered who I am: an unlimited divine being. I choose to change our program now. I choose to release aging and death. I choose to rejuvenate this sacred form. I choose to live forever, in ever-lighter form or formlessness.

We are safe to make these changes. You cooperation is needed. Will you give it?

Look deeply into your feeling now. Can you see if, or how, your unconscious is responding? Allow it to be honest—this is a huge step and it cannot be forced. It may be saying "What?" "No way!" "I need more information," or "I'm thinking about it." You are likely to need patience and perseverance in getting your unconscious mind's full support.

Ask your unconscious to show you its beliefs, memories and emotions which are against rejuvenation or immortality. Those which you are ready to see will come up. Anything you are not ready to see—a particularly painful or horrifying death, for example—will not show itself until you are strong enough to face it. The I Release Death! and I Choose Life! initiations below will help.

When your unconscious shows you something, acknowledge it and honor it. In the chapter "Clear!" see the initiations under the Clear Fear-Based Energy section.

It may take years, even decades, to create full alignment between your conscious intention and your unconscious mind. But once your unconscious aligns with your rejuvenation process, your success is practically guaranteed.

I Release Death!

Before you say these or any words of initiation, go into a silent space and call your spirit. Ask that every level within you be able to hear these words and be changed by them. Gather yourself into a deep and powerful space, ready to speak words imbued with the power of transformation:

I now make "the impossible" possible. I give up death. My body never dies again. I give up any plan or idea, conscious or unconscious, that my body will die at a particular time. I give up all aging of the body, all illness, and any other effect that limited thought has had upon my physical form. I give up the idea of being any age. I am ageless and eternal.

I give up attachment to being "one of the crowd" in pretending that this light form must die. I release all emotional attachments to death and dying in every form, not only in my body but in my mind and feelings. I give up funerals, funeral parlors, and grave sites. I give up speaking about death. I give up the idea of leaving life.

I heal with the light of God within me, and the love of God within me, all previous thoughts, feelings and memories of this and any past life of aging, illness and death. I accept the healing of my conscious and unconscious minds for all of these past experiences. This healing progresses in the time and way best for me.

Call in the violet flame, or the golden flame of your divinity. Ask it to now blaze through every level of your being, clearing as much as you are ready to let go of. Deaths in other lives, including any trauma around them, aging in any life, illness in any life—the flame blazes around and through! Beliefs, fear about aging and death—clear them out! Breathe! Let your hands sweep up your body and above your head, giving up all to your spirit.

You may want to repeat this many times over the years, as you are guided, until it is so complete that you are totally invulnerable to the old limited beliefs of humanity around you.

I Choose Life!

If you choose physical immortality, these statements are for you:

I embrace life in all its fullness—the excitement, mystery and beauty of it, the joy and sorrow of it, this eternal now! My aliveness expands forever. My breath is full and deep. I live on the leading edge of my spirit, and step with courage this day into the new, the unknown.

I choose the ever-expanding joy of the divine, of which I am part. I choose to experience heaven and earth as one, here and now. I dare to fulfill my dreams and be happy, loving, prosperous and fulfilled in the ways of earth and the ways of spirit. There is no reason for me to leave my life on earth for life on a different level.

I Am the perfection of my real self. I Am the ever-expanding life of the divine. My body is divine substance! It is living light. It is everlasting life, wholeness and perfection. It is beauty. It is God/Goddess in expression, now and forever.

My thought, vision, imagination and intention uplift me into immortality, my new reality! I joyously accept the eternal life of the divine as this sacred form.

I live in this body as long as long as is right for me—a thousand years if I am so guided—in ever-increasing beauty, strength, health, aliveness and joy. When I am ready to leave earth, I quicken the frequencies of my body and step into a lighter dimension. No form remains behind.

I am an immortal. Thanks be to God. And so be it.

Clear Barriers to Rejuvenation

You are likely to hold many of these beliefs below, as they have been virtually universal in our culture. Select those you choose to release now. Call upon your divine presence or a favorite master to be with you, go through it with you. Gather your lion heart!

We each have our own way of releasing old beliefs. In the "Clear!" chapter, many different ways of release are given. Below is yet another way. Change this process to work better for you, or create a method entirely your own.

From the list below, choose a limiting belief you recognize as one of yours. Fly or slip into this belief. Feel it and continue moving through it, deeper and deeper. Here it may get complex: the one issue may break down into two or more. If so, you will want to repeat this process with each one. Just pick one of them and begin to move through it. If you really do this, you may find the belief blowing up into space, or that you have come to an outer edge of it and space is beyond. Leap into this space! Now let the belief fall away beneath you, or rise above it until it looks very small below you. Say to yourself:

I created that.

Really get that you are the one who created it for yourself. Get it all the way into your belly. Now add:

It's okay that I created it.

Feel that too. Now, see that the only reason it exists is because *you* put it there. You have chosen to give it your creative energy, so that it would continue to exist. When you withdraw your energy it will begin to disperse or will disappear entirely. Do you want to do this, to un-create it? If so, choose how you want to do it. Here is one way:

Thank it first for serving you, and invite its energy to go into your new creation. Then picture a big red electrical switch that has been up in the "On" position. Taking both hands up above your head, throw the switch downward to "Off," simultaneously saying "Kaboom!" See the belief shrink into a pinpoint and then explode into light.

Now, what is your new creation going to be? Refer to the antidote and let it assist you. Speak it aloud, with great clarity and passion. Feel your new reality, enjoy it, accept it deeply. Give it your energy over the following weeks (or months or years) until it becomes real for you; until it becomes "the way it is."

If you find the old belief returning, recognize that you are still giving it life. This work often peels the issue away in layers. When you feel ready, repeat the process. It is extremely powerful for dissolving something no longer wanted and creating what is wanted.

Here are limiting beliefs common to humanity.

1. God does not love me.

    When we forgot our oneness with divinity, eons ago, we constructed the ego—a trickster—to replace it. So we have feared—unconsciously—that God must be very angry with us. This has birthed the idea of a judgmental, vengeful, angry God.

    Antidote: *God loves me infinitely and eternally. God has never judged me, only I have judged myself. God has understood my belief in separation. He/She has continued to know me as the innocent, beautiful, divine being I am. I welcome and feel this truth now!*

2: I am not worthy of having what I want.

    Our belief in separation spawned guilt and unworthiness. These feelings have multiplied through lifetimes as we have played out our roles, including "persecutor," to develop wisdom.

    We need to forgive *everything*. As we do, we begin to feel worthy of having what our heart desires.

    Antidote: *I am innocent forever, one with all-loving God/ Goddess. I humbly accept this truth. I forgive as deeply as I can now, myself and all others, all events and circumstances. I do not stop until all is forgiven, and I live in a forgiven world.*

    I am worthy of all good, because I am one with the divine. I am the image of God and the worth of God. I deserve only goodness. I accept no lesser truth about myself. I love and honor myself. I am my own best friend. I accept all divine good in my life.

3. Life just isn't this good, and can't be this good.

    We have been accepting far less than life offers us— everything we could want.

    Antidote: *God, the principle of life, is an outrageous giver. Totally loving, It wants me—as part of Itself—to be and express the infinite abundance of the universe. My true nature is so vast, it encompasses all that is; I already include everything I could possibly want. I only need to know this, and claim and accept my desired* *good. I choose to understand this truth in the depths of my being, and thus to live a transformed life.*

4.   Aging and death are real; they are simple facts of life.

To succeed in rejuvenation or immortality, it is crucial to overcome this belief. Our body has no power of its own; it follows our beliefs. But it longs to fulfill its true nature: the eternally expanding life of divinity. (This belief is one that needs deep, patient work to clear.)

Antidote: *I am the image of my divine, beloved Mother/ Father God. I am everlasting, expanding life. Aging and death are illusions that hold no reality for me. My body is God's body, a body of light and increasing beauty eternally. I place God-thought of perfection for this body uppermost in my thought. I am free to regenerate my body, to rejuvenate and beautify it, and let it always live.*

5.   I fear and judge death.

When we identify with the body, this is a natural outcome. Anything we fear, resist, or judge, we attract into our experience. That is why it's important to release these attitudes toward death.

The death of the body is not a bad thing. We've been dying and reincarnating for a long time. At death our higher self gives us loving welcome into a lighter realm, where we expand in wisdom until we are ready to reincarnate.

Dying can, of course, be agonizing, as with painful illness. And sudden or violent death is terrifying. In difficult death experiences, we may have felt so frightened or confused that we were unable to accept the loving welcome from our higher self. If we didn't make this connection with spirit, we got stuck for a time in "limbo:" a non-material being trying to relate to a material world. If you have had such experiences, you have fears of death to overcome.

Antidote: *With the assistance of my divine self, I am freeing myself from all fear of death. I release judgment of death. If death comes to my body this lifetime, I let that be all right. I have plenty of time to choose immortality of form! I am divine and fearless.*

6.   I fear and judge aging.

Some fear aging more intensely than death. It's true that aging is a sad process, intensified by our society's worship of youth. Aging is unnatural for our body. But until we have moved into our unlimited consciousness enough to turn the process around, it is beneficial to accept whatever has taken place, and to accept aging if it continues to happen. To fear, judge, or resist it invites aging to continue.

Antidote: *I let go of all fear, resistance or judgment of aging. I accept and love my body and face exactly as they are. Whatever my physical appearance, I am the infinite worth of the divine. I am totally loveable and loved. I am beautiful! I am wonderful!*

7.   I judge or hate my body, or parts of it.

How many times have we looked in the mirror and judged? The body *feels* this condemnation, and sinks lower in its ability to express its aliveness and beauty.

Antidote: *I give thanks for life in form, a wondrous gift of the creator. I acknowledge, with wonder and gratitude, the amazing miracle of my body. I love my naked body in the mirror. I praise it and bless it. This brings joy to my beloved body, and prepares it to accept rejuvenation. It responds with renewed energy and strength. There is no power greater than this love!*

8.   I identify with how I look. I identify with how old I am. I'm afraid to change that. Who would I be? (A big one!)

Antidote: *Who I am transcends how I look. If I am a youthful immortal, my soul is the same and my identity is the same. Beyond human form, I identify with the divine I Am. I am ageless and eternal!*

9.   Time is real. I feel security in the progression of time, including aging. Changing this would be frightening and confusing.

Antidote: *Time is illusory; there is no time in God. All time exists simultaneously. My security rests in the only place it belongs: the eternal divine in this now moment.*

10. My age is associated with wisdom and power. If I looked young again, people would not think me wise or powerful. They wouldn't respect me.

     This phenomenon is a matter for re-education. Pioneers in rejuvenation will express wisdom and power in a beautiful, youthful body.

     Antidote: *I can look young and be ancient in wisdom and power, spirit and grace. People respond to my being, not my appearance. I can look young and be fully respected.*

11. If I become younger in body, it means I'm going *backward* in time, losing wisdom. (Is it only me that has had this strange one?)

     Antidote: *I move forward through time into my youthful body and appearance. I never go back! Through this process I gain great wisdom and have many gifts to give.*

12. What I am eating or not eating, doing or not doing, is harmful to my body.

     Our thoughts about food and activities are *creative.* If we think something is harmful, it will be. We had best change either the activity or the thought!

     Antidote: *Nothing physical has the power to harm my body. I choose harmless thoughts, and I do what works for me now in wisdom.*

13. My life isn't much fun. Why prolong it?

     Antidote: *I choose to be happy. I align with the joy of the universe! I fulfill my purposes. I heal my relationships. I do only what I love to do, or move into that. I give the gifts I've come to give, and I receive God's infinite abundance of good including financial prosperity. With my life full of joy and meaning, I welcome rejuvenation and immortality.*

14. If I become immortal, I'll be trapped in this body forever! I couldn't stand that!

     Antidote: *I am never entrapped. I am learning how to quicken the frequencies of my body and step into lighter* *realms, leaving no form behind. When I am ready to leave this plane, that is what I will do.*

15. I love my family, my parents and grandparents. If I don't age and die the way they do, I won't honor them.

    We confuse love and honor for our family with being bound to their choices.

    Antidote: *Love and freedom are one. The most loving thing I can do for my family and friends is demonstrate freedom from age and death—to give them that gift! This is what I choose to do.*

16. I will lose the love of my family and friends if I rejuvenate. I'll be too different from them. They'll think I'm crazy or they'll be jealous. I'll be alone! I won't have friends!

    Antidote: *My family and friends are one with divinity. If they aren't yet ready to rejuvenate, that is fine. In their own right time, they will express their mastery over limitation. I do not fear if someone seems to not love me; I understand and forgive. I know love is forever the only truth between us.*

    Whatever I am doing, I have friends who are doing the same. The closer I am with my spirit, the more loving and wonderful are my friends. I am never alone. Most of all, I have God's eternal love and support.

17. In my meditation I get clear on rejuvenation, but during the day when I look in the mirror or think about my body, I slip back into the assumption of aging. (Ah, easy to do!)

    Antidote: *I have patience with my process. Gradually I am able to hold every thought and feeling, and every picture in my mind, to the truth of my eternal divine form.*

18. It can't be spiritually right to rejuvenate. It's just vanity to want to look good.

    Antidote: *As part of the divine, I naturally express as eternal beauty of mind, heart and body. To leave my body out prevents the divine from expressing its natural, eternal beauty as this form. It's fine to enjoy looking youthful.*

19. This body is just gross physical matter. It isn't important. When it has served its purpose, it is sluffed off while my immortal spirit continues on. Physical immortality is pointless.

    This thought is often expressed. It is fine to hold this belief. Here is an alternative.

    Antidote: *I am here to recognize and experience everything as divine. If I leave my body out of divine expression, I will not receive a priceless jewel of wisdom. My experience on earth will not be all it could have been.*

20. I don't see any results! Where are they? This isn't working!

    It is such a tremendous shift from death consciousness to life consciousness that you may continue to age for awhile, with spurts of youthing, gradually shifting over to mostly youthing with spurts of aging, until you come totally into life consciousness and continuous rejuvenation. You may concentrate on projects such as feeling stronger and more alive, and succeed in these, until it all comes together. Patience! You're turning around eons of old belief.

    Antidote: *I choose to remember the truth of divinity as this form. I ignore all illusion! My rejuvenation process may work on a cellular-atomic level long before it becomes obvious. If it truly isn't working yet, I realize that something in myself is preventing it. I have all the patience and perseverance I need to clear my old programming.*

    I place my whole process in the context that whatever is happening or not happening in the moment, I am succeeding! I take each experience, including any appearance of failure—and my reaction to that—as a step forward to ultimate success.

21. I'll never do it! It can't be done! (In other words, nontrust in the unlimited realities of life.)

    Antidote: *I hold to the truth of an all-loving and all-giving divinity which offers me all the good I can possibly desire right here and now. I choose to really, truly accept this on every level of my being. Life is good! Real-*

*ity is beautiful and full of infinite, magical present pos-
sibility. God is the doer, and He/She accomplishes anything effortlessly. I do accept this good. It is happening. So be it!*

22. What if I give this my all, my very best, and it doesn't
    happen?
        This is really the same thought as "What if I trust
    God completely and find out He/She/It doesn't exist?
    What if I swing full out on a trapeze, no safety net, let
    go in mid-air, and no one is there to catch me!" The
    result would be devastation, that is the feeling.
        This question is at the root of life. Most of us have
    forgotten that we are one with the source of all, and
    that when we swing out on that trapeze in daring and in
    faith, *it is impossible* that we would not be caught.
        There's no simple answer for developing this kind
    of trust.
    Antidote: *I go within, and tune to my true nature and the
    nature of the universe. When I do this long and deeply
    enough, I come to know the reality of God and the real-
    ity of good. Also, I begin to feel to the depths of my bones
    my own capacity to create anything I truly desire.*

23. If I do allow myself to rejuvenate, it will be taken away
    from me. I'll be left worse off than if I had never re-
    ceived it. (Belief in loss is an old one.)
    Antidote: *God has never abandoned me—how could It
    abandon Itself? I am eternally loved and provided for. All
    success and fulfillment in my life is mine to keep eter-
    nally. Life's goodness is forever and cannot be taken away.*

24. I can't accept this much joy.
    Antidote: *With the help of my divine self, I let go of any
    remaining resentment and anger, sorrow, judgment, fear,
    confusion, pain and stress—symptoms of feeling sepa-
    rate from divinity. I move into the joy, love, light, trust,
    relaxation, acceptance, forgiveness, power, freedom,
    and knowing that express my oneness with divinity. I
    can and do accept this much joy.*

25. I have to do it right! (An old favorite.)
    Antidote: *If I choose a rejuvenation program or schedule, I let myself flow within it. I take short breaks or long breaks. I am rejuvenating in my own perfect time and way, unique to me, as my knowing guides me. I honor myself and trust my process. Everything happens in the best way for me.*

26. I have to do this myself. I have to work really hard to make rejuvenation or immortality happen.
    Antidote: *All I need do is remember that rejuvenation or immortality is happening, and clear other thoughts away. God is the doer. My divine self and my master friends are aspects of God. I place my trust in the divine, and relax. God's action is effortless and sure.*

27. Immortal life is too much. What will I do? Who will I be? How can I make plans?
    Antidote: *As I am immortal anyway, I might as well be immortal in body. I flow easily from one combination of activities to the next. I need not ever worry about what to do: the divine I Am always knows. It is easy and good to be immortal in form.*

Reprogram Your Body

The body has no will of its own. It follows the commands we give it, commands in the form of our beliefs. But it does desire—as all life desires—to express its divine potential.

Get in touch with your body. Feel its energy flows; feel where it is touching your clothes, your seat. Feel its warmth, its life, your heart beating, your breath. Ground it. Give your love to your body, and open up a two-way channel of communication. Welcome your divine presence, love and power. Say as you will:

My beloved body, I so honor and thank you for obeying my commands of the past. You have served me perfectly!

I want you to know that I have remembered who I am. I am an unlimited divine being, free to choose my path. My beloved divine form, I choose your rejuvenation and immortality. You are divine love, divine light, divine joy and eternal life! You are divine beauty and perfection. You express your divinity more and more! Each day you are stronger and more energetic, more light-emanating, more joyous, more beautiful. You live forever!

I know you will follow this program as lovingly and obediently as you did the old one. Thank you!

Does your body have any reaction to this? Often, it is one of great joy ("Wow! Your finally getting it!"). There may be confusion in the face of the long-time old commands, and resistance from your unconscious mind. Stick with it until all feels clear.

Reverse the Death Hormone in the Pituitary

The pituitary gland has been producing a "death hormone" in response to our belief/command that our body age. I experienced an amazing, spontaneous, spirit-guided initiation in which the death hormone stopped, and life hormones began to take its place. The production of life hormones later expanded to all the ductless glands associated with the chakras. This is a most powerful initiation.

Feel your desire to release the bondage of aging, and express your unlimited potential in rejuvenation. When you feel clear about this intention, gather your passion around it.

Call in your divine self.

Your pituitary gland is about three inches down from the center top of your head; ask it now to "light up" for you. Let your words be filled with the passion you feel, and speak to your pituitary with absolute clarity. Take the time to feel each statement:

My beloved pituitary gland! I thank you and acknowledge you for producing the death hormone in the past. That was exactly what I commanded you to do from my old beliefs, and you have served me perfectly! I want you to know that I have remembered who I am. I am an unlimited being with absolute choice to determine all my life experiences. I have chosen to rejuvenate this beloved body, and to be an immortal.

Therefore, I command you to stop producing the death hormone, and begin producing a life hormone. Do this now!

Now, feel what is happening. Mentally place an egg shape around your body, and see it filled with a liquid lavender light-love, the life hormone. See this flowing, dancing through everything, lighting the divine spark within every atom and cell. See it whirling through every organ, bone, and system. See if you can feel the joy of your cells: "Yeay! Let's *celebrate!*" Feel everything becoming immediately stronger, clearer, and more healthy.

Now, command the other ductless glands of the body, each associated with a different chakra (energy center), to align with your rejuvenation. These glands are:

☆ **Pineal**, associated with your third eye chakra.

☆ **Thyroid**, at your throat chakra.

☆ **Thymus**, above your heart chakra.

☆ **Adrenals**, close to each kidney, with your solar plexus.

☆ **Pancreas**, with your second chakra. Your pancreas is next to your stomach, on the left.

☆ **Ovaries** or **testes** as the case may be, with your first chakra.

Call upon each gland in turn, with these or similar words:

Beloved _____ gland! I charge you now to join this rejuvenation process! Release your hormones and frequencies of love, life, light and joy now into this unlimited body! We are rejuvenating!

With each one, see if you can feel what is happening. Some people feel great joy from these glands, especially the thymus.

After you have done this once, don't insult the intelligence of your body by repeating it like this; call upon the *continuation* and *strengthening* of what has already begun.

This initiation can become an extraordinary part of your rejuvenation process. Here's to your success!

Language of Immortality and Rejuvenation

Harness the power of your spoken word through statements such as these:

Oh, how old do I feel today? About 27!

I'm timeless and ageless. How about you?

I'm immortal.

I'm _____ years into this life, and time isn't real.

Billions of years!

I love him to life!

She's making her transition.

He's gone into a lighter realm.

Age and death are okay, they're just not my choice.

I don't do funerals.

Time is an illusion; we made it up. The sequence of events certainly has no power to affect my body.

I love this body, I don't ever judge it!

I feel tired, but I Am infinite energy!

I am all-powerful in creating the levels of energy in my body.

This body is divine, formed from God/Goddess thought of perfection.

My body is made of divine light and infinite energy.

Any aging I see in the mirror is illusion; the beauty of the divine blue print I am, my light body, is my only truth.

This divine form is transmuting daily into my light body.

All the cells of my body are daily bathed in the perfection of my divine being.

Love Your Body

Stand, preferably naked, before a mirror. Caress your body as you say aloud to it something like this, adding anything you feel:

I love you, my beautiful body. Thank you for being spirit's home in this dimension. You are a sacred form, part of the divine. You were created by divine love, thought and will. If my limited thought has altered you from perfection, you remain in truth perfect, and your perfection will manifest.

I love every atom and cell of you, my wonderful body. I love every muscle, every bone. I love every organ and gland. I love you, amazing heart, for pumping all day and all night. I love you my lungs that work so perfectly. I love you my liver, my kidneys (etc.). I love every blood cell and every nerve. I love my skin, all over. I love you my face and my eyes and my nose and mouth, my chin and neck. I love my arms and hands for enabling me to do so much in my life. I love my legs and my feet, my whole beautiful torso. I love my breasts. I love my waist. I love my stomach. I love my bottom. (If a part is diseased, give it special loving attention, affirming its perfection.)

I love you, my body of light. You are my sacred body of joy. You are more perfect today in every way than you were yesterday. You are younger, stronger, more energetic, more flexible, more beautiful, more light-filled every day. You are healthier, more graceful, clearer, and more perfectly formed today. You are rejuvenating. Any seeming imperfection is healed. Everything functions perfectly and in comfort.

I forgive myself for not liking (this or that) in the past. I know you are perfect and I have only appreciation for you. I praise you, my beloved body! Your frequencies are higher than they have ever been, and you are moving into the expression of my light body, my divine blue print body. So be it.

Your Light Body

Your divine blueprint body—the body you were meant to have in this lifetime, also called the light body (some call it the etheric body)—is a touchstone for rejuvenation, regeneration, and immortality. Though we haven't much felt it, it is—just like God—right here! We can tune into it, see it, feel it, and have it become for us the reality it is. As we become convinced that this light body is real, it is easier and easier to shift our thought of who we are and how we look, into unlimited divine blueprint beauty.

Call in your divine presence. Ask It to help you see your light body. It may help to place a mirror before your mind's eye and see your light body in it.

Most people don't see their whole light body, though you may be lucky. You may catch glimpses of parts of it, or see all of it briefly. If you want a clearer picture, imagine how you would most enjoy looking. Most likely, this is very much how your light body looks.

As you keep working with this, it may become easier to see.

When you have seen your light body as clearly as you can for now, ask it to step into your physical body. *Feel* it, as best you can. It is an effortless body, light, free, joyful. If it has organs, they don't seem to have anything to do. It has infinite energy and strength, infinite ability and infinite life.

Some words:

My physical body is now transmuting into my beautiful, divine blue print light body.

Feel this transmutation begin, or strengthen! See each atom radiating the divine light that is its reality in each area of your body. This light increases in brilliance until it shines like the sun. See it transmuting all into the perfection of divinity. Take time to enjoy the experience of being light, your true essence.

A Rejuvenation Program

Here's a paradox: we work within the illusion of time to arrive at timeless truth! Our own divine presence, infinitely loving and powerful, could shift our body in an instant from the appearance of any age to that of beautiful youth. But most of us are not yet able to accept such a dramatic or sudden change. Therefore we rejuvenate through time.

Rejuvenation for your body can be exactly as you define it. You may choose a slight change in appearance or vitality all the way to major shifts in both. And you may choose a small change now, and bigger changes later.

It is important to feel really ready to accept rejuvenation— your own definition of it—before you undertake a rejuvenation program; otherwise, you set yourself up for a sense of failure.

If you do feel ready, proceed in a balanced way which allows anything that happens or doesn't happen to be fine. If you notice success, wonderful! If you don't, ask your spirit to help you locate the next level of clearing for you to open to rejuvenation. Be a learner eager for the new wisdom you will inevitably gain!

Here is a program of rejuvenation meant for daily or frequent use. Choose the aspects of it which match your own agenda.

You may find attitude to be very important for you. Excitement and enthusiasm! Humility: you are aware that you are not the doer, God/Goddess is. You are rejuvenating *in God,* you are successful *in God.* Joy, a childlike innocence. Shall you adopt any of these attitudes? You may be guided to others along the way.

Become centered and grounded. Breathe deeply and gently. Relax your whole body, part by part. Become detached toward your mind. Relax your feelings. Bless your whole being. Call in your spirit.

With each chakra:

Command it to open; see and feel it open. See its blazing light radiate into infinity.

Ask your spirit to spin your chakras in optimum speed and direction.

Affirm that the gland(s) associated with each is fully cooperating in your regeneration process. The chakras and their glands, from the seventh down:

- ☆ Crown: pituitary
- ☆ Third eye: pineal
- ☆ Throat: thyroid
- ☆ Heart: thymus
- ☆ Solar plexus: adrenals
- ☆ Creative center: pancreas
- ☆ Root chakra: ovaries or gonads

Feel and see your body as divine. Say:

This is God's body. God formed this body, and is reforming it this moment. Without God, I would have no body. God's will, energy, love, intelligence and life are running this body right now, taking care of six trillion transactions each second. God expresses its perfection through and as this body. This is God's heartbeat. This is God's breath. This is God's liver, God's kidneys, God's organs, God's glands, God's bones, God's muscles, God's immune system, God's eyes (etc.).

I give up my old way of defining this body. I give up my old way of looking.

This body is regenerating and rejuvenating now. I put God/my divine self to work in every atom of my body. This body is transforming into my perfect light body, more and more every day. My muscles are becoming stronger. My skin is smooth and clear, my face and neck are young. My eyes are perfect. (Etc.)

I am returning to the ancient, original divine encoding within my cells, the encoding of an immortal body.

The genes within my cells are all reversing action toward divine youthful form.

The chromosome strands in every cell of my body are increasing from 2 to 3, from 3 to 6, from 6 to 9, and from 9 to 12, the original number for god beings in physical form.

My blood is purifying, as is my entire body. Free radicals, toxins, and anything else not harmonious with a divine, immortal form are disappearing from my body.

The telomeres in every cell are increasing to optimum number for my immortal body. Anything else that has appeared to be lacking (name anything you wish) is now easily created by the divine chemist within this body and comes up to optimal, sustained levels.

My spirit told me that because of commands that the body age, sometimes new cells have not come in perfect. Also, the body may actually turn away new cells! Here are corrective words:

My beloved thymus, spleen and bone marrow, thank you for creating 100 million new cells per minute for this body! I command that all new cells come in divinely perfect, whole and strong. I command that they take the place of all old cells that need replacing. I command that this be a continuous process. My entire form now benefits! So be it.

Here's something to look forward to! It seems the body of a master is a different kind of structure than the one we have known:

As the frequency of my body increases, my entire body becomes crystalline energy forms.

If you have a picture of yourself that represents how you choose to appear, study this now; it is close to your light body in appearance and gives a clear picture to work with. Actually touch your body with it, because its frequencies are carried in the picture. Visualize your perfect light body, as above or in your picture. Step into it and feel it. Become it. Especially, emphasize *light* itself—see it totally blazing and brilliant, as and through every atom. This may be the single most beneficial thing to do in rejuvenating. Give yourself time and feel this as completely as you can.

If you feel guided, do the five or six Tibetan rites (see below). As you finish, you may say:

I place my divine self in complete charge of my rejuvenation. It continues all day today, all night tonight, and into the following days, weeks, months and years, as long as I choose. I give thanks for it. So be it.

Give the work of creating the changes to your divinity, God/ Goddess, a chosen committee of masters—aspect(s) of divinity. The changes are not your job. Your job is to *hold the end result in your mind and heart; to focus upon this and give nothing else power:* not the mirror, not anyone's comments about your appearance, or anything else.

It is wise to keep this process secret. The one exception: if you have a friend who is truly ready and desirous of doing this with you, you can support each other. Then you both keep it secret.

As you work with this each day, address the old dynamics in you which have doubted, feared or resisted rejuvenation. Affirm truth.

If you are changing your appearance, you are doing so in a world where this "isn't done." As you move forward, you may want to give energy to keeping harmony with others. When people begin to notice changes, know in advance what your response will be. Plan ahead for the success of your project.

You may find it beneficial to use a mantra, words of sacred sound which you repeat aloud. For women, the mantra *om vir mata* (honor to Divine Mother, of divine love and power) or another mantra to the Goddess may help you feel your oneness with Her. This oneness includes beauty.

For men, the mantra *om namah' Shivaya* (honor to Divine Father in the immortal form of Shiva, divine fire and power) may serve well, or another of your choosing.

It is helpful to repeat your mantra for at least one half hour in the morning and before bed. Steep yourself in the meaning of the mantra, feeling your honor for Divine Mother or Divine Father. You will probably notice greater ease in experiencing your own divinity and beauty.

If you would enjoy creating a schedule for your rejuvenation, see below.

Resolve that while you are doing your rejuvenation program you pay no attention to your mirror, give no power to appearances of age, no power even to the process not seeming to work. Remember that what you continue to intend, *must* manifest. If it takes awhile—though it doesn't need to take long—it's a good opportunity to clear yourself of anything in the way, and to exercise patience and perseverance!

If you begin to feel you are forcing yourself with the process, take a break. Put all work and all rest in the context of eventual success, and it will indeed come for you.

A word about vitality. The frequencies of Earth and all upon her, including humanity, are quickening so rapidly that it is a major challenge for the body to keep up. Your body may often feel tired for no apparent reason as its energy integrates the new frequencies. You may need more sleep than you think you should. This is a matter for patience, realizing that this phase of rapid frequency rise will not last forever! For now, if your vitality is not returning as you intend, recognize that frequency adjustment is the likely cause.

Great success to you in your rejuvenation program!

Plans for Rejuvenating Through Time

We may manifest our timeless, eternal divine light body on schedule!—a schedule of our own choosing. Here are ideas.

Rejuvenate:

☆ One year for each year that passes.

☆ One year per month.

☆ One year per half month.

☆ One year per week.

If you choose a schedule, write it down. If you plan to rejuvenate for instance one year per month beginning June 1st, and you are 65 years into this life, your schedule would look like:

June 1:   65

July 1:   64

August 1: 63, and so forth until you reach the year of your chosen appearance or vitality.

Also, determine how many days you are rejuvenating each day. In the above schedule of one year per month, you are rejuvenating about 12 days every day. A good awareness to add to your process!

If you would like to accomplish your rejuvenation in one year's time, divide the number of years you wish to rejuvenate into the 365 days of a year. For instance, if you choose to rejuvenate 20 years in one year, divide 20 into 365. You get about 18 days for each year of rejuvenation.

Next, write out your schedule. If you are beginning March 1st and you are now 50 years into this life, write down:

March 1: 50

March 18:49

April 5:   48

and so on until you reach age 30 in about one year.

With this schedule, the number of years you rejuvenate within the year and the number of days you rejuvenate for each day are the same. In the process above, then, you would rejuvenate 20 days every day. Give thanks that this day you are rejuvenating your particular number of days for this one day toward your chosen year.

If you choose a schedule, proceed in a balanced and open way as suggested in the process above. Once you get going, for instance, it may be right for you to follow your schedule for only a few months. This is perfectly fine. Be grateful for the wisdom you have gained, do your next level of clearing if appropriate, and move on.

Rejuvenation Through God Alone

One of the masters I communicate with I call simply "Emil's mother." She is a major player in the events from the books *Life and Teaching of the Masters of the Far East,* by Baird Spalding. If her name is given, I have not discovered it. She is well over a hundred years old, yet she is youthfully beautiful.

I asked Emil's mother if she had ever aged, expecting to hear "No," she had simply remained young and beautiful. Instead, she told me that she had indeed aged, and later rejuvenated.

"How did you do that?" I asked.

"Through God alone," she replied. "I had no program, no desire except my oneness with God. In realizing this, the rejuvenation of my body just happened."

This is a most pure and direct way to rejuvenate. May it be your right way?

The Tibetan Rites

A little story about these ancient rites: When I was considering if I should teach them, a Tibetan lama came into my presence. He said nothing, but pure intensity radiated from him. His message was, "These are a true gift to the world and its people. They came to you not by accident. It is our hope that you will disseminate them to the best of your ability." I agreed, as have others who teach them.

The story which accompanies the rites in Peter Kelder's book *The Ancient Secret of the Fountain of Youth* is one that I perceive as true. The book also has a section of testimonials from people who have benefited from the rites.

All the rites are geared to quickening the spin of the chakras, which in the past has slowed down with age. The breath is vital: long, slow, deep, oxygenating breaths to the rhythm of the movement.

Suggested statements before beginning each day:

I give thanks for these rites. I honor them. I am attuned with those who have done them for thousands of years. We do them together.

Repeat each rite only three times a day at first. After a week, add two repetitions of each (to make five); add two more the next week, and so on until you are doing each rite twenty-one times daily (ten weeks). As you do them, know that they work perfectly for you.

First Rite: This is the simplest physically, but perhaps the most important.

With your arms straight out to the side, spin around to the right like a child, quickly. One revolution counts as one repetition. Breathe deeply throughout; no need to coordinate the breath with a single spin. Don't whip your head like a ballet dancer, just let your head turn with your body. When you stop, plant your feet apart, knees slightly bent, and press your hands hard together in front of you as if in prayer. Dizziness stops very quickly. Or raise the thumb of your right hand and focus on that as you spin.

If you can easily begin with more than three rotations, that's fine—don't overdo!

Some have suggested that doing thirty-three revolutions three times a day is all one needs (along with mind change!) to rejuvenate.

Second Rite:

Lie on the floor, arms along your sides and legs straight. Breathing in, lift your legs as high as you can, keeping them straight. At the same time, lift your head and neck (*not* your shoulders) as high off the floor as you can. Breathe out as you bring legs and head together back to the floor.

Third Rite:

On your knees, your thighs are perpendicular to the floor and your spine straight. Place the bottom of your toes to the floor, and your hands on the back of your thighs to brace yourself. Your head and neck are forward, chin close to the collar bone. While inhaling, bring up your head and neck and continue the motion backward, the shoulders also going back, arching your spine as much as you can. (Don't bend backward from the waist.) Then bring them forward again,

breathing out, until your spine is straight, continuing the motion of your head and neck forward to their original position.

Fourth Rite:

This one many people have trouble doing at first. If needed, adjust the exercise however you wish to develop the strength for it.

Sit on the floor, legs straight out in front of you about hip width apart; hands beside your buttocks with the fingers pointed to the front. Your head and neck are forward and down, chin close to the collar bone.

Breathing in, swing your torso up into a "table top" position. At the same time, your head goes back as far as comfortable. Your calves will be perpendicular to the floor over your feet, your thighs in line with your torso. In that position, tighten all the muscles of your body for a second or two and relax them again. Swing back down into the sitting position, breathing out, and bring your neck and head again forward and down.

The most frequent mistake with this rite is moving your feet. *Your feet do not move; you swing up over them, and then back down.*

A slight change of position that may make this easier: turn your hands out rather than forward.

Fifth Rite:

Face the floor with only your hands and the bottom of your toes touching the floor. Your legs and arms are straight, your hands about one and a half feet apart and slightly forward of your head. Your head is back. Your knees are close to the floor but not touching it. Your feet are about hip-width apart.

Breathing in, swing your bottom up as high as you can, and tuck your head toward your collar bone in the same motion. Breathing out, come back to your original position. (It's fine if you need to rest between repetitions.)

Sixth Rite:

The *Ancient Secret* book makes a big thing of doing this exercise only if you are celibate. But I am convinced that if you are sexually active with a partner you love, and especially if you are consciously bringing sexual energies up through your higher chakras to your crown, this rite is good to do.

Stand with your hands braced upon the front of your upper thighs. Take in a breath, and breathe out completely, with a series of short little huffs at the end to rid your lungs of all air.

Keeping the air out of your lungs, suck your solar plexus up as high as you can. Hold for as long as you can. Before you faint, breathe in through your nose, and out through your mouth. Take a breath or two to restore oxygen, and repeat. *This rite is done only three times a day, no more.*

Research and Rejuvenation

It is our approach here, obviously, to rejuvenate and become immortals through our realization of divinity; clearing limited belief from all levels; and harnessing our mind and emotion for positive creativity.

More and more research is available now about the causes of aging, and its reversal, from a scientific point of view. (An exciting book on this is Michael Fosser's *Reversing Human Aging.*) We learn about free radicals and anti-oxidants; about the telomeres that are part of each cell, and how aging accompanies the loss of some of these with every cell division; the mind-body connection; and much more. Natural and newly created substances come on the shelves that help slow or reverse aging.

Science alone is expected to increase life expectancy to 150-200 years in the near future. This is helpful, and it is fine to put to good use anything science has to offer. For one thing, if we are choosing rejuvenation and immortality through consciousness, and we have a lot to clear, longer life can give us extra time to accomplish it. For another, it gives tools to the mind that can assist the transformation of consciousness, and thus the transformation of the body. For instance, now that we know about telomeres—and we are aware of the amazing chemist in our body that can create any commanded substance—we can call upon our body to create new ones.

So, if you choose, make good use of scientific research!

In becoming physically immortal; in rejuvenating completely—all blessings to you, and complete success.

Rejuvenation Initiations in Other Chapters

"The Peak of Health!" chapter:

☆ To Fast, or Not to Fast?

☆ Move!

The "Lighten Relationships" chapter:

☆ Merge Your Right and Left Brain

12
Ascend!

O god! O goddess! Do you not recognize yourself?
Awaken your ancient memory of who you are.
Come home!

The Age of Light

There are still many difficult things on earth, but since the 1960s humanity has been transforming rapidly. The difficulties which remain are on their way out. Some will take longer to de-fuse, but others are like the Berlin wall: solid and strong one day, and the next just a pile of rubble. The oldest, most entrenched and separative practices will transform to serve the whole, or they will fail.

We have already seen so much! People helping and empowering one another as never before; crime rates plummeting; a sea change to honor the individual within many corporations; people working to protect endangered species and environments—the list goes on and on.

There is no need for a coup—this is a revolution from within. The "Aquarian Conspiracy" is conquering, for the good of all! Humanity is moving into the light so quickly that even the masters assisting us look on in awe. Still we need to step carefully, to stay conscious and alert; but from these eyes the day is won, and we are waiting for the full results—the age of light—to roll in.

Ascension

As we are part of the divine, our belief is powerful and creative—and we may believe what we choose. The power of the *entire universe* says Yes! to our belief. Belief in limitation and trouble has created lack of money, energy and time; illness; having to work hard for a living; debt; difficult relationships—and age and death. We have become masters of limitation!

By the same token, we have mastery in certain beneficial ways. Is your home a good shelter—comfortable, warm, well-lit? Do you have enough to eat? A vehicle to get around in? Are some of your relationships happy ones? Do you have a job you enjoy? Are you good at certain activities? Mastery in any area of life is a great boon because that sense of mastery can be transferred to areas of non-mastery until they too are mastered. It is important to recognize the mastery we already have.

When the divine, the universal Isness, the Tao, the infinite—it doesn't matter what we call it—expresses directly in life, it is an amazing goodness. It is love and joy, light and wisdom; eternally expanding creativity and life; infinite power; peace, order and harmony; perfection everywhere now; freedom and laughter. As the image of God/Goddess, we are all these qualities. The first humans knew Eden: perfect health, happiness, abundance of all desired good, beauty and immortality. Paradise is our natural state. We are simply returning to what is natural.

We are coming home! We are sailing into the age of light. It is time to *know* we are unlimited in every area of life. In God and *as* God, all things are possible—without exception.

This teaching labels our return to paradise "ascension." Though ascension has not been an everyday word, it is for everyday life. There hasn't been another term to express it; ascension is at the leading edge of humanity's expansion.

Ascension has a different meaning now from leaving the earth for a lighter realm. Ascension is the process of being our divinity so deeply that all limitation falls away—while we are yet on earth. Ascension is another word for enlightenment, but in this teaching it includes abilities that come with our enlightened state. We will be able to:

- ☆ Rejuvenate our body.
- ☆ Live as long as we are guided upon the earth.
- ☆ Manifest anything needed or wanted from the air.

☆ Travel by thought, taking our body into light and putting it down anywhere we choose.

☆ Step back and forth between dimensions at will.

☆ Quicken the frequency of our body and step into a lighter realm, leaving no physical form behind.

These abilities may sound fantastic and impossible to you. They once did to all of us! And neither I nor anyone I know has mastered these things. But we know of people—people like you and me—who *have* done it. We call them "ascended masters." There are ascended masters from many traditions including Taoism, Hinduism, Christianity and Tibetan Buddhism, and ascended masters from no tradition—they just did it. (For more on specific masters, see *Living Mastery*.) If someone has done these things, anyone can do them. Those of us on this path intend to do it, and we will do it.

Abilities in themselves are unimportant. The only thing of importance is being the divinity we are. But we have so strongly believed ourselves *incapable* of doing these things that ascension directly countermands these beliefs. In ascension we choose to *express* our divine oneness in all the ways that make life joyous, easy and giving.

These teachings are from my spirit. Each ascension teaching is different. The "flower of life" teachings, sacred geometry and other teachings are equally valid for an ascension path.

Here are initiations to explore.

Activation

It is a powerful decision to choose ascension, if you haven't already. Here are powerful words and works to get yourself going or strengthen your process. Change the words if that empowers you.

Tune to your spirit. Ask it to guide and empower everything here.

I recognize that my spirit is guiding me into ascension through my awakened desire for this path. Therefore I, _____, now choose to become an ascended master in the time and way that is right for me.

I choose to express my divinity, my limitlessness; the perfection of my individualized God/Goddess self. I choose to recognize and experience everything as divine: heart, mind, body and earth. I choose to master my body and my environment through love, and experience all ascended master abilities. I choose to use my God-given power in love and wisdom. I choose to have a most joyous, abundant, easy and giving life on earth. I choose to serve others, to help my beloved divine brothers and sisters also awaken to their divinity. When I leave here, I choose to take my form with me and step into a lighter realm. So be it.

Now, here's some head work.

Locate your pituitary gland in about the middle of your head, about three inches down from the crown. Ask it to light up for you. Do the same with your pineal gland, above and behind the pituitary. You are going to open the "rainbow bridge" between these two glands. This will empower your ability to manifest more quickly and easily, and will better balance and merge your male and female energies and aspects. Say:

In the name and by the power of the Lord God of my Being, I now open the rainbow bridge of enlightenment, the antakarana, between my pituitary and my pineal. (Give this some time; intend, feel!) I welcome the balance and merging of my male and female aspects. I welcome, when I am ready, my ability to manifest from the air.

I now command my pituitary and pineal to open to receive unlimited divine thought, and its dissemination throughout my being. (Again, take time; feel it happening.) I welcome divine unlimited thought.

I now open my all-seeing eye, in the middle of my head, to become operative in the time and way best for me. When I am ready, I will be able to see in all directions without need for physical eyes. I will also be able to see clearly into the past and the future. So be it.

Ascension Initiation

This is an extremely powerful initiation, unfolded to me gradually from my spirit back in the early '80s when I was learning about ascension. You may experience some things that could frighten you if not understood:

☆ You may see a light—perhaps blindingly brilliant—in your third eye. Know that you *are* this light; you cannot disappear within it.

☆ You may feel great heat in your body, or cold.

☆ Your heartbeat may speed up or slow down, slightly or dramatically.

☆ You may feel or even see your body, or parts of it, disappear.

Whatever happens, because we are giving the meditation into the hands of your divine master self, you are safe. You cannot go too high, and you will always go "high enough": as far into your divine light as optimum for this time. You can relax and let things happen. Also, if you notice nothing dramatic, you are still doing it perfectly—we each experience the initiation in our own way. Lastly, I challenge you to experience your chakras in a whole new way. Chakra opening is not the same as opening your aura so that unwanted energies may enter. You can think of your chakras as divine light centers. When you expand them, you are actually expanding the protective light around your body.

Although chakra opening is common now, seldom do we realize what it can be. Your divinity encompasses the universe; thus a true opening of your chakras can give the knowing of being *fully alive and present everywhere, in every dimension of the eternal now.* This realization came to me after years of chakra-opening.

Sit comfortably. Close your eyes and begin to breathe deeply and gently. Feel your groundedness from your root chakra area and from your feet: cords of energy into the center of Earth. Invite love energy to flow up from mother Earth or down from the top of your head, as you choose. Continue to breathe gently and freely as you allow the release of tension from all body parts to go deeper and deeper. When you feel as relaxed as you possibly can, send love into all of your body and bless it. Say to yourself:

Divine love and will run this body. This is the heartbeat and breath of the divine. These are the organs, glands, and bones of the divine. Every particle of this body is divine. All the space of this body is divine.

This body is divine light, love, and joy! It has no agenda of its own, but follows thought. I choose to think unlimited thoughts about this body: it is the everlasting and expanding life of the divine; it is the resurrection and the life. This body lives forever. When I am ready to leave the earth plane, I take it up into light and ascend. So be it.

Tune more deeply now, away from the awareness of your body and into awareness of mind. Love and bless your thoughts. "Unenlightened" thoughts and feelings are like our children; we created them, and they need our love. As we love them, they lift into lighter and more joyous expression. Say:

This mind moves now into divine unlimited thoughts. I Am the majestic power of God's pure, divine love. I am divine light. I am divine joy. I am divine freedom. I Am everywhere present and know all things. I Am the beloved of God. I Am That I Am.

Tune still more deeply, away from awareness of mind and into awareness of feeling. Send love to any feeling you notice, no matter what it may be. Bless your feeling nature. Say:

My feelings are becoming the natural feelings of the divine: love, joy, wholeness, abundance, well-being.

Tune now to your spirit. If you are in touch with your inner self, or have a favorite master(s) you know and love, you may call upon these now, or simply ask God to assist you in your ascension process. Tune to your inner love, light, and wisdom—it is being poured out to you right now. Feel as deeply connected and one with it as you can. Some words:

I give this meditation fully into the hands of my divine master self, the love and light I Am, to guide me to the optimum experience of my divine light. So be it!

When you feel ready, begin a chakra-opening. To help you open each one maximally, experiment with one or more of these suggestions:

☆ Awaken in each chakra its beautiful light, like the sun, and allow it to be the color that feels best; or you may try white, gold, or white-gold. Let this sun blaze out to fill your body, your room, your area, your world, this universe.

☆ Use your in-breaths to brighten each chakra, and your out-breaths to expand them into infinity.

☆ Use your hands to touch each chakra area and sweep them outward.

☆ In each chakra feel openness, relaxation, vulnerability, aliveness, emotion.

Now open each one with the help of the above suggestions or your own creativity. The accompanying words assist each chakra to fulfill its function.

First chakra at the base of your spine.

I am safe on Earth. I am abundantly provided for by the divine, which is the entire universe. The Earth is a pleasurable place for me to be.

Second chakra in your abdomen.

I am centered. I am safe and loved to express my creativity, which is welcomed in the world. My sexuality is divine energy and God approves of it.

Third chakra in your solar plexus.

I am safe and loved in expressing my power. My power and my love are one. I use my power wisely and lovingly.

Fourth chakra, heart chakra, in the center of your chest.

I am safe to love and be loved without limit. I am full of love and compassion for myself and all others. My love blesses all of life.

Fifth chakra in your throat.

I am safe and loved to express and speak my truth, my power, creativity, and passion. I am full and free giving and receiving. I am abundance.

Sixth chakra, the "third eye" chakra between your eyebrows and back in your head a bit.

I am safe and loved to BE the light I am, and to know everything.

Seventh chakra, the crown chakra at the top of your head.

I am safe and loved to BE divine. I am unlimited being, everywhere present through all space and time.

Eighth chakra, can be pictured above the head.

I am safe and loved to step through the dimensions.

Ninth through **thirteenth**—open if you feel to.

Fourteenth through **twenty-second**—open if you feel to.

Now create a column of golden light from the highest chakra you opened to below the bottom of your feet, gently re-opening any chakras that may have closed again.

Begin to spin this column. (I see this going around to the right, horizontal to the floor; follow any direction that feels best for you.) It moves slowly at first, and gradually picks up speed. As it spins, it is spinning your chakras, your cells, your atoms, your aura—everything! Here are some statements, silently or aloud:

I am quickening the vibrational frequencies of my body, mind and feelings now. I am merging with my divine self. I am quickening, I am lifting! I am ascending! Ascending is easy, ascending is natural. I lift higher and higher, faster and faster. I am lighter and lighter. I am merging with Light. I am becoming transparent now!

Go back and forth between increasing the speed of the light column—finally to whirlwind speed—and proclaiming your ascension, until you feel you're as high as you can go. Next, to make sure you reach your present optimum level, give your divine self three opportunities to take you higher. You don't have to do it yourself or even think about it, simply trust your spirit to take you up. Say:

One, two, three, Lift—Lift—!

and let yourself go! Do this twice more, and you will probably be at optimum light, optimum speed! Now say:

I am the light of divine I Am. I am one with the divine. I am ascended now. I am an ascended master now! I Am That I Am.

Now you may sit in the great silence and be that which you are. Besides receiving the great gifts of your divinity, you may receive specific messages or a healing of some kind; you may be taken somewhere, or other possibilities. Receive all your gifts.

Come back gently, bringing back your awareness of feeling and mind, body and environment, breathing deeply and energetically. Bring the high frequencies *back* with you—stay in love, stay high and know that you are already combining this wonderful state more and more with your everyday life.

Open your eyes and see only the divine around you, see the beauty of everything. Come all the way back to full alertness and objectivity. Look in the mirror and see the divine.

Give love to your daily tasks, and follow up on insights you received in your meditation.

Do this meditation as often as you enjoy it. Record it with your own voice and follow it, or follow the tape that goes with this chapter. You quicken more every time you do it, and although you still fluctuate around a median, each lifting is permanent.

Blessings to you with this initiation!

Divine You!

Sit in meditation. Ask your divine master self to step in and be felt. Next, ask to feel/see your divine blueprint, the divine that wants to express *as* you in the world. Just see/feel it as deeply as you can. Surrender to the divine you—mind, heart and body. Let your experience of it deepen each time you do it.

Bi-Location into an Ascended Master Retreat

An ascended master retreat is a fine place to visit in meditation. There are a number of retreats throughout the planet, mostly in a lighter dimension than the physical. Here masters live and serve. Visiting one puts us in touch with a deeply happy way of life, full of beauty, abundance, love, friendship and service. With the masters, we can see and feel what we are becoming. We can see if it's a place we would like to live. We can receive spiritual gifts to help us along our ascension path. It's a chance to experience our beautiful light body. And, it's fun!

Whenever you do this, the masters know you are coming—and they wait for you! One or more of them will assist you. This master(s) could be your own divine self, a master you know and love, a master new to you—whoever is best for you at the moment will be there.

When you declare that you are in the retreat, you may feel your etheric body splitting into two. This can feel very weird indeed! But you are absolutely safe.

Do the ascension meditation above. When you feel you are as high in light and frequency as you can go, form your intention to travel in a lighter body into an ascended master retreat.

This meditation takes you into the retreat in a great lone mountain in far northern California, Mt. Shasta. You may instead visit the Grand Tetons in Wyoming, or any other retreat you choose.

There is no space in God—all space is right here—so you don't have to travel. What you do is transfer part of your awareness into the retreat. Your physical body will remain in its original space, and you will probably be aware of both places.

Your *intention* is what takes you into the retreat. If when you speak the words you mean to go there, you will go!

Say now with passion and conviction:

I Am here in Mt. Shasta. **I Am here, in Mt. Shasta!!**

Now quick as a flash, be here in the retreat. If your third eye is pretty much open, you'll be able to see the retreat from your physical body perspective with more or less clarity. If your third eye isn't yet so open, you may not see anything. If that happens, trust that you are there and receiving spiritual gifts from your divine master self and/or ascended masters.

Take a look around: where are you? See the master(s) who have come to be with you. Do you recognize any of them? Go to them and give them a big hug—a joyous reunion! You may feel emotional here!

Now materialize a full length mirror in front of you. You are here in your beautiful light body, your divine blue print body. You are probably wearing gorgeous clothing, though if you wish you may see your light body naked. In your light body, your master self shines through.

Look over the beautiful you. How tall are you? (We're often taller in our light body.) What color is your hair? How is it worn? Is there anything in your hair, such as a crown or jewels? Travel down to your forehead, your eyes and eyebrows. What color are your eyes? Look deeply, deeply into them, the eyes of a master. Now your nose, your mouth, your chin and jaw. Are you wearing anything around your neck?

What color is your clothing, and what is its cut? Reach down and touch the fabric—it may be one we don't have on earth. Are you wearing anything around your waist? Anything upon your feet?

What is your name here? (If you hear one, fine; if not, just let it go.)

When you feel finished with the mirror, go back to the masters. They will take you to wonderful places in the retreat. You may be given a tour. You may find yourself splashing in the round cleansing pool, light and sparkling, where all of your being is cleansed and you don't even get wet! The masters may guide you into the crystal pyramid, hollow inside and pulsing its transcendent colors, for an initiation or healing. Crystals may be placed in your light body, which will help your ascension. You may go to the hall of records, or the hall where inventions are being prepared in advance for the people of Earth. You may enjoy the beautiful terraced gardens or the great forest. You may receive a special message. You may be taken to the gleaming white temple at the very top of the mountain. Or something different from all of these things.

Give time now, and let your journey unfold. Again, if you aren't seeing anything, just be patient and stay centered in your meditation until you feel your visit is complete.

If you have a great desire to serve humanity from the ascended plane, there is a possibility that you will be staying in the retreat in your light body, and becoming an ascended master. If so, you will now have two identical light bodies, one in the retreat and one with your physical body.

When you feel complete, come back again very slowly and gently, again bringing back the high frequencies you've been experiencing into your earth awareness. Make sure you are grounded, alert, and objective before you go anywhere!

Divine Qualities

Take one of these qualities of the divine as expressed in creation, and meditate upon it by feeling and being it, as deeply as you can. God Is/I Am:

> Infinite, eternal love, all wise
>
> Perfection, wholeness, all powerful
>
> All-knowing, perfect freedom
>
> Divine right, action, total joy
>
> Divine right, timing, light

Divine right, order, peace

Everywhere present, abundance

Unity, oneness, effortlessness

Ever-expanding life, infinite being

Eternal, all giving

All-creative, perfect confidence

I Am Everywhere

Go into the basic meditation. At your hara, the center of your body just below your navel, envision an intense light of blazing gold or white. Expand this until it fills your whole body and begins to radiate from you. Now envision your body, blazing this light, expanding to fill the room or your immediate area. Actually feel that your body now encompasses the whole area, and that everything in the room is within your body.

Now feel your body break through the ceiling of your room. As you continue to sit upon the earth, expand until your head is level with the tallest trees.

Now, your head is the height of a tall mountain.

Now place your head at the north of your state or country, and your feet at the south.

Now your head is at the north pole of Earth, and your feet at the south pole. Your body and its aura now encompass all of the planet. Look down at yourself and see what the weather is like in Paris or Hong Kong.

Now place your head at the sun and your feet upon the earth. Now include our whole solar system. Now, our galaxy the Milky Way.

Finally expand your body, blazing with light, until it encompasses all of this universe. Feel the vast space and silence you are.

The vast reaches of space are now the spaces between the atoms of your body. The stars are your body's atoms; the galaxies are your cells!

Look around your universe-body and realize that because you are everything, you can direct your awareness to a certain part of you and know what is happening there. Take a look at a planet so far from

Earth that its galaxy hasn't yet been spotted through a telescope or a space probe. Does it have life? Intelligent beings? What do you see?

Explore anything else you wish.

When you are ready to return, you must first find within your body the Milky Way galaxy. You may have to look a bit—is it in your big toe? Realizing that you remain as the universe, you bring your attention to the Milky Way. Within this galaxy, now you must find the rather small sun of our solar system. Do this, and bring your awareness to it. At last you see the minute speck of a wondrous little pearl of a planet called Earth. Focus in on her now, and zoom down to her. Find your place upon her, and come back into that.

Return to the awareness of your physical body—which is *also* a universe! Perhaps this will be your next exploration!

Chant!

Sanskrit, ancient Hebrew, Greek, and Egyptian, among others, are considered holy languages. This seems to be because their sounds resonate with divine frequencies. Chanting in these languages fills the mind, heart and body with holy sound. It helps counterbalance dissonant, destructive sound (of which there is much in our culture), and helps balance and lift the entire being.

There are many chants of between one and a few words, called *mantras,* which are powerfully beneficial. They are meant to be repeated either silently or aloud, over and over. You may chant on one note, or create a simple melody. Approximations to English sounds: "a" sounds like "a" in ah; "e" sounds like "a" in "hay;" and "i" sounds about like the "e" in me.

Here are just a few mantras. A little research will easily reveal others.

☆ **OM** (can be chanted A—U—Mm): the universal sound of creation. In *Isis Unveiled,* Madame Blavatsky describes the three sounds in order as "creation, conservation and transformation."

☆ **Yod hey vod hey:** the four primary "fire letters" of the name of God, in ancient Hebrew. They are also sung rearranged in every way, such as hey hey vod yod.

☆ **Om namah' Shivaya:** God-I-Am is one translation.

☆ **Kodoish, kodoish, kodoish adonai tsebayoth:** Holy, holy holy is the Lord God of Hosts.

☆ **Om mane padme hum:** a sacred Buddhist chant referring to the "jewel in the lotus," meaning compassion. The jewel also represents the union of the divine feminine and masculine.

☆ **Leyoesh Shekinah:** pillar of light of the Holy Spirit, considered here a feminine energy. "Shekinah" rhymes with "Dinah."

☆ **Om Aim Hrim Klim Chamundayei Vichhe Namaha:** to obtain the powers and grace of Divine Mother.

Sun Salutation

In your mind's eye, see the pillar of light of your chakras along your spine and up through your neck and head. Picture the sun, and see your light pillar as the same light.

The translation is included for your knowledge rather than to be chanted, though it would be fine to do so. "Namaha" means "salutations," or "honor to."

Each of the twelve mantras is a different name for the solar deity.

Salutations and honor! to:

1. Om mitraya namaha—the friend of all
2. Om ravaye namaha—the shining one
3. Om suryaya namaha—one who induces activity
4. Om bhanave namaha—he who illumines
5. Om khagaya namaha—moves quickly in the sky
6. Om pushne namaha—giver of strength
7. Om hiranyagarbhaya namaha—golden cosmic Self
8. Om marichaye namaha—lord of dawn
9. Om adityaya namaha—son of Aditi
10. Om savitre namaha—benevolent mother
11. Om arkaya namaha—he who is fit for praise
12. Om bhaskaraya namaha—he who leads to enlightenment

Finally, here is a form of the "Gayatri Mantra," one of the most powerful of Sanskrit mantras. It means in essence: "I open to the light I Am." Do three or more repetitions.

Gayatri Mantra

Om bhuh

Om bhuvaha

Om svaha

Om maha

Om janaha

Om tapaha

Om satyam

Om tat savitur varenyam

Bargo devasya dimahi

Dhiyo yonaha prachodayat

Affirmations for Ascension

I am the divine image of God/Goddess.

I am completely worthy of love.

I do my best with where I am; I always have.

I am eternally innocent and good, as I arose from spirit.

I am completely loveable, exactly as I am.

I love myself.

I honor myself.

I am loved.

I am love, the infinite love of the divine.

I am clear.

I am happy; I am joy itself.

I am creative, from the passion of my deepest heart.

I am powerful.

I can be anything I choose.

I can do anything I choose.

I can have anything I choose.

Whatever anyone else has done, I can do.

I invite the winds of spirit to blow through my life, bringing all the changes best for me!

I am wise.

I am knowing; I can know anything I choose to know.

I am light.

I am abundant in every good thing.

I am in radiant health.

I choose joyful, supportive, open-hearted relationships.

I live in harmony with others and with the earth.

I give to life my unique gifts, for the benefit of all.

My life is fulfilled!

Beloved Mother/Father God, all that you are, I Am.

Beloved Father/Mother God, all that I Am, you are.

Mastery is my destiny.

My thoughts reflect divine unlimitedness.

My feelings are grounded in deepest love.

My body is part of the divine. It is divine eternal energy and ever-expanding life. It is divine intelligence and divine perfection. It is divine beauty. My body is meant to live as long as I am guided on this plane, in ever-increasing health, strength and beauty. It can ascend into light when I am complete with this plane. I accept these truths.

I choose to be an ascended master.

I honor my choice, and support it with my being and my life.

I have everything I need to experience full mastery and ascension in this lifetime.

I have all the patience and perseverance I need, and the ability to flow with life's ups and downs, placing my whole process in the context of success.

I have the determination and willingness to leave all limitations behind and walk step by step into the new, the unknown, the unlimited.

I am safe and loved to change radically because I am one with the divine and beloved of the divine.

I welcome my ever-growing love, joy, light, and mastery.

I welcome my rejuvenation, and my beautiful light body shining through my physical body.

I welcome immortality, with no transition called death.

I welcome travel by thought.

I welcome instant manifestation.

I welcome my experience of the ascended planes as a fully ascended master.

Ascending is easy.

I am ascending.

I have ascended.

I Am the ascended master _____ .

As an ascended master, I joyfully serve as I am guided.

I Am God-I-Am.

I Am That I Am.

So be it.

Your Home Star

Where are you from? Such a common question may have an uncommon answer. Before we came to planet Earth, large numbers of us knew lives as masters in realms lighter than the physical, on stars or planets known or unknown to our scientists. Sirius, the Pleiades, Orion, Arcturus, or Antares may be our original home.

Of the planets sailing with us around the sun, Venus has been home to many of us. And many Earthlings were once residents of Maldek, the planet in our solar system that blew up long ago. On Earth herself, some have known lives in ancient Egypt, or on the continent of Lemuria or Atlantis, only remnants of which remain today. One or more of these may have been an earlier home for you.

A special note regarding the dolphins and whales. Their spirits came originally from Sirius, and many of them today are enlightened and blissful beings. They have been helping to hold the high frequencies for Earth that our planet once enjoyed.

It can be helpful to know our earlier homes, and especially to realize who we were there and how we lived. We are in the process now of re-calling our ancient wisdom, knowledge and mastery, and these memories can become important. Even if some of them are painful, they help us find our way today.

Tune with your spirit. Ask about your origins and see what you get. Heal any painful memories. Bring memories of mastery forward to now, to help you feel and be your divinity more easily, quickly and deeply. An assist to your ascension!

My Last Life on Earth

Now that the transition into the age of light is full on—finally!—many of us who've been assisting humanity for lifetimes are preparing for a change. This may rightly be our last lifetime on Earth. On a personal level, we have embraced our wisdom enough so that we can clean up any remaining karma and take our final steps in the third dimension. Then, either through leaving the body or stepping into a lighter realm, our play on this stage will be done.

For those of us who become physically immortal, we may stay here as long as that is our joy, and see the planet more fully into the age of light. If we rejuvenate as well, this will be easier!

Initiation

Go into a meditation and ask your spirit about your time on Earth. Is it your soul's purpose and your heart's passion that this be your last life here?

If yes, here is a statement to support this purpose:

I choose, in alignment with my knowing from spirit, that this be my last life on Earth. I am here to clear all birth and childhood experiences, any karma remaining, all past lives, all relationships, everything. Through the light, love and assistance from divinity, and the upliftment taking place for Earth, this is now easier to do. I am doing it!

I choose to know spirit and matter as one, heaven and earth as one. I am here to express my divinity wherever I am. I am here to recognize my body as part of the divine: as light, love, beauty and everlasting, expanding life. I am here to serve, as long as it is my deepest joy. I am here to transcend death, to ascend, to step into new dimensions, to serve, to play, to explore, to grow joyously and infinitely forever! So be it.

Life as a Master

Reaching the master consciousness within is an ever-un-folding process. The further we walk along that road, the more choices we have as to how and where to live, including being on earth or in a lighter realm. In full master consciousness we embody love, light and power of the divine; and the possibili-ties of expression are endless. Do you have a sense of what you would like to do? Stay on this planet, serve her from a lighter realm, disconnect from her? All is available!

If you remain here, you may live openly or anonymously. You may live as a pauper, a millionaire or a "regular person." You can seem to age if you want to blend in, or keep your ap-pearance, or rejuvenate—whatever you choose, however you-as-spirit wants to do things.

If you choose to continue to serve Earth from this or a lighter realm, what is your passion? End hunger? Encourage freedom in every land? Assist the peace process? Work with those who are nearing masterhood? Bring new inventions to the world? Be a divine musician? Again, the possibilities are infinite!

Are there particular masters you will love working with? Or a particular group or ascended retreat?

It can be helpful to think about life as a master. For one thing, it may ease the sense of the unknown that can be scary for anyone. For another, your vision of life as a master can excite and activate you, and speed your process. Finally, the more time you spend feeling like a master, the more quickly you will awaken to your mastery. Repeating the bi-location above with some frequency can familiarize you with life in the ascended master retreats, and help you decide about living there.

Every blessing to you in being an ascended master!

Bibliography

This is an expanded list from the one in *Living Mastery.* The additions are marked with *. As always, when books are channeled, as a few of these are, use active discernment. Accept only what you feel perfectly right about.

A Course in Miracles. Tiburon, California: Foundation for Inner Peace, 1975.

Anand, Margo. *The Art of Sexual Ecstasy.* Los Angeles: Jeremy P. Tarcher, Inc., 1989.

Bailey, Alice. *Initiation, Human and Solar.* New York: Lucis Trust, 1922.

Baroody, Theodore A. Jr. *Ascension: Beginner's Manual.* Waynesville, North Carolina.: Eclectic Press, 1989.

*Berne, Eric. *Games People Play.* New York: Ballentine Books, 1985.

Blavatsky, Helena. *The Secret Doctrine,* Vols. I & II. Adyar, India: Theosophical Publishing House, 1979.

*————, *Isis Unveiled.* 2 Vols. Pasadena, California: Theosophical Publishing, 1991.

*Bly, Robert. *Iron John.* New York: Random House, 1991.

Bonnell, Gary. *Ascension: The Original Teachings of Christ Awareness.* Denver, Colorado: Richman Rose Publishing, 1990.

Boone, J. Allen. *Kinship With All Life.* New York: Harper & Row, 1954.

*Caddy, Peter. *In Perfect Timing.* Findhorn, Scotland: Findhorn Press, 1996. (Peter was cofounder of the Findhorn Community; this is his memoirs, from his conservative upbringing to becoming a renowned leader of the new age.)

Chopra, Deepak, M.D. *Ageless Body, Timeless Mind.* New York: Harmony Books, 1993.

Cota-Robles, Patricia Diane. *Your Time Is At Hand.* Tucson, Arizona: New Age Study of Humanity's Purpose, 1992.

————, *The Awakening ... Eternal Youth, Vibrant Health, Radiant Beauty.* Tucson, Arizona: New Age Study of Humanity's Purpose, 1993.

Cooper-Oakley, Isabel. *The Comte De St. Germain.* London: Theosophical Publishing House, Ltd., 1912.

Craig, Peter. *Soul Merge: The Key to Ascension.* Seattle: Rainbow Bridge, 1997.

Cranston, Sylvia. *HPB* (a biography of Helena Blavatsky). New York: G.P. Putnam's Sons, 1993.

Crockett, Arthur and Beckley, Timothy Green. *Count Saint Germain.* New Brunswick, New Jersey: Inner Light Publications, 1984.

Deng Ming-Dao. *Chronicles of Tao: The Secret Life of a Taoist Master.* San Francisco: Harper, 1993.

Dorris, Pearl. *Step by Step We Climb,* Vols. 1-3. P.O. Box 1290, Mt. Shasta, California: Pearl Publishing, 1977-1983.

Dux, Sharula. *Alchemies for Immortality* (a six-cassette set). Santa Fe, New Mexico: Telos Press, 1994.

————. *Secrets of the Subterranean Cities* (a two-cassette set). Santa Fe, New Mexico: Telos Press, 1992.

*Eddy, Mary Baker. *Science and Health.* Boston: First Church of Christ, Scientist, 1994. (First published in 1875.)

Essene, Virginia, Editor. *New Cells, New Bodies, New Life!* Santa Clara, California: S.E.E. Publishing Company, 1991.

*Estés, Clarissa Pinkola. *Women Who Run With the Wolves.* New York: Ballantine Books, 1992.

*Evans-Wentz, Walter. *Tibet's Great Yogi Milarepa.* New York: Oxford University Press, 1969.

Everett, Julianne. *Heart Initiation.* Livermore, California: Oughten House Publishing, 1994.

*Fossel, Michael. *Reversing Human Aging.* New York: William Morrow and Company, Inc., 1996.

Fremantle, Anne and Christopher, Editors. *In Love With Love:100 of the Greatest Mystical Poems.* New York: Paulist Press, 1978.

Garver, Will L. *Brother of the Third Degree.* Blauvelt, New York: Garber Communications, Inc., 1989.

Gaum, Bill. *My Happiness and Your Happiness.* (A biography of Pearl Dorris). P.O. Box 1290, Mt. Shasta, California: Pearl Publishing, 1997.

Golas, Thaddeus. *The Lazy Man's Guide to Enlightenment.* New York: Bantam Books, 1972.

Grahame, Kenneth. *The Wind in the Willows.* (I just had to put this in!) New York: Simon & Schuster, 1908.

Griscom, Chris. *The Ageless Body.* Galisteo, New Mexico: The Light Institute of Galisteo, 1992.

Haich, Elisabeth. *Initiation.* Redway, California: The Seed Center, 1974.

Hurtak, J.J. *The Book of Knowledge: The Keys of Enoch.* Los Gatos, California: The Academy for Future Science, 1977.

*Isherwood, Christopher. *Ramakrishna and His Disciples.* New York: Simon & Schuster, 1965.

Jasmuheen. *Prana and Immortality.* Brisbane, Australia: S.E.E.A., 1996.

*Keen, Sam. *Fire in the Belly.* New York: Bantam Books, 1992.

Khalsa, Virochana. *Tantra of the Beloved.* Crestone, Colorado: Books of Light, 1996.

Kelder, Peter. *Ancient Secret of the Fountain of Youth.* (The five Tibetan rites). Gig Harbor, Washington: Harbor Press, 1985.

Kenyon, Tom and Essene, Virginia. *The Hathor Material.* Santa Clara, California: S.E.E. Publishing Company, 1996.

King, Godfré Ray. *The Unveiled Mysteries.* Chicago: St. Germain Press, Inc., 1934.

King, Godfré Ray. *The Magic Presence.* Chicago: St. Germain Press, Inc., 1935.

Kornfield, Jack. *A Path with Heart.* New York: Bantam Books, 1993.

Leadbeater, C.W. *The Masters and the Path.* Adyar, India: The Theosophical Publishing House, 1927. Second Edition recommended.

MacDonald-Bayne, Murdo. *Beyond the Himalayas.* New York: Gordon Press, 1973. (If you can get it!)

Mafu. *The Journey Home* and other videos. P.O. Box 458, Eagle Point, Oregon: The Foundation for God Realization, 1987.

Maharaj, Sri Nisargadatta. *I Am That.* Durham, North Carolina: The Acorn Press, 1973.

Markides, Kyriacos C. *The Magus of Strovolos.* London: Penguin Books Ltd., 1985.

————. *Homage to the Sun.* London: Penguin Books Ltd., 1987.

McDonald, John. *The Magic Story/The Message of a Master.* Oak Harbor, Washington: Robert Collier Publications, 1952.

Mercie, Christine. *Sons of God.* Marina del Rey, California: DeVorss & Co., 1954.

Meyer, Ann P. *Woman Awareness.* San Diego: Dawning Publications, 1968. (Order from the Teaching of the Inner Christ; see References.)

———— and Meyer, Peter V. *Being a Christ.* San Diego: Dawning Publications, 1975. (Order from the Teaching of the Inner Christ; see References.)

Mt. Shasta, Peter. *"I AM" the Open Door.* Peter Mt. Shasta, Mt. Shasta, California, 1978.

*Osborne, Arthur. *Ramana Maharshi and the Path of Self Knowledge.* London: Century, 1987.

Patterson, Stella Walthall. *Dear Mad'm.* Happy Camp, California: Naturegraph Publishers, Inc., 1956.

Paulsen, Norman. *The Christ Consciousness.* Salt Lake City: The Builders Publishing Co., 1980.

*Ponder, Catherine. *The Prospering Power of Love.* Marina del Rey, California: DeVorss & Company, 1984.

Price, A.F. and Wong, Mou-Lam, Translators. *The Diamond Sutra and The Sutra of Hui Neng.* Boston: Shambhala, 1985.

Price, John Randolph. *A Spiritual Philosophy for the New World.* Carlsbad, California: Hay House, 1990.

Prophet, Mark L., Recorder. *Dossier on the Ascension: Serapis Bey.* Livingston, Montana: The Summit Lighthouse, 1967.

*Ram Dass. *How Can I Help?* New York: Alfred A. Knopf, 1996.

Rama, Swami. *Living with the Himalayan Masters.* Honesdale, Pennsylvania: Himalayan International Institute of Yoga Science and Philosophy, 1978.

Reichel, Gertraud, Editor. *Babaji The Unfathomable* (108 Encounters with Herakhan Baba). G. Reichel Verlag, Reifenberg 36, 8551 Weilersbach, West Germany, 1988.

Robbins, Anthony. *Awaken the Giant Within.* New York: Simon & Schuster, 1991.

Robinson, James B., Translator. *Buddha's Lions: The Lives of the Eighty-Four Siddhas.* Berkeley, California: Dharma Publishing, 1979.

Sandweiss, Samuel H. *Sai Baba: The Holy Man and the Psychiatrist.* San Diego: Birth Day Publishing Co., 1975.

*Scott, Cyril. *The Initiate: Some Impressions of a Great Soul.* York Beach, Maine: Samuel Weiser, Inc., 1991.

*Shyam, Radhe. *I Am Harmony.* Crestone, Colorado: Spanish Creek Press, 1989. (A book about Herakhan Babaji.)

*Simonton, Carl. *Getting Well Again.* New York: Bantam Books, 1992.

Skarin, Annalee. *Ye Are Gods.* Marina del Rey, California: DeVorss & Co., 1952.

Spalding, Baird. *Life and Teachings of the Masters of the Far East,* Vols. I-V. Marina del Rey, California: DeVorss & Co., 1924-1955.

Stone, Dr. Joshua David. *The Complete Ascension Manual.* Sedona, Arizona: Light Technology Publishing, 1994.

Stubbs, Tony. *An Ascension Handbook.* Livermore, California: Oughten House, 1991, New Leaf, 1999.

Talbot, Michael. *The Holographic Universe.* New York: Harper Collins, 1992.

Thomas, Eugene E. *Brotherhood of Mt. Shasta.* Marina del Rey, California: DeVorss & Co., 1946.

*Twyman, James F. *Emissary of Light.* New York: Warner Books, 1997.

Van Gelder, Dora. *The Real World of the Fairies.* London: The Theosophical Publishing House, 1977.

Weinberg, Steven Lee, Ph.D. *Ramtha: An Introduction.* Eastsound, Washington: Sovereignty, Inc., 1988.

Weischedel, Randall. *The Joy of Ascension.* Marina del Rey, California: DeVorss & Co., 1982.

Wright, Machaelle Small. *MAP: The Co-creative White Brotherhood Medical Assistance Program.* Warrenton, Virginia: Perelandra Ltd., 1990.

Yogananda, Paramahansa. *Autobiography of a Yogi.* Los Angeles: Self Realization Fellowship, 1946.

References

Iris Jackson and her husband, Jerry, produce a wonderful, up-lifting television show called *Miracles Happen! Dreams Do Come True!* If your area is not already carrying it, you can be instrumental in bringing it there. Iris will send you a tape of a show. You may also purchase the videos simply for your own enjoyment.

Iris & Jerry Jackson
P.O. Box 903
Alamo, CA 94507
Phone: 510/831-3608

Teaching of the Inner Christ (offers some fine books and classes)

4444 Zion Avenue
San Diego, California 92120
Phone: 619/283-4444

Jasmuheen (author of the inspiring book, *Prana and Immortality*, about living on prana alone)

Self Empowerment Education Academy
P.O. Box 737
Brisbane 4069
Queensland, Australia
Phone: (outside Australia): 61 7 3878 2446

Sharula Dux (from Telos, the city beneath Mt. Shasta)

AWE
500 N. Guadalupe, Suite G 200-A
Santa Fe, New Mexico 87501

Ramtha Dialogues (a master speaking through JZ Knight)

P.O. Box 1210
Yelm, Washington 98597
Phone: 360/458-5201
Order Phone: 800/347-0439

Mafu (a master speaking through Penny Torres Rubin)

> The Foundation for God Realization
> P.O. Box 458
> Eagle Point, Oregon 97524
> Phone: 541/830-0380

Blanca Bozic (creator of first-quality, wonderfully scented, natural creams and lotions for the body)

> Blanca's Natural Products
> P.O. Box 783
> Nowra 2541
> New South Wales, Australia
> Phone (outside Australia): 61 44 236 499

Norman d'Harlingue (healing himself of multiple sclerosis; offers to share his process if it may help others)

> 660 College St.
> Shreveport, Louisiana 71104
> Phone: 318/226-5692

Rev. Matt Garrigan, of the Universal Endowment for Human Empowerment, gives soul-stirring, enlightening Sunday talks in San Francisco, and workshops in many areas. His "Radiant Light Sunday Celebration" is held at 10:30 AM, at

> Swedish American Hall
> 2174 Market St., at 15th
> San Francisco, California
> Phone: 415/863-4157

Sharon Callahan not only tunes in to an animal and sees what's going on; she has created flower essences that restore balance and wholeness.

> P.O. Box 1056
> Mt. Shasta, CA 96067
> Phone: 530/926-6424

For a do-it-yourself colonic which is safe, effective and pleasant:

> Colema Boards of California
> P.O. Box 1879
> Cottonwood, California 96022.
> Phone: 916/347-5868.

For Robert Crombie's tapes about Pan, and information about the Findhorn community:

> Findhorn Foundation
> Forres, IV36 ORD
> Scotland
> Phone (outside UK): 44-1309-673655

About the Author

Joanna Cherry is Founder of Ascension Mastery International (AMI), an organization based in Mount Shasta, California. AMI helps build the consciousness that we are part of the divine, unlimited and free, and that our natural state is one of happiness, fulfillment and mastery.

With Master's Degrees in Education and Speech, Joanna has taught at public school and university levels. She has a Master's Degree in Ministerial Science from the Teaching of the Inner Christ, a non-denominational teaching based in San Diego. She has also explored Zen and Tibetan Buddhism, and became an internationally certified rebirther with Leonard Orr. In 1986 she was guided to work independently, and formed AMI.

As part of AMI, Joanna is guided to offer beautiful images of masters and deities from many traditions. She also offers audio tape sets she has created, and awareness guides on crystals, chakras, aromatherapy and other subjects.

Joanna has articles in numerous publications including *Sedona Journal of Emergence, Mt. Shasta's Directions, Connecting Link, Ascending Times*, and *New Times* of Seattle. She has a chapter in Virginia Essene's book *New Cells, New Bodies, New Life!*

She has presented her work at Whole Life Expos, the World Congress on Illumination, Astara Mystery School, World Symposium on Interspecies and Interdimensional Communication, and numerous international conferences. She is listed in *World Who's Who of Women*.

Ascension Mastery International

Products

with Joanna Cherry, Founder

Living Mastery, by Joanna Cherry, the companion book to **Self Initiations** and the first of the set. Filled with true and inspiring accounts of people discovering their mastery, plus the understanding which fleshes out every subject of **Self Initiations**. $12.95.

Audio Tape Sets

The Ascension Process Workshop Set: A live workshop with Joanna! Expand with processes on Ascension, Rejuvenation, Relationship healing, Forgiveness, Prosperity, Sexual healing, Marriage of the inner male and female, and much more! Six 90-minute tapes, $44.95. (This set plus *The Rejuvenation Set* span most of AMI's offered work.)

The Rejuvenation Set: Open your inner doors to the reality of regeneration and rejuvenation! Clear old beliefs, release aging and death. Reverse the death hormone in your pituitary gland, and replace it with life! Bring forth your light body. Shift your DNA. Practice with a rejuvenation process of great power. A pioneering 4-tape set to lift you into a new way of being! $34.95.

The God-Oneness Set: Connect and merge with your own inner Self. Listen for the name of a divine aspect or guide. Receive a signal from your spirit through your body. Recognize a true or false message, and receive clear guidance. Experience the bliss of being your divinity! A 2-tape set, $19.95.

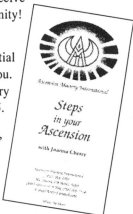

The Relationship Set: Embrace your own essential innocence. Forgive yourself and all who are close to you. Love yourself as part of God/Goddess. Transform every important relationship in your life! A 2-tape set, $19.95.

Steps in Your Ascension: This is now a 3-tape set, to include the tape Bi-Location! Ascension is completely possible for you! Lift into your own God-Light through a dynamic ascension technique. Master each step of your ascension. And bi-locate into the ascended master retreat of Mt. Shasta. A powerful 3-tape set! $24.95.

Purpose & Prosperity: Find your life's purposes, and fulfill them. Shift from unwanted work to a joyous, creative life! Follow your heart and your joy, abundantly giving and receiving. God/Goddess wants you entirely happy and abundant—accept it! A 2-tape set, $19.95.

Pictures of Great Masters & Deities

AMI has been guided to offer these, the most beautiful pictures of masters we have gathered over the years! Here is a sampling.

▲ indicates color

Mother Mary, who volunteered before her birth to bring Jesus to the world. ▲   **M6**

Vishnu the preserver, one of the Hindu divine triumvirate. ▲ **K7**

Krishna, the incarnation of the Hindu deity Vishnu, the Preserver. ▲   **K1**

Babaji, the immortal master of the Himalayas written about in *Autobiography of a Yogi.* ▲ **BJ2**

Quan Yin, the great goddess and Mother of Compassion, loved and revered throughout Asia. ▲**QY3**

Hathor, the Goddess who represents an ascended civilization, assisting Earth from the fourth and fifth dimensions. ▲   **E1**

Kuthumi, a great teacher from 19th Century India, channeled writings to Mme. Blavatsky.   **KU3**

Sri Rama, an incarnation of Vishnu and the ideal of heroic man. ▲ **K19**

Count St. Germain, the great ascended master known as the "Wonder Man of Europe" in the 1700's. ▲   **SG2**

Sanat Kumara, the Ancient of Days who has served Earth for millions of years. ▲ **SK**

Shiva, the destroyer, transformer and rebuilder of the Hindu divine triumvirate. ▲ **K12**

Djwal Kuhl. also called "The Tibetan." A beautiful, profoundly learned master. **DK1**

Sai Baba, a great living incarnation of God (avatar), living in Puttaparthi, India. ▲ **SB**

Jesus the Christ, a great way-shower for humanity. He proved that death has no reality. ▲ **M4**

Lady Nada, said to be the twin flame of Jesus. ▲ **NA**

Lord Gautama the Buddha, born in 550 B.C. and one of the world's great wisdom teachers. ▲ **BU2**

Mother MarY, a bold and coura-geous spirit! The origin of this picture is unknown. ▲ **MM2**

Ganesha, the Hindu god who is the breaker of obstacles. ▲ **K14**

Avalokiteshvara, revered as a Buddha of infinite compassion. ▲ **B23**

Lahiri Mahasaya, a great teacher of enlightenment through Kriya Yoga, and a direct disciple of the Himalayan master Babaji. ▲**LM**

Herakhan Baba, a great Indian master visited by people from all over the world until he left his body in 1984. **HB**

Lakshmi, the goddess of beauty and abundance, and the consort of Vishnu. ▲ **K13**

Medicine Buddha, a bodhisattva who teaches mind-body healing and shines the blue color of beryllium. ▲ **B9**

Paramahansa Yogananda, Indian yogi came to America and wrote *Autobiography of a Yogi*. ▲ **YO1**

Dalai Lama, head of all sects of Tibetan Buddhism. ▲ **DL**

Ramana Maharsh, one of the great modern sages of India. **RM**

White Tara, one of the most revered goddesses of Tibetan Buddhism. ▲ **B17**

Saraswati, the divine teacher who embodies wisdom and inspires art and science. ▲ **K16**

Krishna and Radha, divine masculine and feminine counterparts. ▲ **K11**

Dolphin of Sirius, a being of divine intelligence and unconditional love. ▲ **DO**

Maitreya, known to Buddhists as the embodiment of loving kindness. **MT**

To Order

Order directly from Ascension Mastery International, by mail or through the web site: **www.shastaspirit.com/ami**. Books may be ordered through AMI, or purchased or ordered at any book store. Send $2.00 for the complete catalog (except retailers).

AMI	Telephone: 530/926-6650
P.O. Box 1018	Fax: 530/926-1828
Mt. Shasta, CA 96067	
USA	

Let us know clearly your name and address, and please include your **telephone number** in case we have questions about your order. Thank you!

Californians, please add 7.25%.

Shipping & Handling: Americans and Canadians, please include $4.00. Other countries, please include 25% of the total order cost. (International mailing is so expensive!) Thank you.

Credit Cards: Master Card, Visa, American Express and Discover are all accepted. Just give your Card Number and Expiration date, along with your address and phone.

Retailers: The books and tape products are available at the usual 40% discount. The Master Pictures are available at a 50% discount! AMI was so guided. Send for a free catalog.

Please include your Resale Number in your first order. Thank you.